DO IT... AND UNDERSTAND!

THE BOTTOM LINE ON CORPORATE EXPERIENTIAL LEARNING

Christopher C. Roland
Richard J. Wagner
Robert J. Weigand

Editors

KENDALL/HUNT PUBLISHING COMPANY
4050 Westmark Drive   Dubuque, Iowa 52002

CONTENTS

Chapter Eight
TRANSFER ISSUES AND CONCERNS   **201**
Richard Wagner, Christopher Roland

Chapter Nine
MOVING FORWARD WITH EXPERIENTIAL LEARNING   **205**
Christopher Roland, Richard Wagner, Robert Weigand

ACKNOWLEDGMENTS

This book would not have been possible without the contributions of the twenty-nine authors: Dr. Michael Black, Heather Brown (Australia), Dr. Camille Bunting, John Campbell (United Kingdom), Dr. Christine Clements, Madeline Constantine, Warren Cohen, Leonard Diamond, Elaine Hatala, Dr. Donald Kirkpatrick, Dr. David Kolb, Dr. Mario Kölblinger (Germany), Sergeant Ron Lewis (Canada), Dr. Tock Keng Lim (Singapore), Michael Main (Botswana), Tom McGee, Rita Miller, Russell Millholland, Dr. Todd Miner, Dr. Rod Napier, Iris Randall, Rosanne Ryba, Dr. Pennie Seibert, Dr. Tom Smith, Dr. Paul Stoltz, Mark Sullivan, Mary Teeter, Dr. Betty Van der Smissen and Charles Wolfe. We applaud their commitment to write, their willingness and diligence to remain on various time lines. Contributors' biographical sketches can be found in Appendix A.

For their contributions to the International & Multi-cultural chapter we also thank: Steve Coleman (Australia), Dr. Ton Duindan (Netherlands), Roger Greenaway (Scotland), Dr. Darl Kolb (New Zealand) Trevor Laurance (New Zealand), Dr. Luc Lefebvre, (Belgium), Dr. Victor C.H. Lim (Singapore), Willie Marais (South Africa), Munehiro Mitsuzuka (Japan), and Shinta Suliswayati (Indonesia).

Our gratitude is extended to the following individuals who assisted us in various capacities:

- ◆ B-J Diamond for her copy editing and attention to detail;
- ◆ Sandra Zenga, for her word processing and coordinating the "disc exchange";
- ◆ John Campbell for his help with developing and editing the International & Multi-cultural chapter;
- ◆ Ann Hilgendorg, Julie Nason and Gail Ryan for their significant assistance with developing the International & Multi-cultural chapter;
- ◆ Kendall/Hunt Publishing Company for their support and patience.

We are also indebted to our families, colleagues and friends who gave us the support and encouragement to begin, to persevere and to finish this exciting project.

CCR, RJW, RJW

INTRODUCTION

"Experiential" learning, teaching and training have been around since the days of fire discovery. But not until the 1930s did the "learn by doing" philosophy become popular in education circles. Contributions and teachings of John Dewey helped guide students away from the rote memorization methods to more involved and exciting "get-off-your-seats-and-on-your-feet, learn by experience" methods. Unfortunately, the work of Dewey and other experiential advocates has often been misinterpreted. Controversy about these "new-fangled" teaching methods continues today. Two motion pictures indicate the time span of this debate: *Passion for Life*, the 1960 film depicting the "idiotic ideas" of a young teacher full of experiential enthusiasm, and the 1990 movie, *Dead Poet's Society*, showing how an innovative, creative, experiential teacher can stir up more than a few hornets' nests while infusing his students with energy and a love of learning.

Experiential learning in corporate America is nothing new either. Trainers have used experiential methods to enhance individual, team and organizational change for a long time. The Association for Business Simulation and Experiential Learning (ABSEL) was founded in 1974 to promote the use of learning-by-doing in both higher education and corporate settings. For several decades training professionals have used experiential activities including simulations, games, role plays and skits with varying degrees of success. For the most part, these methods and procedures have been accepted eliciting little or no controversy. The widely-published works of David Kolb, best known for his Experiential Learning Cycle, add to the legitimacy of traditional experiential methodology.

Controversy concerning the effectiveness of experiential training and development can be linked to the psychological movements that spawned "Encounter Groups," "T-Groups," and "Sensitivity Training." Since 1975, these movements have increased in popularity, with thousands of believers expounding the value of the experience. But there are as many nonbelievers and skeptics as well. The use of these experiential methods remains controversial even today. Nevertheless, an ever-expanding contingency of individuals and organizations have embraced this latest experiential movement.

The 1980s brought new momentum to corporate experiential training and development including the use of various components of "challenge" and "adventure" education. Challenge education and adventure education focus on experiential risk-taking, trust-building, and collaborative problem-solving using innovative "initiatives" adapted from traditional high school physical education curricula. These delivery systems often highlight the outdoors as an alternative classroom: from corporate lawn, to mountains, lakes and oceans.

The variety of acronyms associated with this movement adds to the confusion. Some of the ingredients in the terminology soup include:

CAT:	Corporate Adventure Training
EBTD:	Experience-based Training and Development
EMT:	Experiential Management Training
ET:	Experiential Training
OAT:	Outdoor Adventure Training
OBT:	Outdoor-Based Training
OCT:	Outdoor Challenge Training
OET:	Outdoor Experiential Training
OMD:	Outdoor Management Training
OMT:	Outdoor Management Training

In order to minimize confusion, we will use Corporate Experiential Learning (CEL), and "experiential training" to refer to this innovative methodology with the following definition:

> CEL represents models, methodologies and processes that focus on individual, team and organizational development. CEL utilizes both indoor and outdoor learning environments with action-oriented activities, exercises and simulations which incorporate review, feedback and action planning. CEL includes but is not limited to "outdoor adventure" models and methodologies, such as ropes courses, rock climbing, rappelling, mountain climbing, sailing and rafting.

During the last six years, each of the editors, representing providers, academia and consumers, have faced frustrations in attempts to explain experiential training to colleagues, students and future clients. It has become increasingly clear that many people focus on the outdoor adventure models (rock climbing, "ropes courses," rafting, sailing and mountain climbing). The media has promoted this view with its emphasis on the "showy" and "glitzy" parts of CEL.

Unfortunately, little attention has been given to the real payoff for organizations: how experiential training can transfer to the work place. Thus the idea for this book was born: to help corporate managers, trainers and other professionals learn about CEL. While our collective experience in this field is significant, we realized the magnitude and complexity of the task we faced and invited some of the best and brightest providers, academicians and consumers to join us in our efforts.

This book is designed to be more than just a collection of papers under one cover. The sections and chapters flow from one to another with particular attention to the direct relationship between Chapter I—Theory & Application, Chapter 8—Transfer Issues &

Concerns and Chapter 9—Moving Forward with Experiential Learning. Brief introductions appear before Chapters I, II, III and IV to assist the reader.

Do It . . . And Understand! The Bottom Line on Corporate Experiential Learning was created to give the reader an initial glimpse of the broad scope of experiential learning. After reading this book we hope that those who have visions of executives swinging in the trees, hugging each other and sharing their deepest emotions, will have an altered sense of what CEL can be. Unless and until the training and development profession recognizes the true nature and scope of experiential training, there is a good chance that this methodology will fall out of favor and, in time, be viewed as just another fad. We hope that you enjoy the perspectives and insights about a training process that began in the '70s and '80s, developed credibility in the '90s, and will be used in some fashion well into the twenty-first century.

Christopher C. Roland
Richard J. Wagner
Robert J. Weigand

CHAPTER ONE

THEORY AND APPLICATION

Robert Weigand begins with a brief history of CEL and then outlines the components of the Kolb Learning Cycle. This is followed by an in-depth analysis of "Turning Experience into Learning" by Mark Sullivan and David Kolb. Paul Stoltz continues with leadership, team development, communication, decision making and problem solving in "Developing Leaders Experientially." Stoltz presents several subtle elements often overlooked and yet essential for learning and transfer of learning.

Stoltz introduces a number of topics that will be discussed in greater detail in subsequent chapters: needs assessments, follow-up strategies, the use of ropes courses. "Ten Deadly Sins of CEL Providers" may cause one to rethink the question: How does/can experiential training transfer back to the work place?

Todd Miner, in a later chapter, notes that many CEL providers/consultants use the "Kolb Experiential Learning Cycle" as a theoretical foundation. Our experiences support Miner's conclusions, and we therefore use this theory as the framework of this book.

Experiential Learning: A Brief History

Robert Weigand

Many theories and concepts have added to the evolution of experiential learning as applied to adult learning and organizational development. In particular the concepts of John Dewey, Carl Rogers and Albert Bandura have direct links to the philosophy and theories underlying the experiential learning profession.

Dewey believed that problem-solving calls for new responses; especially situations involving conflict or challenge. Habitual actions and thoughts do not solve these problems, but active experimentation and trying out new processes might. Dewey opposed the traditional methods of learning by memorization and advocated a "hands-on" learning approach.

Rogers highlighted the need for congruence, empathic understanding, unconditional positive regard as well as active listening and valuing self worth. These ideals are incorporated into virtually every successful experiential learning process. Those "conditions necessary for client change and growth . . . are congruence (to be real, 'open and honest' in relationships); (and) empathic understanding (to understand the feelings and thoughts of others and to communicate this understanding . . . " (Frick, 1990, p. 105).

Furthermore, modeling these behaviors is typically the goal of the experiential process for the client participants. The social-cognitive theories of Albert Bandura stress the interaction and integration of behavior, personal variables and environmental events through observational learning and modeling (Frick, 1990, p. 72).

The first attempts at creating experiential challenges for groups and for personal growth are generally credited to Kurt Hahn, a German noble who fled Hitler's Germany in the 1930s. Hahn first developed the Gordonstoun School in Scotland which was dedicated to the development of a student's inner resources via physically and mentally demanding outdoor experiences. With the outbreak of World War II, Hahn started a school on the Welsh coast for young British sailors. The curriculum was a one month course in seamanship and survival training. Hahn took the name of the school from sailors who spoke of themselves as "outward bound" as they left the safety of the harbor.

Corporate-based adventure training in Germany dates back to the 1970s. The German Institute for Business Administration, in Munich, made the first attempts at launching a management seminar using the outdoors to improve leadership and teamwork (Mertes,

1973). The goal of the program was building a genuine charcoal burner's log cabin in the Black Forest within five days, which, upon completion, was given to the local community. The educational approach was based on a group dynamic concept, focused on reality-based problem solving, and team performance of a non-intact high executive work group from various corporate strands (Kölblinger, 1994).

Further international exploration reveals several different roots of experience-based training from various countries. Other countries including Australia, Belgium, South Africa and Singapore have roots in an Outward Bound tradition.

Experiential education in the Netherlands traces back to 1784 when Jan Nieeuwenhuyzen from Edam started the Society for the Arts & Science to improve the public welfare. This movement used "actual possibilities" (experiential activities) to expand the knowledge of the citizens. John Stewart Mill, (1806-73) a British philosopher, wrote about experiential methods of learning. John Dewey of the United States also published *Experience and Education*, (1934) a work which provided a philosophy useful to experiential educators. Paulo Friere, a Brazilian educational philosopher, also explored the issue of active learning outside the classroom.

In the United States, Hahn's model was adopted by the Civilian Conservation Corps, a New Deal program of the 1930s that engaged unemployed men to work on the restoration and development of public lands. In the early 1960s the Colorado Outward Bound School was formed, focusing on the personal development of adolescents by providing wilderness experiences, sometimes under stressful conditions.

In 1971, Project Adventure in Hamilton Massachusetts, began to offer an on-site Outward Bound type of experience for high school sophomores. During the late 1970s and early 1980s outdoor-based programs for corporate personnel proliferated and formal presentations began at both the American Society for Training and Development (ASTD) and the Association for Experiential Education (AEE) conferences. One of the first university-based CEL programs was known as "Executive Challenge" at Boston University's Sargent Camp, in Peterborough, New Hampshire (Roland, 1991). Since 1985, there has been an explosion of interest in experiential training, and a growing debate on its effectiveness as a corporate training tool.

In 1975 David Kolb introduced the Kolb Experiential Learning Cycle identifying four stages in the cycle of experiential learning:

1. Concrete experience
2. Observation and reflection
3. Assimilation into a theory
4. Active experimentation

Apply these four stages to a practical example: the process of learning to drive a standard transmission (stick shift) automobile. Is it possible to learn to drive by listening to

Figure 1-1   Kolb Experiential Learning Cycle

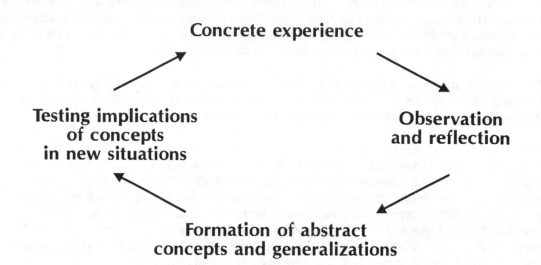

(Kolb, Rubin & Osland, 1991)

a series of lectures and watching videotapes? There is a good chance that these methods would not be completely effective. If an individual really wants to learn how to drive a stick shift car, it is imperative to get behind the wheel (*concrete experience*) with a teacher/coach.

Once behind the wheel, the first few attempts at shifting may result in a quick bucking motion followed by an agonizing stop. With the assistance of the teacher/coach the (possibly frustrated) student now has to think about how to smoothly coordinate the clutch and the accelerator (*observation and reflection*). The student leaves the learning environment to think about his/her experience and how to improve performance (*assimilation into a theory*).

After some weeks of practice, practice, practice (*active experimentation*), the student discovers the proper coordination between gas pedal and clutch; in other words he/she will "get it." As the old Chinese proverb says, "I hear and I forget; I see and I remember; I do and I understand."

Learning new management and leadership techniques at work can be more complex (and frustrating) than learning to drive a car. Kolb's model organizes most learning activities into a framework that improves the understanding of why particular skills are learned, as well as why other skills are not learned.

Turning Experience Into Learning[1]

Mark Sullivan and David Kolb, Ph.D.

Inside the Experience: Anybody Home?

Willy Loman, in *Death of a Salesman*, is portrayed as an ailing, outdated, merchandise salesman, struggling even after many years of calling on a number of accounts. Unfortunately, all of his experience could not translate into new, much needed knowledge about ways of engaging a changing clientele in an unforgiving marketplace.

In this case, it seems that the old adage, "experience is the best teacher," is a bit short in delivering on its promise. Having experience is unquestionably touted in many circles as a prized commodity. Yet experience alone, is not the key to learning. New and intense experiences often yield a flood of new ideas, images, and feelings that swirl with illusory disconnected meanings, half digested, and inappropriately linked to fleeting truths. For some there is a sense that something happened, but it is not clear exactly what that was. Or, perhaps, one knows what happened, but is unable to integrate such new knowledge in a way that has application or intrinsic value.

At times, "specially crafted experiences" (e.g., simulations, fish bowl, group process, gaming sequences, and interactive, multi-media programming), as well as more physical experiences (e.g., indoor/outdoor initiatives, ropes courses, whitewater rafting) may create the illusion of learning, only to find such learning short lived or irrelevant in other applications. Insights generated from meaningful experiences do not always guarantee a change in behavior, or a transfer of knowledge to other contexts.

Training seminars often create insights but do not always produce the desired changes. This can be true for diet workshops, twelve step programs, spiritual and career-life retreats which may vary in the degree to which there are any lasting effects. Experiences that generate passion, purpose, or insight do not, by themselves, guarantee the integration and implementation of thoughtfully planned, heartfelt resolutions. What is beyond the traditional formulaic tips, tools and techniques that draws learning out of experience? Why is an experience at times construed as growth filled, while at other times merely a stirring up or blurring of activity?

There are six processes which help transform experience into learning:

[1]The title has been inspired by Baud, D., Keogh, R., and Walker, D. from their book, *Reflection: Turning Experience Into Learning*.

1. *Perception*—a self-interpretive processing of experience and a critical dimension to the relativistic nature of what is experienced;

2. *Deep Experiencing*—embracing the fundamental essence derived from an organic, holistic spirit;

3. *Following the Learning Cycle*—experiencing learning in concrete, reflective, abstract, and active ways.

4. *Reflection*—gaining perspective over time from the first three steps;

5. *Inside-Out*—engaging the dynamic interplay of the inner world of self in a social system; and

6. *Conversation*—verbalizing and communicating leading to further insight and understanding which reinforces the learning, i.e., making sense through public discourse and community dialogue.

Perception: Barriers and Bridges to Experiential Learning

How we interpret experience and what we learn from it, reflects the way we make sense of, and grow from our experiences. What we attend to, and how we attend to it, forms a foundation for that which is drawn from the experience. The perceptual and process lens through which we focus determines the outcome to a great extent. What we see is often just what we look for. What is most visible in the "here and now" is often linked to what was meaningful in the "there and then." Also, what we perceive as individuals, is often shaped by the collective context of our social milieu.

People often frame their relational context based on previous experiences, perceptions, and projections of social characteristics such as race, gender, religion, sexual preferences, etc. In diversity workshops, for example, this is heightened with participants forming groups according to same and/or mixed categories to work through a variety of issues. Whether individuals conform to the assumed attributes is questionable.

However, what becomes meaningful is what is perceived, not necessarily what is factual. Understanding the underlying significance of how these perceptions become truths helps define one's identity within the context of feelings, facts, and fantasies.

People sharing an experience might interpret the same events in varying ways. Staff meetings, project teams, group discussions, and training seminars often present multiple truths that compete or conflict with each other. Debriefing these groups often reveals just how different the interpretations may be. When verbalizing these perspectives some frustrated participants may question whether the others were even at the same event! Coming to terms with these varying realities, and to what is actually learned, gives insight into the participants and their influences.

In addition to perception, learning from the experience requires *intentional* effort to attend and assimilate the interrelated thoughts and feelings generated by the situation (Boud, Keogh, and Walker, 1985). One needs to be fully present in the situation. The intentional effort involved in real learning is crucial if the learner is going to progress from the known to the unknown to the newly known. New ways of perceiving directly challenge underlying assumptions, values, and beliefs (Rogers, 1969) and enhances the possibility of new behavior. However, this possibility of new behaviors may create dissonance within emotional, intellectual, physical, spiritual and/or communal dimensions of the learner.

An example of this dissonance is dramatized in the play, *My Fair Lady:* the story of a young lady from the streets of London temporarily cast squarely into the social elite of British society. In the process, she is torn between two worlds, the familiar and the unfamiliar. Professor Higgins wagers that he can take *"a common ordinary gutter snipe from the streets, and in six months time, pass her off at the Queen's Ball as royalty."* Eliza Doolittle, the crass-speaking, hunched-over, poor flower girl from the streets, accepts the professor's tutelage. She receives intensive instruction in everything including etiquette, language, dance, dress, posture, and table manners. At the appointed time, Eliza, the (now) poised, stunning, social sophisticate, makes her appearance at the Queen's Ball and is enthusiastically received as royalty by the court. Yet Eliza's new behaviors viscerally conflict with her basic values, attitudes and interests.

Eliza soulfully questions whether she is still really the poor flower girl, a British socialite, or something caught in between. For Eliza, this learning experience involved a fundamental shift in meaning-making structures and processes. In a new way, she painfully and purposefully asks *what makes sense, what feels right, what is possible, and what is not.*

Carl Rogers (1969) indicates that learning from experience involves a continuing openness to the event and an incorporation of oneself into a process of change. This change is one of self organization in the perception of oneself. This change tends to create various kinds of resistance due to the inherent threat perceived in altering one's perceptions. Learning involves a willingness to change (one's view), to change expectations, to change what is comfortably normal which requires a well-developed sense of self in order to grapple with the conflicts between old and new ways of being and doing. Therefore, one needs to be strong enough to be vulnerable, stable within a dynamic environment, able to stretch, or to venture out. Being open to new ways of perceiving involves a willingness to travel deep within the experience.

Deep Experiencing

Frequently, people respond to learning events in an habitual and unquestioning manner (Candy, Harri-Augstein, Thomas; 1985). Regularly meeting the experience engaged only in the familiar or safe often yields no new insight or behavioral change. Repetition of experiences will not make the explicit link between "theory in use" and "actions in use" (Argyris & Schon, 1974). Transforming ideas into action requires a willingness to get inside what is new, try it out, play with it, and give it space expand the edges of what is known. Specifically, this involves:

1. identifying and connecting the new experiential data to what is already known,
2. organizing and relating the data in ways that make sense and
3. testing or validating it followed by incorporating the new insights (knowledge).

This identifying, organizing, testing, and incorporating of experiential data contributes to, and further anchors the integration of new learning. It intrinsically involves new and different kinds of *thinking, feeling, sensing, acting*. At first, the experience may create a sense of imbalance, out of sync with what is known. The novel parts of the experience must eventually link the new with the old, conceptually and affectively.

For example, when one attempts to learn a foreign language the experience continues to be foreign until the deep structure of the language (the underlying meaning, spirit, and rationale) is internalized in addition to a working sense of grammar, syntax, vocabulary, and pronunciation. Foreign language instructors say that until you *feel* the romance and excitement in the language, *sense* its rhythm, *think* in it, even *dream* in it, the language is not yet yours to keep. Hence, learning involves many aspects of self in order to fully mine its multi-faceted offerings.

Follow the Learning Cycle

This process of making sense out of experience, learning on a deeper, more integrated level, is further articulated in the Experiential Learning model (Kolb, Rubin & Osland, 1991). According to the Kolb model, all learning is experiential in nature, involving four stages in a cycle: (1) *concrete experience*, which is the basis for (2) *observation and reflection,* that is then organized or (3) *assimilated into a theory*, from which new hypotheses or implications lead to (4) *active experimentation*. Each of these four stages in the learning cycle represent an ability to engage in the experience in a particular way: concrete, reflective, abstract, and active.

These four stages can also be viewed as contrasting elements of cognitive and affective growth: concrete versus abstract dimension and the active versus reflective dimension. Individuals can be stronger in particular elements (or stages). In order to more fully draw learning from experience there is a need to develop the other elements. For example, one may have a concrete experience but not absorb all that happens (observe and reflect upon the event). Others may be able to watch and reflect on an experience but not develop a theory or set of related ideas (abstract concepts and generalizations) from the experience. Some people build the theory but are tentative in actively experimenting with it. Kolb has developed a Learning Style Inventory to assist learners in discovering their own characteristics within these dimensions of the learning cycle.

Reflection

Reflection is frequently the overlooked or undervalued dimension in the learning cycle. Cultural or societal influences often value the quick fix and the bottom line (Wolfe, 1989), where tangible results, speed, decisiveness, predictability, immediate returns/ gratification are prized.

Stray thoughts, circular reasoning, open-ended dialogue, inner urges, intuition, feelings and hunches are often unclassifiable. Inquiry is sometimes disdainfully reframed as "academic." Therefore, reflection is not valued either publicly or privately given the pressure to respond quickly. The popular re-phrasing "Ready, Fire, Aim," while often the source of humorous reflection, is still standard practice for many.

Reflection, by its very nature, requires additional time, intentionality, intellectual curiosity, suspension of judgment, capacity to tolerate ambiguity, risk, empathy, accountability, and willingness to be vulnerable to the unknown. It requires head, heart, body and soul.

This certainly is not easy; reflecting on the sensations, feelings, thoughts, and behaviors (actions) associated with experience opens the self to transformations of many kinds. Reflecting on experience can move one beyond mindless action, appearance management, and the illusion of change toward active mind, purposeful engagement, and real change. Reflection leads to the "Aha" in life, the recognition or discovery of something new (for the individual). Peak moments emerge as insight linked to action, and the unknown is connected to the known.

However, genuine self reflection is not always a smooth, natural or positive experience. Habermas (1974, cited in Grundy and Kemmis, 1982, p. 87), stated: *"The self-reflection of a lone subject . . . requires a quite paradoxical achievement: one part of the self must be split off from the other part in such a manner that the subject can be in a position to render aid to itself . . . (furthermore) in the act of self-reflection the subject can deceive itself."*

The learner may be so deeply involved in the experience that it is impossible to step back and gain perspective, or to view it from a different angle. This multi-positional scan is much like controlling a descending airplane on a glide path, requiring both the hands-on data from the cockpit, as well as the more distant visual data from the control tower, in order to appropriately gauge the bearings and characteristics of the runway. Being both *of the experience*, and *in the experience*, demands the delicate balance of participant-observer; subjectively-objective and objectively-subjective.

Inside-Out

Frequently, the reflective dimension of experiential learning involves boundary issues. For some, looking inward to an ambiguous, or ever fleeting world of thoughts and feelings may be unpleasant or unrewarding. Or in doing so, one's intrapsychic findings may be discounted by the external world. Varied interpretations of the experience may be renegotiated without full understanding or awareness of the context's influence on the content. Often, defenses (particularly interjection, projection, and denial) provide a safe, comprehensible framework for the new experience. For example, at the beginning of one stress management workshop for sales managers, participants were asked to describe the stresses they experienced in their respective organizations. One manager immediately snapped back in a rather volatile, high-pitched voice that *"My office doesn't have any stress, I personally make sure of it!"*

Heron (1982) states that the experiential learner may use affective barriers when confronted or threatened. This may disable or numb the ability to comprehend the experience. Such barriers create rigidity which further retards readiness levels. The learner becomes less flexible, creative or open to what is occurring. Further, boundaries can contract, blur, or become engulfed, actually distorting the experiential path. Alex Main (1985, cited in Boud, Keogh, and Walker, 1985), builds on this, inferring that some learners do not do their own work. They abdicate responsibility to draw from their own experience:

> "Some learners are over-conscious of the 'otherness' of knowledge, of the external nature of the subject they are studying. What they have to learn originates outside of themselves—in a teacher, a book or a television program. They regard themselves as vessels into which information and knowledge are poured. They seem to sense themselves as vehicles for replication and perpetuation of what is 'taught' to them. These students are often rote-learners because they have little confidence in internalizing or 'owning' their learning—or little experience of so doing . . .
>
> Many are under pressure from the outside world to accept the values and opinions of elders and betters, teachers or advisers, parents or spouses, subject specialists and potential employers. To them there is a low apparent value to their own inner world."

The learner needs to be as attentive to the influences of others, as well as the discounting of one's own perceptions. Rejecting one's inner musings in order to accept the interpretation of others is personally and emotionally costly.

Grundy (1982) emphasizes how reflecting on experiences must involve the freedom to make genuine choices. For this to happen, particularly within a social context, Grundy argues that: *"there must be a structure which allows equal power relationships between group members, including the teacher or facilitator, if the freedom to choose is to be a valid one."*

Paulo Friere points out that, within any social context, participants must be empowered to choose their personal view. He adds that conversation is not only a relational act, but a co-equal process where all have the chance to name their own experience.

To reflect and grow from such an experience is to enhance contact with the experience regardless of the power dynamics surrounding it. Directives from a supervisor or significant figure on how to interpret a given experience needs to be acknowledged, but should not rob the individual of doing one's own work in reflecting on the event. Ultimately, events are most significant when viewed from the genuine emotive and cognitive perspective of each individual participant.

Experience unfolds in a microcosm of a larger environment. Individual perceptions are actually culturally induced within a unique social and political context (Friere, 1970). Individuals bring both a social and solitary "I" to experience. Their nature is indicative of particular membership in ethnic, social, cultural, political and gender groupings. The politics of experience and reflection is an active, political, psycho-social statement in time (history). While the individual's perceptions and reflections are central to the learning process, these influences provide a broader context which frames the experience and adds further meaning to it. Therefore, integrating meaningful experiential learning must reflect these many perspectives ranging from intra-personal to planetary.

Development of Community Norms

In many ways, experience-based learning is cultivated within the context of both thought and action; both individual and group. Each polarity serves the other within each set in the effort to find meaning. For the intentional learner this effort may include private reflection, public dialogue or some combination thereof.

While reflection may be considered a solitary matter, it is interesting to see the power and presence of private thoughts shared in community (public reflection). Conversation focused on a singular or shared experience can be a catalyst for new learning about the subject, self, and community. One often enriches the other as they become more relevant and related.

Learning from experience leads to informed action, which "emanates from a socially responsible sense of consciousness" (Habermas, 1974). Value is found by relating the critical intent (or purposeful dimension), of the experience to the human spirit and knowledge-base of the community. Learning from an experience affects the individual and all who encounter that individual as well. Communities add to their knowledge base through the experiences and reflections of its individual members. Individual knowledge is tempered by the collective context while public knowledge is interpreted individually.

The subtle processes by which people learn can be improved by consciously attending to the components of the processes: perception, reflection, communication with others and within oneself. Changing habitual responses and validating personal interpretation will often open new doors that will transform experience into learning.

Developing Leaders Experientially

Paul Stoltz, Ph.D.

Leadership development is undoubtedly the most frequently requested CEL goal. Such popularity has led to major opportunities that have been made and missed. What is spurring this popularity of leadership development? Why is this all about leaders not managers? What is this special opportunity for CEL providers? We will examine the results of a key study on the effectiveness of CEL and discuss the Ten Deadly Sins of CEL Providers, designed to help both client and provider.

Why Leadership Development?

Why is leadership development so hot? In an informal poll more than 50 executives and corporate managers tried to describe the new found importance of leadership in today's turbulent marketplace. They described the need for a visionary guide or coach able to direct an organization through the most devastating weather. This group's responses seemed indicative of larger changes occurring in the work place. There is a deeply felt need for a new breed of effective leadership.

In a recent survey (Froiland, 1993) conducted for the American Society for Training and Development (ASTD) more money is invested in leadership development than any other training area, more than team skills, sales training, even more than the currently popular Total Quality Management!

The growth of leadership development is also reflected in the increasing numbers of consultants, training companies and publishers addressing this area. Ten years ago it was a major event if more than one significant book emerged on this subject each year. Today, dozens of leadership related works appear every year. One need only be on the mailing list for training and development materials to note the incredible pervasiveness of leadership development providers and resources.

Clearly, something is going on. Everything is faster, better, and more difficult to fully grasp. Perhaps Tom Peters said it best in *Liberation Management* (1992): " . . . the definition of every product and service is changing . . . no corner of the world is exempt from the frenzy." Traditional organizations are changing, customer expectations are fickle and uncompromising. Increased employee and customer diversity, quicker cycle times, overnight global competition, an indecipherable global economy, daily technological breakthroughs, revolutions in personal life-style choices, and an endless sea of consumer options has deepened the overwhelming confusion. In times of unprecedented turbulence, we seek leaders who can make sense of it all, articulate an inspirational vision and guide us through the fog.

Leaders Versus Managers

Stephen Covey (1989) describes the difference between managers (out of favor) and leaders (very much in favor). Managers provide the jungle expedition members with machetes and food. They provide jungle cutting seminars and health benefits for machete wielders so they can cut through the jungle as quickly as possible. Leaders climb the tallest tree, look out over the jungle and proclaim, "Wrong jungle!" Leaders provide direction, managers provide support for the direction. Which comes first? When direction is increasingly difficult to discern, leaders become increasingly valued.

The Case for the Great Outdoors

Of the many resources and approaches for developing leaders, CEL providers have a special opportunity. The marketplace is demanding creative, powerful and effective techniques for developing these much needed leaders. Old models and methods often fall short, pointing to a genuine opportunity for CEL to do it right. CEL providers approach leadership development with a different viewpoint.

Although not all CEL activities and programs take place outdoors, a large part of the CEL "magic" derives from simply being outside, i.e., outside the box, or corporate office, or simply, the building. The psychology of this magic is often as simple as getting managers away from neckties and telephones and placing them in a completely nontraditional environment for getting things done. It is important to consider the *power* dynamics in trying to create change, especially among a mixed-rank group. Being outside removes the traditional trappings of power, from clothing to desk size, resulting in a refreshing opportunity for work teams and individuals to demonstrate other (natural) skills and abilities.

Perhaps the magic of the outdoors-as-training-room is enhanced by pleasant childhood memories. Words describing associations with "outdoors" often include: open, fun, wild, summer camp, sunny, games, hide-and-seek, unknown, unpredictable, freedom, and vacations. Some of the associations with the word 'office' might include: cold, sterile, uncomfortable, comfortable, efficient, professional, structured, fluorescent-lit, technological, fast, and stiff. There are certainly offices that are clear exceptions to these descriptors. Nevertheless, which is more conducive to exploring leadership capabilities and developing the potential of the work team? Which is more likely to bring out risk-taking, paradigm-breaking, transformational leadership behavior? Which is a more apt context for testing and developing one's ability to determine and articulate direction? Given that expectations have a tremendous impact on learning, which setting is more likely to create an environment of positive anticipation? Although not universally accepted, there are some clear advantages to creatively integrating the outdoors into experiential learning programs: the positive association with childhood, the open environment without the trappings of status or power and the natural setting.

A second major strength in CEL programs is the harmony between CEL philosophy and the needs of the client. Philosophically, CEL providers come from a more holistic viewpoint than traditional business. CEL providers tend to think more globally and less linearly. They consider the environment, the system, the entire person, including each person's feelings and reactions. This approach can help today's changing organizations face systemic problems in a more holistic way. Furthermore, CEL providers are typically high energy, collaborative individuals who enjoy sharing the transformational power of experiential learning. These professionals create positive, meaningful change in the definition of leadership.

CEL Measured: Promises Versus Practice

The results of a recent study (Stoltz, 1989) can provide some insights. A content analysis of the promotional materials of more than 40 CEL providers shows a clear and consistent promise to develop leaders. In addition, CEL providers promise to develop teams, enhance communication, promote change-management, decision-making and problem-solving skills.

A problem arises in defining key terms, such as "leadership." The definitions and usages of "leadership" are as varied as the number of providers who promise to develop it. It is essential for both client and provider to share a clear understanding of terms and the essential qualities thereof. Without consensus, confusion will almost certainly occur. An example of this can be found in analyzing one of the most critical leadership skills, communication.

Communication encompasses a vast spectrum of skills including (but not limited to): interpersonal, team, presentation, conflict management, listening, and writing skills. If a client means "team facilitation" when thinking of communication and the provider means "listening skills," there is likely to be significant problems throughout the process, from design through transfer of learning.

In 1992 a well known, major CEL provider also made these popular promises. An indepth, qualitative and quantitative analysis indicated that Provider X had difficulty answering some basic questions (Stoltz, 1992). When asked how they develop leaders, or what skills are necessary to be an effective leader, each facilitator had a different answer. When asked how they develop these various skills, the course designers and facilitators responded with non-specific answers. When discussing a specific, completed program design, Provider X had great difficulty clarifying content, processes and goals. The objectives were broad and vague. Provider X had no workable definition of the basic terms of "leadership" or "communication." This ambiguity appears to be quite common among CEL providers, certainly a major concern for the industry.

Clear definitions shared by client, participants and provider, drive the successful consulting process from contract negotiation through learning objectives, program design and transfer-of-training. Vagueness in these terms results in vagueness throughout the change effort. Providers and clients must help each other in the definition of key terms and their translation into desired actions or process changes. The success of CEL depends upon careful planning, focus and shared terminology.

Lesson plans, participant-centered learning objectives, theoretically-based development strategies and client-centered program design are typical of the traditional trainer. This specificity and detail have not traditionally been a strength of some CEL providers, but, as these elements provide an opportunity for refinement in focus and improved program results, they are more frequently utilized.

The relationship between learning-centered detail (objectives, design, methods, etc.) and program results were the subject of a specific study. Two programs were analyzed using pretests, post-tests, facilitator interviews, observation, questionnaires, follow-up participant interviews and document analysis.

Both programs had similar designs including a thorough briefing, a number of team-centered activities, most of which were followed by a debriefing session. Facilitators selected those initiatives most appropriate for each group combined with available resources based on time demands, logistics, equipment, number of facilitators, facilitator expertise, and weather.

Based on thorough pre- and post-assessments, not one area of leadership skills was improved upon over time. Through multiple data-gathering methods, it was clear that certain individuals appeared to learn and improve, despite the program. It is important for trainers and clients to note that this failure to achieve overall improvement in client's skills directly contradicted feedback received on course evaluation forms. In fact, many participants stated that they perceived improvements not identified by their peers and followers. In other words, good feelings expressed in glowing post-course evaluations did not result in real change in leadership behavior. Thus, participant evaluation forms are not always an accurate measure of program success. Neither group showed statistically significant improvement in the desired skills.

Given the real results, little, if anything, was working or worth repeating. Similar results have been witnessed, using less rigorous data gathering methods, in other CEL programs administered by other providers. So, while everyone had a good time, there was no real improvement in leadership as perceived by their most important constituents, their followers.

Unfortunately, this is the result experienced by many CEL providers. So, in the middle of the magic of the outdoors or other non-traditional settings, given the holistic philosophy, the positive sense of expectancy, the powerful promotional promises, the hype and the energy, what happened to change? A successfully operating business would not settle for less than clear terminology, specific objectives and real, measurable results that equal positive, meaningful and enduring change in leadership behavior.

This study is a wake up call for many providers and potential clients. It is a solid validation of the demand for clarity, shared expectations and measurable results. Consider the reality of what providers deliver versus what clients receive. The clearer the understanding between contractors, the fewer the problems and the more successes achieved.

We can learn from the problems and practices identified in this study and we can learn from the Ten Deadly Sins of CEL Providers.

The Ten Deadly Sins of CEL Providers

1. *Using "Granolas" To Facilitate Leadership Development and Organizational Change*

A reverence for the outdoors or a solid background as a "rock tech" (those to whom we trust our lives when scaling sheer granite walls or hanging suspended between trees sixty feet in the air) does not make an effective facilitator or agent of change. One of the great weaknesses of the experiential training industry has been the criteria for hiring facilitators. Outward Bound uses outdoor skills experts to lead their outdoor courses. This practice makes perfect sense to meet the needs of their clientele.

However, what works for troubled teenagers does not necessarily work for marketing executives. Outward Bound slammed into this reality when they began to expand their course offerings to include "Professional Development" and corporate programs. The industry is heavily populated with outdoor skills experts having limited or nonexistent expertise in organizational issues, communication, psychology, human performance theory, facilitation skills, course design, evaluation, transfer of training or organizational change.

There is hope for improvement as more and more forward-thinking providers begin to use qualified experts in organizational areas. These providers value and therefore seek out, those experts having organizational development skills with some experience in outdoor skills over those having only outdoor skills experience. Outdoor skills experts cost less than organizational behavior experts who have years of education and training in their fields.

This is not to downgrade the importance of techies. Quite the contrary, their importance has grown as safety and legal concerns continue to be integral to these programs.

In fact, knowledgeable and experienced techies can make or break those programs that use more advanced outdoor adventure exercises. The ethical and technical expertise of these individuals maintains the integrity and safety of the industry.

However, some of the best-intended but worst facilitation occurs when a "river jock" or a "rock tech" facilitates an executive team development. The standard debriefing questions "What just happened?" "How did you feel?" "What did you notice?" "What worked?" What didn't work?" and "How does this relate to your organization?" are not enough for most groups to experience meaningful and enduring change. These are merely the outer layer of debriefing. In order to be effective, CEL facilitators need deeper expertise in the context, content and process issues confronting each client group.

2.   Fitting the Customer To the Program

Putting participants through a pre-set program may be effective for the youths for whom Outward Bound was originally intended. However, every learning experience needs to be adapted to each client's needs, culture, language and objectives. This might conflict with program selection and design that is based on client or provider personal favorites or situational variables.

Customization of the program needs to begin with the very first client-provider meeting and continue through every phase of the change process. Just as we tend to be unmoved by a canned speech, we are likely unmoved (to change) when channeled through a canned program. Every customer has unique characteristics that must be accommodated and integrated into every aspect of program preparation, design, delivery and follow-through. This ability to customize, both planned and spontaneously (in the field), is a strong characteristic of the high quality CEL providers and a major drawback for many others.

3.   Putting Events Before Learning

No doubt CEL initiatives, games, activities, trips and events can be fun and enlightening. How and when are these activities selected?. Often providers choose an activity and then ask what could be learned. Clearly the learning objectives are the bottom line for the entire experiential intervention or program. The client's learning objectives are primary and should be the guidepost for the entire process, including location, facilitators and their expertise, duration, pace, design, and specific activities. Learning objectives drive the entire change process. CEL providers must have the ability to identify and clarify, define and design learning objectives, then determine the best way to fulfill those objectives. These learning objectives are the client's ultimate expectations. The successful CEL provider sets out on Day One to find as many possible ways to not just meet, but to exceed, those expectations. The provider must never let the activity drive the learning. Such a sin is as deadly as letting the auto mechanic's tools decide which repairs to perform, ("I know your water hose is blown, but all I have is a tire kit, so let's patch your tire instead").

4.   *Assuming Culture is Distinct From Learning*

Techies are taught about equipment, safety procedures, first aid and technical skills. The more advanced CEL consultants are taught to work through the action research model in implementing change. Trainers are taught to assess, design, deliver, evaluate, and transfer a learning experience. All of these backgrounds and knowledge sets are invaluable to the successful CEL provider. But, how do providers learn about organizational culture and its impact on achieving results?

An organization's norms, rules, beliefs, values, attitudes and behaviors determine everything about that organization. In a sense, these things define the organization. How can meaningful change be implemented without seriously considering these cultural variables?

The young, energetic, "can do" sales force perceives themselves as invincible in the face of competition and the best at what they do. Are their needs, program pacing, activities, experiences, and results going to be different than the senior-level engineers working for a recently restructured airline recovering from Chapter 11?

Are the processing needs of the Madison Avenue advertising group that thrives upon internal competition different from the nonprofit, highly collaborative social services organization?

How are gender and minority issues handled within each organization? How are things communicated, to whom, in what direction, and in what ways? Who has the power and how is that power manifested? How are people rewarded for their efforts; and who controls those rewards? What is the climate of the organization? What are the rules, both implicit and explicit, that govern organizational behavior? These are but a few of the internal variables that will dramatically effect the shape and flavor of any change effort.

The more familiar we become with the culture of the client organization, the more focused and successful results will be. A thorough needs assessment conducted through a cultural lens is essential for the delivery of a "when can we hire you again?" change effort, and helps to avoid this deadly sin.

5.   *Using words like "leadership" without knowing what they mean to the client*

We must begin with a common understanding of key terms. Asking the client "what does that mean to you?" or, "what do you mean by . . . " are effective ways to make sure that you are hearing and acting upon what the clients are saying, and more importantly, what the client means explicitly and implicitly. This technique not only clears the cobwebs of ambiguity away (from terms like "communication," "effective," "productive," and "leader"), it also serves as a way for clients to clarify their own thinking, and demonstrates respect for their culture and concern for their results, a most valuable investment.

As a scholar and an CEL professional, the term "leadership" is defined differently in varying contexts. Vagueness in terminology is a challenge for CEL providers and their clients as they develop leaders in an ever more demanding world.

6.   Confusing Excitement With Change

Part of the appeal of CEL programming is the rush of excitement experienced when overcoming an individual or team obstacle in an outdoor challenge activity like rock climbing or completing a "nitro crossing." These moments are the high points of many programs! Many providers' brochures and bulletin boards are covered with photographs of ecstatic teams, in identical T-shirts, giving each other high five's, hugs and triumphant grins. As opposed to many traditional programs, CEL workshops often conclude on an emotional high.

Are these photographs, blatant displays of emotion and the powerful, participant testimonials evidence of change?

Studies have shown that these manifestations of human exaltation do not equal meaningful and enduring change. In fact, there is even a clinical name for the excitement so often seen at the end of a program: Post Group Euphoria (PGE) (Marsh, et. al., 1984). Like any brand of euphoria, PGE wears off over time.

Post Group Euphoria is analogous to what is experienced on a truly exceptional vacation. The soaring peaks, quintessential old-world charm, turquoise rivers and endless hikes on a trip to Innsbruck, Austria, made my spirits explode. My college pal/travel companion and I made a pact that we would move there, whatever it took. We promised far-reaching change that would last forever. To date, neither of us has moved to Innsbruck. When we returned to our real lives, we regained a perspective different from our "peak" experience that altered our internal motivation for change. Likewise, for participants, once the hugs, euphoria, and cheers wear off, what remains? What learning endures? What changes after the party is over?

It is often a lot more fun to stage an event, to host the party, to put on the show, than it is to clean up after the horses, pick up the beer cans, or, in our case, do the unglamorous task of follow-up and transfer of learning.

But our "show" will be just that if learning objectives are not considered primary. Although transfer of training may not appear as glamorous or dramatic as facilitating a program, there is considerable excitement in creating real change and future jobs. Transfer of training creates the semi-permanent alterations in behavior that result from these objectives. Despite the best of intentions, real change will not happen without considerable investment in this critical portion of the change process. Only a few CEL providers are really enlightened when it comes to putting these efforts into practice.

7.   Confusing a "Thank You" Note With Transfer of Training

Good CEL providers accumulate their share of thank you's and personal testimonials. Many participants will describe intense moments of personal revelation and change. Attitudes do affect behaviors, but until there is a change in actual behavior that is observable and measurable, training cannot be considered successful. It is easy to be confused. These testimonials and expressions of gratitude are deeply genuine. However, the leader who describes herself as "much more visionary" immediately following the program, may demonstrate no improvement in her ability to inspire others.

In fact, in the previously discussed study, participants' perceptions of change were quite at odds with their followers' perceptions. People were poor judges of their own behavior and level of competency. Many participants described themselves as improved in certain communication-related leadership skills, only to have their followers describe no discernible difference. There is a significant difference for example, between understanding empathic listening skills and demonstrating them. The true judges of leadership effectiveness are the participants' followers. Let them evaluate their leaders' development. Our results and other studies suggest that we cannot trust participant evaluation of their own behavior.

8.   Failure to Capitalize on Environmental Applications

The ability to anticipate and respond to major trends is a necessary skill for CEL providers. Three relevant trends are: 1) outdoor programs; 2) people are taking to the wilderness in unprecedented numbers. Our national parks and forests are experiencing ever increasing levels of popularity; 3) conservation and preservation of the environment has grown from a mild plea to a loud demand. Organizations and politicians are actively promoting and marketing themselves as "green" in response to this demand.

These three trends of outdoor programming, outdoor interest and "environmentalism" create a powerful opportunity for the program that uses the outdoor context to rekindle or inject a sensitivity to and concern for the environment while meeting client learning objectives. We can leverage our outdoor expertise and context as a tool for awakening environmental awareness in our clientele. What a nice perk, (and learning objective), for any organization that seeks to address the environmental demands of its customers. Furthermore, implementation is simple: demonstrating, teaching and integrating healthy environmental practices and philosophy into programs can make a difference. Executives, managers, professionals typically spend their work lives inside. The higher the management level, the more insulated from the natural world. Placing them in an outdoor learning mode can quickly create significant attitudinal change. The key is to make environmental sensitivity a proactive component of program design.

9.   *"Learning Objectives? I Thought You Said Burning Directives!"*

Objectives should be **S**pecific, **M**easurable, **A**ligned with the organization's mission, **R**ealistic (and Relevant) and **T**imely (able to be completed within a reasonable time frame). These foundation stones of traditional training should be integrated into every CEL program. The **SMART**er we are, the better our programs will be.

Saying "we will make you more effective leaders," is too broad, vague, perhaps unrealistic and tough to measure. Rephrasing this as "participants will practice and demonstrate five ways to delegate to a follower," is specific, measurable, aligned with mission, realistic and can be completed within a few hours.

Without effective, **SMART** learning objectives CEL providers sabotage their own efforts. If providers understand and communicate clearly what to expect and what each person intends to do, there is a better chance of meeting those expectations. Moreover, **SMART** learning objectives focus our thinking, and channel decisions toward the fulfillment of those objectives, giving them the necessary priority over other criteria such as fun and facilitator preference.

We need to be familiar with the language of change and integrate it into leadership development practices in order to effectively compete with other methods of training and intervention. Design expertise that recognizes and builds leadership development characteristics around learning objectives is essential. The most enthusiastic facilitators and innovative equipment (e.g., ropes courses) simply cannot replace **SMART** objectives.

10.   *Seeing Themselves as Program Providers Rather Than Change Consultants*

Upon completion of a workshop, as the participants boarded the busses, a well known CEL provider said, "Well, another batch done and over with." It is this "done and over with" mentality that endangers the industry and the results. It is time that CEL leadership development programs move beyond a purely intervention or event-based mentality to an overall change process paradigm. This change process must begin with a thorough needs assessment, from which providers derive and decide the learning related detail including learning objectives, teaching methods, course length, activities, pacing, environment, etc.

The culture of the client organization, as mentioned in Sin Four is one of the key forces acting upon the change effort. There is no guarantee that the client organization will be amenable to the changes in leadership behavior that participants learn. To further complicate matters, the organization may state one objective and act upon another. They may profess a desire for specific changes, when in reality, they fear and resist those changes. Client participants should have their behavioral changes bolstered through on-site follow-up sessions and continuing efforts to provide information (such as a newsletter), and resources (books, tapes, seminars, information packets, articles) to reinforce and solidify the change. Ideally, these follow-up strategies help the client to institutionalize the changes by integrating them into their language and incentive system.

The list of possibilities for the transfer of learning is endless. Learning is ongoing, change is constantly in motion, and there are forces that can make it extremely difficult to try new behavior back on the job. It is the provider's responsibility to recognize these factors and work with them to turn the thrill of leadership development (programs) into measurable results.

Concluding Thoughts

Recently, there has been a surge in the demand for leadership development. Current work place chaos makes it imperative that CEL providers recognize and capitalize on some of the opportunities that come with this demand. The CEL industry's affinity for and skill in outdoor programming (and holistic approach to people and change management), all point to distinct, competitive advantages.

Past studies have shown that we can not rely on the "happy sheet" evaluations as meaningful measures of program quality or of real change. We must not mistake participant or client enthusiasm and gratitude for meaningful change.

The Ten Deadly Sins of CEL Providers confirm that the CEL industry must mature, learn and harness the power of meaningful change processes driven by clear terminology and specific learning objectives derived from a thorough needs analysis. Honest assessment will upgrade the transfer of learning to create enduring behavioral change. CEL providers must avoid the Ten Deadly Sins and seize the opportunity to develop some truly innovative approaches to develop future leaders based on our philosophy and expertise.

CHAPTER TWO

POPULAR METHODS
AND METHODOLOGIES

This chapter examines various models of outdoor and indoor CEL where participants have opportunities for various experiences and challenges. Tom McGee writes about "The One Day Ropes Course Model" detailing the development and implementation of an on-site ropes course program designed primarily for intact work teams at a military installation. These one day programs where employees, including executive teams, are "taking to the woods", are quite popular in the United States as well as other countries.

Elaine Hatala and Madeline Constantine present multiple-day programming at "outdoor centers." These facilities are typically comfortable conference centers, though often on the more rustic side. Bunk beds, family style meals, and shared bathrooms characterize with these facilities. Corporate groups sometimes enjoy the change from the more luxurious conference centers and resorts.

Michael Black presents a third model involving the wilderness environment where participants spend the majority of the program outdoors. These "Outward Bound" types of programs can focus on intense action-based activities such as hiking, mountain climbing, tenting and sailing.

Finally, Chris Clements discusses the advantages and disadvantages of indoor and outdoor experiential training, suggesting that it is not the setting, but the programming that determines training effectiveness.

THE ONE-DAY CHALLENGE COURSE MODEL

TOM McGEE

It may be hard to imagine that the U.S. Navy has an installation in a rural, wooded area in the heartland of America. The Crane Division, Naval Surface Warfare Center, is located on 63,000 acres 80 miles southwest of Indianapolis. It was commissioned by the Navy in 1941 as an ammunition production and storage facility and currently employs approximately 4000 civilians. Crane's present day mission is the provision of engineering, technical and material support to the Fleet for various weapons systems. Crane has a highly technical work force and is the largest employer of engineers in the state of Indiana.

Crane has always been committed to employee training and development. In 1987, an initiative to revamp management training began. An in-house team was selected to completely redesign the 5-day basic management theory course for new supervisors that had been taught by an outside consultant.

The first step in the program development process was an indoor pilot program for new supervisors. The indoor teambuilding module was designed to introduce concepts, and get the class thinking and working as a team. This module was developed in 1988 by a firm specializing in experiential training programs.

The sixteen supervisors attending this pilot program were surprised by the experiential approach which definitely took them out of their comfort zone, unused to the "off your seat and on your feet" approach. Overall feedback from this new module was positive, though guarded.

Based on this modest success, the experiential teambuilding module was closely scrutinized. Should this module continue and in what format? Could it be a stand-alone course available to any employee? This led to the idea of building a low, outdoor challenge course on-site.

Since Crane was initially established to store ammunition, there are many storage bunkers on the premises. Each bunker has an "explosive arc," an area in which nothing else can be located. It therefore took considerable effort and the interest of the Public Works Officer, to locate a suitable, unrestricted five acre site.

The Public Works Officer, the Executive Director and other high level managers were taking a graduate course in the design of training delivery systems. During the course, these two key people investigated outdoor challenge courses. Their research helped speed the approval of the course and the site.

The actual construction of the course required careful planning and outside expertise. The consultant who had designed the pilot module returned for this purpose. During the planning phase, objectives were developed, and needs which were not satisfied by traditional classroom training were identified. The consultant also determined that a low-ropes course was appropriate.

The low-challenge course plan included eight to ten "stations" for team exercises. The site was nicely remote, yet only a quarter mile off a main road assuring easy access. The first program using the new site was a train-the-trainer program for in-house facilitators. The course construction and training of eight facilitators was completed by the fall of 1988.

The initial success of this training project emanated from the enthusiasm and effectiveness of the in-house facilitators who quickly became champions of this type of training. Their knowledge of the people, corporate culture and business issues were invaluable when debriefing groups after an exercise. They were also available after training to address concerns. Since their salaries were not charged back to the students, the training was quite cost-effective.

The first group of facilitators faced the immediate challenge of achieving a balance between a normal workload and additional facilitating. This seemed to produce a high incidence of burnout among facilitators resulting in a high turnover rate in this group. Initially, facilitators trained groups from May-October when it became apparent that some type of relief was required. Additional in-house facilitators were recruited and trained, while outside consultants were retained to co-facilitate with the new facilitators. Even though this was an unexpected additional expense, it helped bring the new facilitators up to speed more quickly. As the consultants learned more about the business from the in-house facilitators, they were able to customize the program, focusing on key corporate concerns. Outside consultants now lead all experiential programs at Crane. While the budgeted expense is greater for additional consultants, the overall program is more consistent.

After five full seasons using the outdoor challenge course for both mixed groups and intact work groups, the original five-day course for new supervisors dropped the experiential outdoor component because teambuilding appeared most effective with intact work groups. Using experiential learning to teach the principles of teambuilding to a class of new supervisors from many areas of the organization can be accomplished indoors as well as outdoors.

Follow-up results were much more positive with the intact work groups (Wagner, 1990). Presently, the outdoor program is only used for intact work groups, with the required participation of the group supervisor. Surprisingly, many supervisors felt that they did not have to attend a teambuilding program involving their team.

Typically, one week before the outdoor program, there is a half-day meeting with the team and facilitator to explain the program, answer questions and generate discussion about team issues that need to be addressed. The facilitator normally selects the exercises to be used based on the issues discussed at this meeting. The actual outdoor portion of the program is usually a full day. These exercises can and often change during the program if other issues surface. Ample time is scheduled for discussion and debriefing throughout the day, and at the end of the program. The objective is not the completion of a certain number of exercises, but addressing teambuilding issues. At the end of the day an action plan is cooperatively developed to be implemented by the team at the work place.

Follow-up consists of at least one half day with the team after about one month. This session explores the progress of the action plan as well as obstacles and successes experienced by the team in applying what they learned. Early follow-up meetings featuring the viewing of videotaped outdoor exercises were discontinued due to cost considerations. However, videotaping is an excellent teaching and debriefing tool which is highly recommended if the budget allows. Interestingly, while follow-up was not discussed in the original program design, or even included as part of the minimal one half day meeting, its use appears to have maximized the extended learning and reinforcement, and was a definite enhancement to the overall program.

The Program in Review

The first three years of the program at Crane had an abundance of groups seeking this type of training. The past two years have experienced a significantly lower demand. This decline is somewhat perplexing in light of the Divisional commitment to the Total Quality Leadership philosophy incorporating teaming as a major foundation.

A key factor for this decline may be the lack of an in-house facilitator, involved in the entire process including the necessary planning and logistics coordination that make the outdoor portion successful. This type of facilitator can be a "champion" of the training program adding credibility and enthusiasm that a mere program administrator cannot.

It is also likely that the marketing strategy needs to be updated in light of program and funding cutbacks in the Department of Defense that have caused much change and upheaval. Outdoor experiential learning is something that teams could repeat periodically. An annual retreat, for example, can be a forum to air out issues, look at goals, obstacles, and opportunities. In these unsettled times often there will be new team members or fewer team members, which tend to re-configure the dynamics of a team. These key issues can be addressed, discussed and demonstrated in an outdoor forum.

A large advantage of outdoor challenge courses is flexibility. A team can use the course for as many hours or days as it takes to achieve their objectives, reinforcing classroom methods or standing on its own. Many outdoor activities can be adapted for the indoors, a concept that must be further explored in light of the hot summers, cold winters and the resulting hesitation of some employees to "do the outdoor challenge course."

The Future

The outdoor experiential learning program at Crane is at a crossroads. After experiencing a high degree of initial success which surpassed expectations, the program must be adapted for a smaller organization with a reduced budget where team training dollars compete with technical and skills training. We know CEL can make a positive impact, but educating the public and marketing the programs is essential. The next few years will be challenging in efforts to keep experiential learning at the forefront of corporate survival strategy.

MULTIPLE-DAY EXPERIENTIAL LEARNING AT OUTDOOR CENTERS

ELAINE HATALA
MADELINE CONSTANTINE

Utilizing outdoor centers for training is becoming more widely accepted in the business world. Outdoor centers are typically conference centers with comfortable yet somewhat rustic accommodations: cabins with wood stoves, bunk beds, community bathrooms and family style dining. There are also meeting rooms with basic audiovisual equipment available. Although one day programs are popular, multiple (2-5) day programs have many advantages.

Multi-day programs increase the time allotted to working on both individual and group skills. This is true for programs which take place on consecutive days or those that are planned for several days spaced out over a period of time. Participants have the chance to get to know others more fully and see the strengths and weaknesses each possess. Individuals not only have the opportunity to learn new skills but, more importantly, the time to practice and refine these skills. The longer time frame also provides more time for participants to "bond" with the group and reflect on their roles therein, i.e., to form a more cohesive group. Sharing in an extended common adventure including debriefing time brings the group together as a unit.

Another advantage of the consecutive multiple day program is sharing living quarters, where learning can take place in non-structured times. Feelings are often shared and ideas exchanged freely in an open atmosphere.

Goal Setting

Goal setting includes establishing overall training goals, daily goals and individual goals which reflect work place issues and skills. Continuous evaluation of goals is important during the program and should be discussed with the client (supervisor, human resource professional, or other representative of the corporation) as well as the group itself. Redefining daily goals is often necessary as indicated by observation and feedback that the group is having difficulty meeting objectives. Evaluation of daily goals helps refocus the group by highlighting specific behaviors, approaches, skills and techniques that were used to meet goals and those behaviors that significantly inhibited the achievement of goals.

When groups/individuals begin to meet established goals, the resulting fulfillment enhances confidence, commitment, eagerness and willingness to attempt more challenging and complex goals. Bandura's (1977) research on self-efficacy supports this concept of increased self-challenge. Skills mastered in training can be cornerstones for transfer to the work place.

Debriefing

A distinctive advantage of a multiple day program is the opportunity for work-related discussions (debriefing). These typically occur after each exercise, at the end of the day and sometimes well into the evening to summarize the group's functioning, focus on the learning and evaluate individual and group goals. At the end of the day concrete strategies can be formulated to transfer back to the work place. By the end of the program, specific action plans and personal participant commitments are developed and agreed upon. One experiential exercise to reinforce commitment and accountability (a critical step) is the "Wild Woosey."

> *Wild Woosey:*
>
> Two partners each attempt to walk along one of two cables a few feet off the ground. At the beginning the cables are close together and gradually move farther apart. The partners hold hands and must lean on each other in order to accomplish the walk without falling off.

This can also be the time for participants to give each other individual feedback. These daily debriefs serve as a vehicle to bring the group back together and reinforce shared commitment.

The final debriefing on the last day of training takes place after the action plans are finalized and serves as a summary of the daily debriefings. Action plans based on these debriefing sessions should be distributed to each participant prior to the end of the program. It also affords the group an opportunity for closure as well as reinforcement of the skills, tools and conclusions that were made during the training. This is also a time to reiterate the overall goals of the training and evaluate the group's status or current level of functioning and performance. Emphasis is placed on using the new tools and skills in the work place and reminding participants that although the formal training program has concluded, it should not be the end of the learning process.

Formulating the Program

There are many aspects to developing a multiple day experience-based training program. It is important to have a written program plan reviewed by one or more representatives of the corporation prior to the training. This becomes the blueprint for the training. But trainers must be flexible and skilled in adapting specific activities prior to or during the program if the needs of the group differ or change from what was expected and originally planned for. Ideally, the representative of the organization is an integral part of the planning team and is willing to identify and/or discuss possible changes. This type of partnership is critical in order to meet or exceed goals, expectations and outcomes.

Activity mix can include active and passive, indoor and outdoor, discussions and activities. Group demographics is one determinant of activity selection. It is important to acknowledge any and all limitations of group members. For example, activities involving a high degree of physical involvement (e.g., high ropes course), must consider the ability of participants to handle the physiological and psychological demands.

Sequencing

Appropriate sequencing of the activities in multiple day programs is essential. Typically, in a team development program, the complexity of the activities increases over time. Relatively easy tasks are presented first, building confidence and trust in oneself and the group. Sometimes, more difficult challenges are presented early in the training as a way to engage individuals or a group who may not be fully invested in the training process. Overcoming these challenges early in the program can also give the group a needed boost of confidence, or clarify weaknesses in a group that might be overconfident or unaware of existing limitations (within the group). Sometimes a group will attempt a challenge at the end of a multiple day training that they could not complete earlier in the training in order to experience the progress made during the program. The key to activity sequencing is that each day provides opportunities for the group to grow in the direction of the stated goals.

There are a wide variety of exercises and activities; each is a vehicle for the group or individuals to work on improving work-place functioning. The sequential approach often begins with warm-up activities which facilitate interaction. Physical warm-up (stretching) exercises are often used, especially if subsequent activities involve physical exertion. The second phase of the program usually includes spotting and trust activities designed to establish guidelines for challenge by choice, valuing, risk taking and safety. These activities set precedents for actions, language and gestures that will be acceptable during the training, enabling individuals and the group to feel safer emotionally and physically, as they begin to tackle the issues that the training is designed to address. For example, important discussions about how trust, or lack of it, in the work place affect efficiency and quality, can begin in these activities.

Subsequent segments of the training program can blend individual challenges with group problem solving activities. During this phase of training, the group explores individual and group strengths and weaknesses, evaluates their efficiency and quality of work and practices enhancing these qualities. The activity mix during this phase can have an individual or team focus and may include passive thinking activities, low and/or high ropes course activities. A skilled trainer must choose from the multitude of possible activities and sequence them in such a way that the group will stay challenged and progress towards their goals. If a training group is split into smaller teams, each small group should experience some of the same activities so that debriefing achieves similar learning and transfer opportunities for all of the groups.

High ropes course challenges have sometimes been treated as "peak experiences" in which little discussion takes place about the relevance of the experiences to the work place. While the challenges presented by high ropes are typically more individual in nature, a corporate group will have the opportunity to support and acknowledge individuality if the experience is framed in a group context. Spotting teams can serve as a support metaphor with group members learning the skill of supporting others. Conversely, this also provides individuals being supported with the opportunity to experience being the center of attention. Teaching group members to belay or anchor each other can also increase trust, support and commitment between group members. It is often during group-oriented high ropes challenges that the power of the group is reinforced from previous lower-level activities.

Dual High Experiences (DHE), are high ropes course challenges in which two or more people attempt a high ropes challenge together. DHE can provide individuals with an opportunity to depend on and trust each other, reinforcing the type of environment necessary for effective, quality work. A reality of the work place is that individuals have to frequently work together on projects they would just as soon do by themselves. DHE can give individuals the opportunity to process the implications of tackling a task together.

The high ropes course can be rich in work-place metaphors when the challenges are presented within the framework of group tasks. Time should be devoted to explore and discuss work situations which are brought to light by the group experiences and observations on the high ropes.

The final segment of the program is the closing or debriefing of the day. Debriefing was discussed earlier relative to customizing the program, but warrants additional explanation because it is the catalyst for the learning that takes place, and is crucial in making the activities relevant to the work-place. If the group is split into smaller activity groups for the training, debriefing should begin in the small groups, followed by processing as a large group. In this latter stage, small groups share their observations and conclusions for each day with the larger group. Observations, conclusions and skills that the group wants to take back into the work place should be recorded and distributed to each group.

Journal writing can be a useful debriefing tool in a multiple day program and in subsequent post-training follow-up experiences. Journals are vehicles for individuals to express personal thoughts, feelings, observations, and experiences that may be awkward or inappropriate to share in the group, but important to express. Journaling assists in the exploration of individual work performance and personal training goals.

Feedback

Trainers must provide feedback to each other as well as share feedback with participants in order to effectively monitor program skill development. Especially during multi-day programs, trainers must periodically discuss program logistics, group progress, dynamics, obstacles, etc. Often, a client representative would participate in these meetings as well. Due to the ever-changing needs of groups, designs must be changed (sometimes on the spot) in order to truly meet clients' goals and objectives. There are often times when a part of the program must be redesigned and, given the tight schedule of most CEL programs, trainers find themselves working on revisions until one or two o'clock in the morning. Yet this flexibility and dedication are perhaps the most important trainer requisites for relevant experience-based training programs.

Multiple Groups in Multiple Day Programs

It is not uncommon for an organization to send thirty or more participants to a multiple day CEL program. Group size is dependent on desired outcomes. If a client is interested in creating a general awareness of important characteristics of effective teams, elements of creative problem solving, leadership styles, etc., then it may be appropriate for training groups to have 20 to 30 participants. If, on the other hand, a desired outcome is to begin transforming a group of individuals who work closely together into a more effective team, then a group of eight to twelve is more appropriate.

CEL providers often contract with independent trainers to staff multiple group programs. Fortunately, they select from a pool of highly qualified facilitators throughout the world with rich backgrounds in business, training, human resources and experiential technology. However, some CEL program outcomes have undoubtedly been compromised because just one facilitator failed to meet expectations. Thus, the importance of "qualifying" potential facilitation staff cannot be minimized. Some providers require any facilitator with whom they are not familiar take the role as assistant or co-facilitator, regardless of the person's education and experience. This allows the provider to evaluate each and every new trainer in an environment that does not jeopardize client expectations and adds to the provider's "stable" of qualified trainers.

To Tape Or Not To Tape

Videotaping of the training experience can be useful in some situations and a hindrance in others. Realistically, everything that happens in a multiple day training cannot be taped. It should be determined prior to the training whether the taping will be used for follow-up training or for more informal reinforcement as a "souvenir." It is also important to determine prior to the training who will do the taping. If participants take turns taping, their participation in activities is interrupted or limited and the development of the group is hindered, unless it is agreed upon to process the impact on the group of losing a resource to other responsibilities. Alternatively, it may be best to assign an individual who is not participating in the training to videotape.

Videotaping a multiple day training program has some distinct advantages. As an evaluation tool, participants can observe group functioning. The tape provides accurate, objective information that "may allow them to move from the level of awareness to that of more responsibility" (Nadler & Luckner, 1992, p. 53). Conclusions and strategies that were successful during training can be reinforced at a later date. Videotape can also serve as a method of reliving the experience and energizing the group after the training.

Videotaping also has some distinct disadvantages. Individuals may feel inhibited or self conscious if they know they are being taped and be less spontaneous. Videotaping sometimes catches embarrassing moments. Also, since it is impossible to tape everything, key positive moments in the group's progress or success may not be captured. Similarly, unsuccessful or frustrating moments might be captured too often, causing more of a negative focus and possibly misrepresenting the real attributes of progress of the group. Varying skill levels when rotating volunteer videographers can result in a tape which may be difficult or distracting to view.

Follow-up

The training experience is an arena for exploring, defining, and practicing skills and behaviors that promote efficient and effective work. It cannot be expected that the level of skill and motivation at the end of training will automatically be maintained in the work-place following the initial training. Employing some form of follow-up training enables continued application and reinforcement of the insights, skills and conclusions to the realities of the work place.

Summary

The multiple day CEL program can be a powerful method of increasing the effectiveness of a group and improving the quality of work it produces. The time invested in a multiple day program exponentially expands the learning that takes place in the training. The outdoor setting provides a relaxed atmosphere and presents unique opportunities for meaningful training. Overall, a well planned, flexible multiple day outdoor-based experiential training program can provide work groups with unique opportunities to acquire and practice skills necessary to function effectively in a changing world.

WILDERNESS-BASED CORPORATE EXPERIENTIAL LEARNING

MICHAEL O. BLACK, PH.D.

> You cannot stay on the summit forever; you have to come down again. So why bother in the first place? Just this, what is above knows what is below, but what is below does not know what is above.
>
> One climbs, one sees. One descends, one sees no longer, but one has seen. There is an art of conducting oneself in the lower regions by the memory of what one saw higher up. What one can no longer see, one can at least know.
>
> —Rene Daumal

Wilderness: The term connotes high adventure, risk, and the unknown. It may conjure remote mountains, raging rivers, pristine lakes, arid deserts. Our knowledge of experiential training with a wilderness focus is akin to the wilderness itself, largely unmapped and unknown. Some adventurers have journeyed into the region, but much of the landscape awaits exploration.

This introduction to Wilderness Experiential Learning (WEL), includes a framework for deciding when to use this type of training, clarifies similarities and differences relative to other types of experiential learning, and highlights WEL's unique benefits and disadvantages. Essential factors for evaluating the quality of WEL programs are also discussed. Many of the ideas were gathered from seasoned WEL experts, and the author's personal experience.

What is Wilderness Experiential Learning?

WEL is defined as: Participation in outdoor adventure pursuits within the context of an extended expedition into the wilderness for organizational and/or individual enhancement.

"Outdoor adventure pursuits" include climbing, kayaking, orienteering, caving, white-water rafting, expedition-style backpacking and canoeing. Priest, Attarian, and Schubert (1993) suggest that these wilderness adventure activities develop confidence, leadership, judgment, and help participants to resolve conflict and cope with change and uncertainty.

" . . . extended expedition into the wilderness . . . " implies that a WEL program must be long enough and remote enough to allow participants to disengage from civilization and immerse themselves in the enriching, transformational milieu of the wilderness environment. Optimal duration and remoteness vary depending on individual and organizational needs, but programs generally last between 5 and 10 days.

Participating in an extended expedition creates opportunities for self-sufficiency and interdependency. Participants eat, sleep, and conduct their daily activities away from civilization, relying on personal and group effectiveness. WEL participants do not always engage in spartan survival exercises or "live off the land." Tents, sleeping bags, camp stoves, etc., are almost always used. The relevant parameters are the extent to which individuals are removed from civilization and the extent to which they rely on themselves and their companions for sustenance and success.

" . . . for organizational and/or individual enhancement . . . " indicates that WEL programs are results driven. The deliberate development of organizations and/or individuals is at the core of all CEL programs and wilderness programs in particular. The goals of WEL programs can vary, but in general seek to enhance processes associated with business success including leadership, teamwork, problem solving, goal setting, decision making and risk taking.

WEL Examples

WEL programs take many forms ranging from complex, staged, rescue and retrieval scenarios to simple wilderness journeys. Programs may include a wide array of activities and milieus including alpine mountaineering, desert canyoneering, white-water rafting, and flat-water canoeing.

For example, in a complex, staged program, an intact management team might be placed in a Rocky Mountain lodge where they receive a "communiqué" from the CIA. The communiqué indicates that a federal plane carrying canisters of a highly toxic nerve agent has presumably crashed in the mountains near the team's lodge. The highly durable canisters are probably not damaged. There were five military agents on board, but the CIA has learned that one of them is actually a double agent for a hostile, third world country. The likelihood of passenger survival is unknown at this time, but the CIA fears the double agent's cohorts will seek to retrieve the canisters. Because of the management team's locale, they have been asked to utilize their skills and resources to retrieve the canisters before the third world agents.

The management team receives further information throughout the multi-day scenario, but their task is to quickly form an organization, inventory their resources and skills, design a plan of action in the midst of ambiguous circumstances, and modify the plan as events unfold. Within a different context, the processes associated with accomplishing this task are akin to the everyday business environment in many significant ways.

Throughout the scenario, participants stop to debrief their experience. They make observations about their newly formed organization, focusing on what is working well and what is working poorly. Based on these observations, attempts are often made to enhance the effectiveness of their efforts. Most importantly, participants reflect on how their learning applies to their everyday personal and professional lives.

A simpler WEL program may place a management team in a situation where the team learns high-country camping and orienteering skills, and then engages in a variety of activities including rock climbing, a peak ascent and a solo (a period of time alone, generally including at least one night). There are many rich metaphors found in each of these activities and regular debriefing sessions enable this metaphorical learning to be transferred to the work place. These programs provide more flexibility than the more complex, staged experiences, allowing an effective facilitator to spontaneously adjust to the immediate needs of the group.

A WEL Framework

WEL shares many characteristics with other models. Participants are placed in challenging situations that require the application of a broad range of skills. Situations require groups to use creative problem solving with uncertain outcomes. Participants interact on fairly intimate levels and often have significant emotional experiences. Generally, program goals promote transferable learning which focus on business related intrapersonal, interpersonal and group processes.

Levels of Program Challenges

In order to understand how WEL fits into the broader spectrum of experiential learning, the following framework defines the levels of challenge within various CEL programs. This framework suggests how to optimize learning conditions by understanding the connection between participants' thresholds of interest, excitement and skill levels interacting with the levels of program challenge. The degree of challenge is defined by many factors including task complexity, physical demands, specialized skill requirements, climate and program duration. An indoor experiential exercise conducted at the office is likely to offer less challenge than a 10-day wilderness trip. These two examples are at nearly opposite poles of the challenge continuum. Many programs overlap their range of challenge (Figure 2-1), so that two programs adjacent to each other on the continuum may offer similar levels of challenge. Taken as a whole, a progressive increase in challenge occurs as one moves across the continuum.

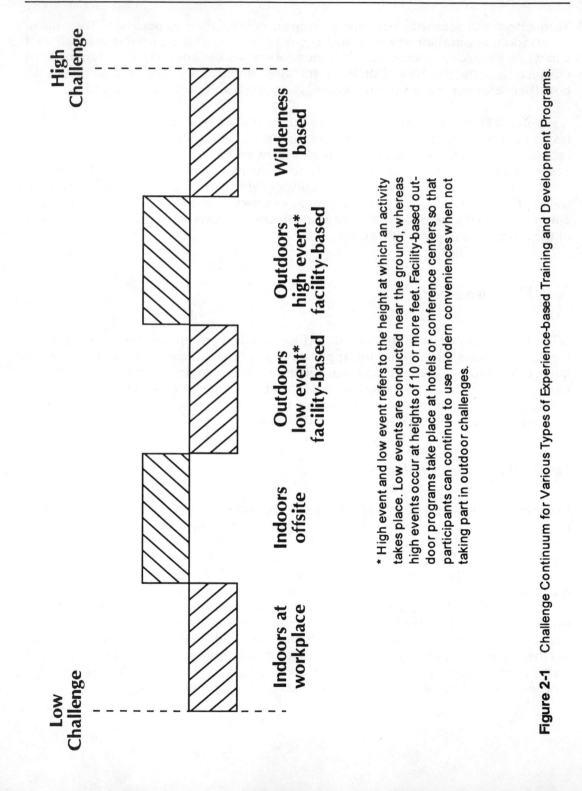

* High event and low event refers to the height at which an activity takes place. Low events are conducted near the ground, whereas high events occur at heights of 10 or more feet. Facility-based outdoor programs take place at hotels or conference centers so that participants can continue to use modern conveniences when not taking part in outdoor challenges.

Figure 2-1   Challenge Continuum for Various Types of Experience-based Training and Development Programs.

Interest/Involvement Levels

All experiential programs are intended to promote some measure of learning. Learning is, in part, a function of attention, interest and, most importantly, involvement. Moderate levels of involvement yield optimal levels of learning, while low or exceedingly high levels of involvement limit learning (Kahneman, 1973; Yerkes & Dodson, 1908). In order to optimize learning in CEL programs there must be a concerted effort by program designers to include activities and exercises that ensure opportunities for sustained interest and involvement. When participants are in the wilderness trying to stay warm, trying to find their way from point A to point B, etc., the focus is on the basic needs of food and shelter. This usually keeps participant interest and involvement levels exceedingly high.

Skill Level

In wilderness programs, one must assess the skill level of individuals and groups and choose a program with a challenge level that matches these skills. Effectively matching program challenge with participants' skills enhances learning potential. Csikszentmihalyi and Csikszentmihalyi (1988) suggested that learning, attention, memory and motivation can all be enhanced by finding the optimal match between skill and challenge (see Figure 2-2). If the level of challenge is too low for a given level of skill, individuals feel bored; if the challenge is too high, they feel anxious. Boredom and anxiety are to be avoided when attempting to optimize learning conditions. Higher levels of skill necessitate more challenging CEL programs.

Skill assessment needs to include interpersonal and group skills (leadership, communication, group process, etc.) as well as specific outdoor skills (camping, orienteering, boating, etc.). These skills should be evaluated for both individual participants and the group as a whole. Participants' previous exposure to experiential learning may provide generalized skills for group problem solving. Participants who possess these skills may require a higher level of program challenge in order to derive optimal learning and even higher levels of challenge in subsequent programs.

The CEL Framework

Figure 2-3 represents the evaluation of participants' levels of involvement and learning which can help prescribe the appropriate level of CEL program challenge to achieve optimal results. The appropriate balance between skill and challenge optimizes learning paralleling a continuum of challenge levels for various CEL programs. This conceptual model for choosing a level of program challenge optimally matches participants' interest/involvement levels and skills. At the extremes this framework indicates that

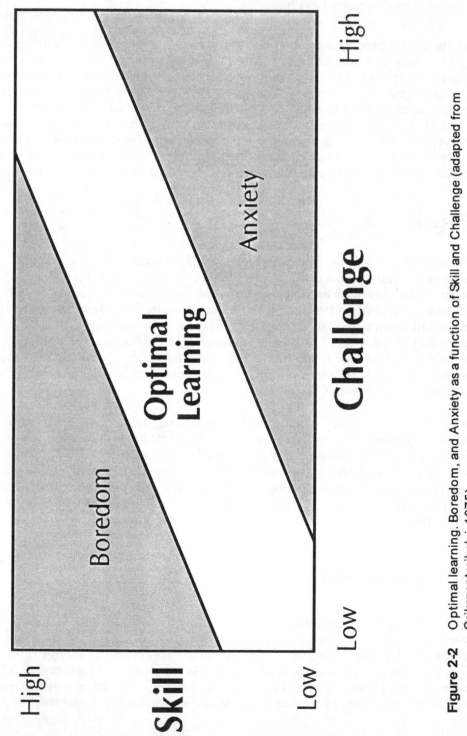

Figure 2-2   Optimal learning. Boredom, and Anxiety as a function of Skill and Challenge (adapted from Csikszentmihalyi, 1975)

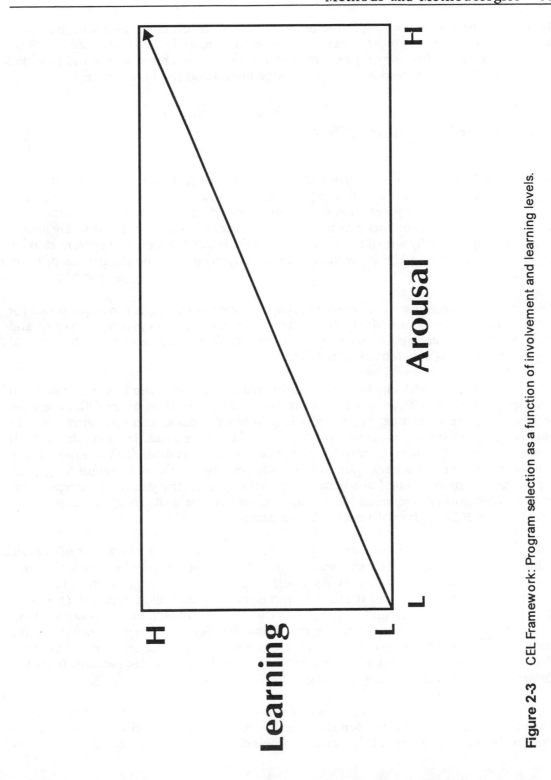

Figure 2-3   CEL Framework: Program selection as a function of involvement and learning levels.

individuals or groups with high interest/involvement levels combined with high skill levels, would derive the most benefit from high challenge CEL programs, such as WEL. Conversely, individuals or groups with low interest/involvement levels and low skill levels might be best served by a low challenge program at the work place.

What is Unique about WEL?

WEL might be considered the Ferrari of CEL. It is potentially faster, more powerful, and higher performing than the other experiential learning methods. A Ferrari can yield incredible results or be potentially dangerous, depending on the skill of the driver and the quality of road conditions. Regardless of outcome, a ride in a Ferrari is rarely forgotten. WEL is potentially one of the most vital and meaningful training experiences available. However, if improperly or inappropriately applied, may be dangerous or detrimental.

Why do organizations want a Ferrari? Perhaps they do not. WEL is not appropriate for every organization or individual. Like a ride in a Ferrari, WEL can promote anxiety, and its broad, but not universal range of applications can be limited, in part, by the skill and arousal thresholds of potential participants.

The uniqueness of WEL lies in its level of intensity and in specific features associated with environment. WEL programs tend to be more intense than other CEL programs. Activities are very exciting, engaging, and insight provoking; and outcomes are very meaningful and transformational. A WEL mountaineering or rafting expedition with competent facilitation, is likely to be more emotionally, physically and interpersonally stimulating than many other experiential learning endeavors. Other distinguishing qualities include environmental aesthetics and challenges. Authenticity of interpersonal connections and intrapersonal transformation, and richness of emotional experience are qualities WEL shares with other CEL programs.

The wilderness environment can be a favorable training milieu because it offers tangible and compelling realities that arouse participants' attention and awareness. Sometimes the wilderness provides uplifting aesthetic experiences (e.g., encounters with wildlife, beautiful vistas) and at other times dispenses challenging hardship (e.g., sudden storms, unexpected frigid temperatures). In the wilderness, success is not assured, and the environment may provide immediate and significant consequences for positive or negative performance. For example, if a tent is pitched improperly, people get wet. This authenticity precludes any tendencies to "check out" or disassociate from the program, and fosters enduring learning.

Metaphors in the wilderness are abundant and very potent. Sunrise, sunset, and changing weather can be the focus for allegorical learning. Observation and thoughtful reflection lead to insights that transcend the immediate circumstance and apply to many arenas within civilization. For example, observing lush moss and spry, little plants growing from a decaying tree may prompt one to contemplate the inevitability of change and the need for transition in one's organization or personal life. However, these metaphors rarely surface by themselves. A talented facilitator is usually the guide who helps participants see and understand business or personally focused metaphors.

WEL is considered by some to be more reality-based than other training environments because the programs are authentic, uncertain, and inescapable—in many ways similar to the corporate environment. Wilderness mirrors the unpredictable, volatile nature of business. Individuals cannot ignore the reality of their circumstances at work or in the wilderness without consequences. In both wilderness and business, people are more effective when they work closely together, react to a changing environment, fulfill leadership roles, resolve problems, and achieve goals. Leadership in both includes taking risk and forging ahead into unknown territory. The impact of team dynamics is powerful in both settings.

In wilderness programs there is a fluid, harmonious progression toward one inclusive, unified experience. Activities and the linkage between activities are more natural than contrived. WEL participants test their skill and teamwork in mountains and on rivers, as opposed to group juggles or ropes courses. In some CEL programs, teams cross rivers as a learning exercise. In WEL, teams cross the river because, after consulting their map, they recognize that the river lies between their current location and the high camp they want to establish before tomorrow's peak ascent. WEL activities are completely integrated into a larger unifying natural scheme.

Authenticity

Promoting more authenticity within and among participants is partly a function of sustained interest/involvement and skills. A wilderness experience often disengages participants from usual patterns, roles, and conveniences. This disengagement often spawns some vulnerability, requiring facilitators to maintain an atmosphere of interpersonal safety resulting in an environment that encourages participants to engage in authentic, genuine interactions with themselves and others. On the other hand, some participants, often with fewer skills, may experience the wilderness as so threatening that they are unable to fully commit to the experience. These individuals are likely to receive limited benefit from a WEL program and may gain more from a less demanding experiential program.

Individuals who benefit the most from WEL are able to raise their self-awareness and engage in personal transformations that benefit them privately and professionally, often clarifying what is most important in their lives. For example, during some reflective time alone, a leader may reaffirm a core value of treating coworkers with dignity and respect, recognizing that this value often gets lost in the chaos of managing daily operations. The leader can emerge from a wilderness program with enhanced motivation and strategies for implementing these core values. Illuminating the essence of one's character allows the individual to recognize personal strengths and how best to offer them.

Wilderness experience promotes considerable interdependency among team members and magnifies the dynamics of the team. After a few days in the wilderness, conversations often become more personal and relatively free of pretense. With this increase in authenticity, teams gain an unobstructed view of their interactions and operations. They are able to observe more objectively and critique processes, including leadership, problem solving, decision making, utilization of resources, communication skills, and interpersonal relations.

Emotional Experience

A rich, emotion-laden experience means that participants are likely to apply what they learn with more enthusiasm and remember their learning longer (Baron, 1983; Glass & Holyoak, 1986). Relationships forged and/or tempered in a WEL experience are firmly rooted in rich, emotional soil promoting greater resiliency back in the work place. Coworkers understand each other better, have greater awareness of strengths and weaknesses, and consequently have better working relationships.

Some Drawbacks of WEL

While there are many compelling reasons for using WEL, it is not for everyone. Several factors may preclude an individual or group from undertaking this type of adventure. WEL programs are conducted in remote wilderness areas with limited medical and evacuation resources. Such programs require the presence of top-notch safety and technical staff who are experts in outdoor living, expedition leadership, and wilderness emergency medicine.

The remote location and physical activity of WEL necessitates careful consideration of participants' physical health. This is not to say that participants must be in ideal cardiovascular health and demonstrate superior athletic prowess, but it is important for program designers to prudently consider health status and integrate it into the design accordingly. In the case of severe health problems, some groups or individuals may be advised to pursue an alternative form of training. Sometimes, when team development is a primary goal, and even one team member cannot participate, it is best to choose a less intense option.

WEL programs can be costly, both in terms of time and money. A week or more is generally required for participation in a wilderness program. For some groups, this is too much time away from the office. Wagner, Baldwin, and Roland (1991), reported that WEL programs cost between $1500 and $4000 per person with an average cost of $2800 (plus transportation, lodging, food, equipment rental, government permits, subcontracts, insurance and the labyrinth of logistical detail). If the program is supported by an outfitter, who handles most of the logistics, the outfitter's competence and understanding of program goals and outcomes must be assessed. A well-intended outdoor guide, accustomed to helping patrons, may occasionally spoil important learning opportunities by offering assistance too quickly.

Critical Elements in WEL Effectiveness

There are several common but critical elements that contribute to the effectiveness of training programs in general. Each of these critical elements requires a unique slant when applied to WEL. Before committing to a particular program, training and development personnel should consider how the provider of that program handles assessment, design, delivery, and follow-up.

Assessment: In evaluating potential providers of WEL, organizations should scrutinize the provider's assessment efforts. "What are your organizational needs; strengths and weaknesses of the group and individuals?" is one of the first questions competent WEL providers ask. Answering this question is often not simple and may require sophisticated assessment methods and technology (i.e., individual and group interviews, focus groups, surveys). Once needs have been established, another question is directed toward the provider: "Can WEL effectively address these needs?" For example, if organizational difficulty originates from a primary lack of shared information, then WEL may not be appropriate at that time and training should first focus on distributing needed information. Other issues such as leadership, trust, communication, decision making, and teamwork are often effectively addressed in a WEL format.

In addition, providers must be capable of assessing the interest/involvement and skill levels of potential participants. This can be accomplished via interviews and observation of group process. Accurate assessment provides the foundation for successful WEL programs.

Design: WEL program designers must be able to develop compelling metaphors that address the important issues of the client organization, while insuring that the design accommodates the interest/involvement levels, physical limitations of participants, amount of time, and cost. Activities must be selected based on compatibility with the needs of the organization, rather than the interests of the planners. The dynamics of the program should be similar in structure and form to the usual dynamics of the organization (Bacon, 1983; Black, 1993). For example, if a team's work environment is fast paced and requires crisp, clear communication and immediate responsiveness, then white-water rafting would be a compatible activity. As a crew, the team would be required to respond to the commands of the captain with an immediate and coordinated effort. The team's efforts on the river may serve as a powerful metaphor for their actions at work. Regular, timely, river-side discussions regarding the metaphoric link between white-water paddling and business operations will contribute to transferring participants' learning back to the work place.

Delivery: The program facilitators must be capable of delivering a program that directly applies to the work place. Facilitators need a familiarity with both the organization and the wilderness milieu, as well as significant skills in teaching and group/interpersonal processing. Technical and safety staff need to be experts in wilderness medicine and outdoor expedition leadership. The physical and emotional safety of participants must be foremost in the minds of all staff.

Follow-up: Follow-up is critical to all experiential learning programs and is essential in transferring learning from WEL programs to the work-place. It is extremely important to assist participants as they strive to apply their learning and integrate it with their organizational culture. The best CEL providers recognize that the proof of their work lies in the transferability of learning back to the work place. Therefore, they are invested in comprehensive follow-up.

Conclusions

Many corporate experiential learning models share many of the advantages of the wilderness models but the wilderness often has a particular draw of its own. If properly implemented, WEL is a compelling and powerful training experience which can serve a variety of organizational needs. Choosing such a venture should be undertaken with careful consideration. WEL providers must be capable of assessing the organization, designing and delivering programs that appropriately address organizational needs, and conducting follow-up integration and evaluation sessions. Judiciously applied, WEL can offer many benefits to individuals and organizations.

EXPERIENTIAL LEARNING: INDOORS VERSUS OUTDOORS

CHRISTINE CLEMENTS, PH.D.

Scenario One: As an employee of Company A you have just been informed that you will be involved in a corporate training program all day Friday. "Not again," you think to yourself. "We'll spend half the day listening to some consultant drone on about how exciting work can be, watch a movie showing a completely unrealistic situation that has nothing to do with me and collect 30 pages of hand-outs that no one will ever look at again. Why don't they just let me do my job instead of wasting my time?"

Sound familiar? This scenario represents perceptions of a typical indoor training program, the type that has been used for the last thirty years. These programs have generally failed to invigorate or motivate employees, or to bring about successful changes in work behaviors. Trainers have struggled to improve the quality of corporate training, and many have focused on the use of experiential learning techniques.

Experiential learning, or learning by doing, first gained popularity as a management training method in the 1970s. Research has shown that people tend to learn most when they are actively engaged in the learning process, rather than being passive, as they would be in the traditional lecture presented in Scenario One (Gilley & Eggland, 1989; Morgan & Ramirez, 1983). Experiential learning can take a number of forms. Recently, outdoor-based experiential training programs have proliferated. The typical perception of an outdoor training program differs markedly from the first scenario.

Scenario Two: As an employee of Company B, you have just been told that next Friday you will begin the second phase of your management team development program. "Great," you think to yourself. "We get to leave the office, go outside in the fresh air and be physically and mentally challenged. Nothing energizes me more, or makes me feel better about my and my work partners. We ought to do this more often.

On the surface, this certainly sounds like a more appealing and effective model for corporate training. But, is Scenario Two a realistic picture of outdoor training? And what about Scenario One? Does indoor training necessarily follow the model presented?

What's Special about Outdoor Training?

Outdoor programs are generally used to improve the effectiveness of management employees in "soft skill" areas such as teamwork, problem solving, risk-taking, building self-esteem and improving interpersonal communication. Programs may take on a variety of forms, but more common outdoor formats include:

1. Wilderness/Adventure Training—where participants live outdoors and engage in such activities as whitewater rafting, sailing and mountain climbing.

2. Low Impact Programming—where structured activities rarely get above eye level. Equipment can include simple props or permanently installed low ropes courses.

3. High Impact Programming—where structured activities take place well above the ground; e.g., a 40' high "ropes course", rock climbing, rappelling.

While advantages and disadvantages may vary based upon the type of program selected there are some distinct benefits associated with simply being out-of-doors and engaging in physical activity. One benefit is that physical risk forces participants to actively engage in the training program. An individual walking across a cable or falling from a table into the arms of teammates is likely to pay close attention to the experience at hand. In typical indoor classroom programs, there is nothing to force individuals to actively engage and participate because they remain within their comfort zones (Flor, 1991).

Another benefit to outdoor programs is that participants often experience heightened awareness of feelings and emotions, and when faced with risk, often must confront their limitations and understand their behavioral choices. This level of personal involvement is difficult to achieve in an indoor, low-risk environment. Because participants are placed in situations that reveal behavioral norms, they return to the work environment with a recognition of ineffective patterns of behavior, allowing for alternative choices.

Finally, because the situation is unique and novel, individuals are forced to break out of their old patterns of thinking and experiment with creative problem solving (Nadler & Luckner, 1989; Priest & Baillie, 1987; Thompson, 1991). There is no single, right answer against which they will be judged and the outcomes are uncertain for all team members. In summary, typical outdoor-based experiential training programs appear to create an environment that is more conducive to real learning than the traditional indoor classroom program. Participants outside their normal environment are more likely to engage with the program, experience activities at an emotional level and take risks in their problem solving behavior. Empirical studies show some support for the effectiveness of these programs in improving group awareness, acceptance of change, communications and interpersonal relations (Wagner & Fahey, 1992; Wagner & Weigand, 1993). But many of the characteristics of outdoor training that contribute to the learning environment may also create danger, emotional distress and, perhaps, legal liability.

Some Concerns about Outdoor Training

Perhaps the most serious questions about outdoor-based experiential training to date have to do with the areas of potential legal liability for companies using physically and emotionally demanding team-building and risk-taking exercises in a rural or wilderness setting (Kezman & Connors, 1993). These include negligence claims for personal injury, intentional infliction of emotional distress, invasion of privacy, false imprisonment and wrongful discharge. The recent American's With Disabilities Act (ADA) raises questions about training providing equal access and fair treatment of employees based on ability.

Another concern are activities that require people to touch each other. For example, the commonly used "Spider Web" requires a team to lift their fellow members one at a time and pass them through a hole in the web. While some people absolutely love this activity, others have refused to participate due to the amount of physical contact required.

A third concern with outdoor programs is the outdoor setting itself. Most people prefer to learn in an environment that is *not* in the rain or snow, or at 90 degrees above or 10 degrees below zero. Even when the weather cooperates, participants may be distracted during the actual activity, and even more so during the all-important debriefing, where the critical links to the work setting are made.

What about Indoor Training?

Indoor-based experiential training programs, also focus on the "soft skills" areas of team work (interpersonal relations, problem solving, etc.) and can take a variety of forms including:

1. Paper & Pencil Exercises—such as self assessment questionnaires.
2. Role Plays & Simulations—which may include brief two-person interactions, in-basket exercises or more elaborate behavioral simulations.
3. Group Projects—where team members work together on cases or real problem solving issues using, for example, affinity diagrams or nominal group process.
4. T Groups—sensitivity training based upon self-disclosure and openness such as the encounter groups of the '60s and '70s.

Due to the wide variation of methodologies used, an evaluation of the outcomes from indoor programs suffers the same weakness as attempting to evaluate outdoor programs; the effectiveness of each program is unique in terms of goals, group needs, skills and commitment (Buller, 1986). Indoor programs as a group, pose a greater problem because these include both experientially-based, and non experientially-based segments. The traditional indoor training model is thought of as either lecture or film. In fact, many of the concepts used in outdoor programming can also be used indoors. The benefits of the indoor-based training discussed here refer to indoor experiential programs. Depending on the type of program being employed, the following advantages may be found:

Physiological and emotional safety. Even in low impact outdoor programs a certain level of physical risk exists. Individuals with special health concerns may be unable to participate in many outdoor programs. Some individuals are simply uncomfortable with physical activity (perhaps due to physical or age constraints), and may be skeptical, frightened of or unwilling to participate in outdoor programs. Everyone can participate in an indoor program. These programs are less likely to violate ADA legislation, nor do they discriminate against employees with reduced physical capacities.

Ease of work-place transfer. Indoor activities may appear more closely related to on-the-job behaviors because the setting is so similar, and specific activities can be created that directly address work-place behaviors, thereby making a clear connection between learning from the program and applying to actual work activities. The point of training, is to teach skills and change attitudes and behaviors of people at work. When people leave the training and return to work, the tendency to fall back into old behaviors is still quite strong. Indoor training may more effectively address systems or context factors by dealing more specifically and directly with the work place patterns.

Relatively low cost. Most outdoor training requires participants to leave the work place and travel to a conference center that has special equipment available, e.g., ropes/challenge courses, orienteering courses. Indoor training can be done anywhere in any weather, and may require no more than pens and paper for equipment. In addition, there is no need to absorb liability insurance costs that are often included in outdoor training fees.

Finally, many options for indoor-based learning can be employed that elicit very real emotional responses. Some of these may be in the form of games built around power or competition issues, or the activities may be real, involving work-related feedback. The emotional impact from these activities can be quite meaningful as it can be directly relevant to work place behavior.

Limitations of Indoor Training Models

Even when considering experiential training models only, limitations do exist for indoor models. Generally, indoors is not as engaging as outdoors. This is especially true when the training is held in the normal work place. The stage is not set for change. Trainees may find themselves in the same place, with the same people, and even the situations may not be dramatically different from those that are part of everyday work life. It is much more difficult to promote change, when the environment remains the same. This makes it difficult to adapt new patterns of behavior, to discover and recognize what needs changing, and nearly impossible to uncover new ways of interacting. In addition, many trainees expect indoor training programs to be similar to Scenario One and whether true or not, this causes them to disengage from the process even before it begins. The environment is not different enough to catch their attention or to open their minds to new possibilities.

One exception is the emergence of several indoor experiential simulations that do, indeed, get people more involved, engaged and interactive. Indoor programs can produce significant improvements in group effectiveness, as well as individual behaviors (Buller, 1986; Buller & Bell, 1986). They may do a better, safer and more cost effective job of addressing specific job-related issues, and virtually everyone is able to participate. Given the many legal concerns associated with outdoor-based training, at the very least, indoor training should be an available option to those who are uncomfortable with outdoor approaches (Kezman & Connors, 1993).

The following table summarizes the advantages and disadvantages of indoor and outdoor-based experiential training.

	Typical Indoor Experiential	Typical Outdoor Experiential
Advantages	1. Open to all, non-discriminatory 2. Can be done anywhere, no matter what the weather 3. Learning transferred more easily to work situation 4. Relatively less expensive	1. Physical aspects promote engagement 2. Reality-based 3. Novel situations 4. Promote experimentation with problem-solving 5. Positively affect group awareness and trust
Disadvantages	1. Less engaging environment 2. Simulated versus real situations 3. Less likely to reveal behavioral norms 4. May not break traditional roles	1. Increased safety concerns (adventure) 2. Transfer of learning more difficult 3. Relatively more expensive 4. Requires participants in reasonable physical condition 5. Contingent upon weather conditions

Indoor or Outdoor?

So, which training model is more effective, indoor or outdoor? The specific training objectives, the clientele's skills, needs and concerns must be addressed. There are some general conclusions about when each type of program is best utilized.

Outdoor-based experiential programs are excellent vehicles for early team-building, especially with newly-formed work teams. The activities tend to force initial engagement with the group, and have a positive affect on the cohesiveness, trust and homogeneity of the group (Wagner & Fahey, 1992).

Outdoor-based programs are also very effective in improving the effectiveness of the interactions of existing work groups (Wagner & Roland, 1992). Non-threatening setting and high involvement activities have the group learn to deal with each other in more personal, and non-threatening ways.

Outdoor-based experiential programs can be particularly effective in improving group cohesiveness and trust. Outdoor-based activities offer unique learning settings which focus attention on improving group interactions, rather than task accomplishment and individual achievement, more typical of indoor programs. The outdoor environment encourages participants to deal with other participants as real people, without the usual facade which hides their emotions and feelings in most indoor programs. This honesty has been found to enhance the development of these team skills.

However, the participants ought to have the option to attend, not attend, or participate on a limited basis. Personal safety issues and issues of group cohesion must be resolved in the needs assessment and design stages of each program. These decisions affect the objectives, and outcomes of the programs.

Potentially, the best training program might consist of a combination of indoor and outdoor programming. Neither outdoor nor indoor-based experiential programs are panaceas for achieving individual, team or organizational change. Care should be taken to select a custom designed program based on specific organizational needs and objectives. In addition, careful consideration should be given to selecting facilitators who are the right "fit" for a particular organization and program.

Chapter Three

Designing the Experiential Training Process

For an experience-based training and development process to successfully meet corporate objectives, there are a number of key factors or elements that must be a part of the design process. The five elements comprising effective CEL programs are: needs analysis, (expert) design, (quality) facilitation, meeting the customer's needs and expectations, and follow-up.

Russ Millholland describes the evolution of a successful CEL program in his organization using these five key elements. Pennie Seibert then takes an in-depth look at the needs assessment, an important first step in determining program goals and outcomes. Next, Rod Napier discusses the whys and hows of program design, and offers a model for training facilitators in design techniques. Rita Miller and Mary Teeter then discuss how trainers develop good facilitation skills.

Roseann Ryba shares her views, as a customer, on the importance of partnerships between customers and the CEL trainer/provider/consultant. With the focus on customer service in business today, CEL program orientation is shifting from the one-size-fits-all program to a more customized format. This customization relies on constant communication between client and consultant.

Chris Roland, Mario Kölblinger and Len Diamond discuss the importance of follow-up in CEL programming. "Learning Partnerships" are highlighted as a technique to enhance the learning process and improve the transfer of training to the workplace.

Experiential Training: Spanning a Decade

Russell Millholland

In the late 1970s, Saint-Gobain, formerly Norton Company of Worcester, Massachusetts began using Corporate Experiential Learning (CEL) as a regular part of Quality Circle efforts. Methods of doing business were changing. Traditionally, supervisors had managed the work of their employees, but the environment was evolving toward individual empowerment through team work and consensus decision-making. Demands for higher productivity dictated a reduction in the number of management and staff positions, along with this new way of doing business. To meet this demand, a new philosophy was required along with an understanding of how work was accomplished. Ownership of decision-making and responsibility for follow-through needed to be pushed further down into the organization.

Considerable time was spent developing training department programs and materials. Outside consultants were first used to assist in developing quality circle techniques. This gave us a solid foundation in the traditional teaching methods, but we were still not comfortable that these traditional methods would allow us to change from individuals workers into successful work-teams.

One person from the Materials Division attended a facilitator training session on Quality Circles, and gave us the technical-know-how we needed to improve team coaching. Yet, we were still unsure of how to successfully present this team-work concept to the factory employees.

A model was developed that combined traditional classroom instruction with outdoor activities specifically designed to allow trainees to practice what had just been taught in the classroom. This combined knowledge of the company with aspects of an executive challenge program (taken earlier at Boston University's Sargent Camp). Sixty different team-based exercises are used to improve group problem-solving; and all forms of training use some outdoor activity to help reinforce the classroom instruction. Separate programs are also held at a local YMCA camp with both low and high ropes programs. These programs at the YMCA camp are used only for teams which already have established the high level of trust and cooperation necessary for this unique adventure.

All outdoor activities are carefully designed to support the total learning objective. The teams are primarily intact work units and cross-functional work teams having common work objectives that require them to come together to achieve a common goal.

It was important for employees to be responsible for their own success or failure. The Company's goal was to change the style of running the business. While we could see many examples of successful teams (e.g., sports teams), the concept of teamwork in the work place was difficult to discuss and demonstrate. While traditional classroom techniques provided a conceptual framework for learning, they did not allow trainees to practice an abstract concept like team work.

Determining Training Needs and Meeting Customer Expectations

While the goal of all of our training is to transform old behaviors into new work habits, each training program is specifically designed to meet the needs of the participants. Before any training program can be successful, the need for training must be determined. The first step is specifically identifying customer objectives, i.e., what the team is to do differently after (each) training session. Although we have many standard topics (e.g., leadership, communications, problem solving, developing trust, meeting skills, quality management) the participant interview defines the opportunity.

Designing the Program

Before the formal training sessions began in the factory, management practiced on themselves. Considerable time was spent preparing examples from our own operations. The purpose of this was to make the learning real for everyone. Supervisors, managers and selected hourly employees were the customers during these practice sessions. The objective was helping the trainers insure that the materials were applicable, reasonable and understandable for everyone.

The actual training process began with four teams from each department. Programs were kept small, 8-12 people per team, and focused on basic problem-solving skills. The location was either a local YMCA camp or the regional Boy Scout reservation. All the sessions combined outdoor and indoor activities.

Facilitation

This design helped the in-house facilitator keep a close watch on how the leader and the team progressed. All team members were trained at the same time. As the teams grew in skill, knowledge and ability, the facilitator could handle more teams.

It was important to have all of the supervisors trained prior to the training of the factory employees to insure that the supervisors knew what to expect when their own teams were trained and for supervisors to participate as team members and understand the presentation of the material. The supervisors were part of the training so that their direct leadership could be modified to allow the team to take more direct ownership. This would help them to understand the objectives of the training, and the expectations of the new company philosophy. Their support and direct assistance were needed so that the CEL techniques would be reinforced. No team was trained until the supervisor was fully committed to the process.

In a few instances people were replaced because they had difficulty accepting the new concepts, but only after efforts were made to change their management style.

Projects and training were directed toward improving the general quality of work life. The teams identified these projects. Here, management demonstrated the objective of having the teams set their own priorities. As time progressed, the teams moved to more cost-saving ideas, thus sharing objectives with management.

At times, management specified projects that were vital to the business; most were less than one year; several extended 12 to 15 months. The intention was to keep the projects short in order to minimize frustrations and more importantly, to experience successes more frequently. This reinforced the teams' efforts and was very important to the success of the training. It also enhanced the self confidence of the participants.

Eventually, all other manufacturing and staff areas in the Strategic Business Unit (SBU) were trained using the CEL model. Division management participated in both separate and departmental sessions. The complete process encompassed six years of continuous learning and updating of the CEL methods.

A preliminary training agenda reviews the rationale for all outdoor events and demonstrates how they compliment overall course objectives. The experiential activities help the participants learn by practicing. All experiential activities are debriefed. In this most important part of the entire learning process, participants identify what they learned from the activity. Debriefing provides trainees with the opportunity to identify what they did well, what they think they could have done differently and how to transfer what they learned back to their work.

The Facilitator and the Debriefing Process

How the facilitator performs the debriefing of each exercise is critical to the success of the CEL process. Training sessions utilize two facilitators: the unit's leader (or manager), and the in-house team facilitator. The in-house facilitator has primary teaching responsibility, particularly for all the outdoor exercises. The unit manager is involved in all sessions to reinforce management's commitment to the process.

During the debriefing segment of each activity, the value of the training becomes real. This is where the seeds are sewn for future learning, where people remember what did or did not go right for the team, and make linkages back to the workplace. Some teams lose all faith in the learning process when they believe they are only playing "silly games," and fail to make the connection with improving their effectiveness. If this happens, then debriefing has not accomplished its purpose. Observers are often used to help in debriefing. They must be skilled in identifying behaviors that help or hinder group dynamics, but must be careful not to cast blame upon a group member if something has gone wrong. Observers are asked to watch and write what they see, but to remain silent during the experiential activity.

The real value of CEL techniques comes from the doing and understanding, which is essential for any new behaviors to become new habits. Recently, the debriefing process has been modified to bring people inside immediately after the activity. This has led to an immediate improvement in the following exercise stemming from debriefing in a more comfortable and slightly structured environment.

Follow up: A Critical Component for Transfer

Weekly post-program meetings are required for all the factory teams. During these follow-up meetings, teams really begin to transfer their learning from the experiential training program to the workplace, and the team facilitator is the key. The facilitator will help the team and their leader develop a better understanding of how to work differently by providing opportunities to practice learned skills and behaviors in the work setting.

Follow-up also takes place annually for factory teams and every eighteen months for office and cross-functional teams in the form of *Continuous Renewal Training*. These off-site CEL sessions often incorporate some outdoor experiential activities and provide participants with the opportunities to learn new skills, refresh old ones and evaluate "how we are doing." Follow-up outcomes include improved communication and trust.

Workplace Realities and Benefits

Team members will say, "Why should I change the way I now work ?" The answer is simple: company survival. Jobs will be lost without improvements in productivity and profitability. People will ask "what's in it for me?," or will want to know if the company is going to share the gains with them. While the CEL program is based on non-financial incentives for productivity improvements, it is becoming apparent that some form of financial gain sharing on a percentage or dollar basis will be needed to further motivate teams. Training and reward systems must compliment each other to minimize the inevitable conflicts. The overall goal of accomplishing a task, regardless of position in the organization is reinforced as part of CEL training.

Corporations are increasingly questioning the incremental value of training programs to the "bottom line," creating pressure to measure the return on the investment of all this time spent on training. Successful training blends team projects at the organizational level with strategic, company-wide initiatives. The credibility of training can be compromised if organizational programs are out of sync with overall company philosophy.

The Environment for CEL to Flourish

Trust, respect and fairness, necessary for survival in any business environment, are also fundamental for the success of CEL methods. Cooperation and communication are necessary to achieve realistic training expectations. It is also important for management to demonstrate a belief in and commitment to the training. Depending upon available budget and training resources, a pilot program can be used to evaluate and modify the training and/or desired outcomes prior to launching a major program.

Impact of the Training

In addition to lowering costs and improved quality, the Materials Business received its ISO 9000 certification at three separate locations after their first evaluation. Remarks by the auditors following recertification speak to the strong team commitment to quality and the role of the CEL program in helping us achieve these results.

However, the long term benefits are in the attitudes of the people. At Saint-Gobain, teams are using consensus decision making, and team members are developing a personal desire to take ownership of their work. Since the implementation of CEL methods, employees have developed a shared sense of responsibility and teams have demonstrated an awareness of just how much they really can accomplish themselves. Hourly employees perform basic engineering tasks and complex financial calculations; identify process improvements and interact with outside vendors and suppliers. Teams review monthly budgets and financial statements to keep current on the health of their operations. In some cases, they prepare capital requests. CEL training has been fundamental to our current level of team and business success, and a critical tool for transforming the attitudes of our people by showing them what they are capable of doing themselves. Traditional classroom techniques alone could not have provided these results.

The Importance of a Thorough Needs Assessment

Pennie S. Seibert, Ph.D.

The experiential approach creates an atmosphere where the most powerful training and development programs will flourish. However, even the finest programs can be quickly reduced to a useless state of irrelevance if the programs do not meet the needs of the participants. Imagine a skillfully conceived training program titled *Computers and Performance* and further imagine that a large national corporation enrolled fifty of their employees in this program.

This group of employees differed dramatically in their experience with computers; indeed some had never even turned on a computer while others had designed sophisticated computer software. The first two days of the training program were devoted to experientially learning the basics of computer function. This approach was wonderful for the novices but it did not take long for the experts in the group to feel annoyed that not only was their time being wasted but so was their expertise. Why were the experts included in this group?

This example may seem far fetched, but it is quite common for organizations to commit errors such as this one that result in serious loss of time, money, and sometimes morale. The good news is that these types of problems are avoided when organizations engage in a thorough needs assessment prior to embarking on any training and development programs.

A needs assessment is the conscientious investigation to determine the specific requirements of both the trainees and their organization. It then defines the type of training and development program needed to meet these requirements. A thorough needs assessment is the critical first step in any training program and can be thought of as the insurance for successful training and development programs. The following discussion outlines a generic needs assessment procedure.

The Plan of Action

Create A Guidance Group

This group should represent the population targeted for training and development, those who requested it, and those affected by the outcome. In some cases all of these people will belong to the same group and in some cases they will not. For example, if the executive staff of a manufacturing company requested a training program for their line personnel, the guidance group could contain representatives from: (1) the executive staff, (2) line personnel, (3) direct supervisors of the line personnel, (4) and employees whose jobs are affected by the line personnel. The guidance group relates to the nature of the request, the scope of the training program, the range of needs within the target group, the effects the change will have on co-workers and the organizational philosophy regarding employee involvement.

The guidance group's role and mission includes: (1) providing input, (2) maintaining focus, and (3) facilitating the program's acceptance. The input provided by this diverse group provides a solid foundation ensuring that the needs of the target group will be accurately reflected. This input should include characterizations of both causal factors and expectations. The group's diversity also provides the expertise required to drive the data collection and to analyze and interpret the results. Finally, an appropriately formed guidance group dramatically increases the likelihood that the resulting training and development program will be widely and enthusiastically embraced.

Establish A Data-based Approach

Key here are the words "data-based." Training and development are essential parts of organizational wellness, so it is important to avoid the mistake of getting so enthusiastic over the *concept* and ignoring the *mechanism*. Successful needs assessments are based upon verifiable data rather than instinct or intuition (Cline & Seibert, 1993; Kaufman, 1987; Rosset, 1989; 1990; 1991). People routinely assume they know the needs of others. When carried to an organizational level, incorrect assumptions will compromise training program effectiveness. Relying on a verifiable data base of information increases the likelihood of program relevance.

Formulate Criteria and Goals

Ask a series of questions that will identify the criteria and goals that will drive the assessment process and its focus. Examples of questions are: Who is requesting this program? What is the attitude of potential trainees? What outcomes are you seeking? What is the scope of the need? Who is involved in this program? Do all of the trainees have the same requirements or is there variation within the group? Are the needs well defined at this point? Can one training program accomplish the goals or are several required? What are the time constraints involved? What are the financial constraints?

Research the Area of Concern

Familiarity with industry trends, organizational changes, competitor information and recent developments is imperative (Cline & Seibert, 1992; Kaufman, 1987; Schneier, Guthrie & Olian, 1988). These target areas can provide the background to develop a strong design. Written materials such as journals, texts, employee surveys and reports contribute useful information that will advance knowledge and prevent oversights. Other important resources for research are personal interviews, observations, and, of course, the members of the guidance group.

Identify Data Sources

The guidance group is an excellent resource for developing the sources of data collection. This can be accomplished by asking questions such as: what are the current strengths and weaknesses shared by the employees targeted for training and development? Are there individual differences? Are there special areas of concern within this employee group? Who can best answer these questions? Are the needs readily observable?

It is safest to approach each question or issue from more than one direction. In other words, do not limit the data collection to merely asking one person a question and ending there. For example, the people who perform a particular job may view their training and development needs differently from their supervisors. Multiple sources should always be sought along with reports and documents such as job analyses.

Design the Data Collection Format

A variety of data collection methodologies including interviews, surveys and group discussions provide a wealth of information. It is important to construct the areas of interest and formulate the approach for obtaining the information *prior* to actually gathering the data so that resulting information will be succinct, timely and relevant (Stowell & Smith, 1991). The task for the guidance group at this point is to develop the data collection format. Deliverables from this task include a listing of the interview and survey questions, a procedure for conducting the interviews, on-the-job performance observations and the agenda for group discussions.

Gathering Data

Buy-in is Crucial

It is essential that needs assessment participants are informed about the assessment process, have the opportunity to have their questions answered and feel comfortable with its potential outcomes. If the participants understand that the needs assessment is designed to find out what is needed to help them grow and develop, they are more likely to become positively and actively involved in the project than if they believe they will be adversely evaluated or even discharged if they do not answer in some artificially prescribed manner. If trust is not established from the onset, the data gathered will be worthless. Finally, it is vital to recognize and thank all of the participants for their contributions.

Interviews

Interviews of those who will either participate in, or will be affected by, the desired outcomes of the training and development program, are excellent resources for learning about the organization. The actual interview should be held in an uninterrupted block of time. The purpose of the interview and, if necessary, the assessment process, should be reviewed to establish a comfort level for answering the interview questions. The list of questions developed by the guidance group provides a framework, but should not preclude asking additional or clarifying questions. The interviewee may have important areas of concern that have not been addressed. Interviews are useful but subjective in nature, so it is important to use interview data in conjunction with data collected from other sources.

Observations

In certain situations, on-the-job performance observation provides additional relevant data for program design. For example, an organization seeking to improve skills of employees who regularly meet with clients might have observers sit in on an actual meeting with clients. It is essential that the employees being observed are not intimidated by the process. Careful assurance and reassurance usually mollifies this potential problem.

Group Discussions

This approach provides a format to involve a large number of people in the needs assessment process, and allows for gathering a wider range of information. An added benefit is that group discussions tend to elicit a sense of cohesiveness between members of the group as well as a feeling of commitment to the desired goal. An assertive, trained facilitator is recommended for group discussions to guarantee that the discussion goals are achieved. Glorioso (1991) provides the following helpful guidelines for group discussions: select a representative group, limit the number of participants to a manageable size, provide and follow an agenda, prevent one or two people from monopolizing or controlling the group.

Data analysis

Compile the Data

This can be a tricky part of the needs analysis. At this point there is a plethora of information in a wide range of formats. The guidance group should be used to divide the data into topic areas and to evaluate (e.g., describe, categorize, quantify) each topic area. Findings then can be organized into an integrated report.

Statistical Analysis

In most cases simple descriptive statistics such as mean, median, mode, and range are adequate to describe results. Inferential statistics such as Chi-square, ANOVA, T-tests, correlation, multiple regression, factor analysis and path analysis may be useful for comparing group scores relative to variability within groups, predictions and trends. This latter set of statistics are needed to provide necessary documentation for obtaining resources, and comparing program results (Bowman, 1987; Neuber, Atkins, Jacobson & Reuterman, 1980). The level of statistical analysis will depend upon the range of functions and outcomes addressed by the needs analysis.

Final Report

This report should be written in language that all readers can understand: omit jargon and spell out acronyms. The text should flow in a sequential fashion starting with a statement of the purpose and continuing with guidance group formation, methodologies, data sources, analysis techniques and results. The needs should be clearly defined, described, and justified. Charts and graphs are always helpful. This report provides the basis for decisions and recommendations about the type of training and development program, including specific areas of focus that will best address the needs of the organization.

Conclusions

A thorough needs analysis provides the necessary knowledge to select an experiential training and development program that will effectively satisfy the requirements of the organization and its individual members. Unfortunately, there are providers of experiential training programs who convince their clients that a one-shot, one-program-serves-all approach is appropriate. These providers may produce a fun and exciting experience, but relevance to organizational objectives is achieved only by chance. Participants return to work refreshed, but the actual needs of the organization are rarely met because the design did not utilize data from a needs assessment. In essence, the client is left with employees who may report a nice experience but no change, improvement, or growth that is beneficial to the organizational needs has occurred.

Thus, experiential training programs are most effective when designed in conjunction with a needs assessment. Beware of providers who claim that they can offer a program without the accompanying needs assessment. Rosset (1990) uses the analogy of sending a person into space without thoroughly researching what was necessary to get him/her there and back safely.

THE ART OF DESIGN: THE KEY TO MEMORY AND LEARNING

RODNEY NAPIER, PH.D.

As a young university professor with no training and little knowledge of either instruction or of the course I was designated to teach, I felt incredibly vulnerable and inadequate. I had been asked to teach a course in, of all things, learning theory. My only experience in this subject had been years before when I had taken what turned out to be one of the most boring and least memorable courses I could remember. But, as a new Ph.D., it was assumed that I would have no trouble teaching a group of thirty-five graduate educators. The problem was that I remembered virtually nothing from my past experience. Somehow the "learning" part of the learning theory had not penetrated. To make matters worse, the course was being offered for three hours from 4-7 on Thursday evenings after the participants had spent a full eight hours in school and several hours commuting. It was a disaster waiting to happen.

My response to the threatening situation was to do exactly what I had been taught in my own "learning theory course": to lecture on and on interminably about learning theory. After all, I was a professor wasn't I? And that is what professors did—lecture. It mattered little whether or not people remembered anything, or whether they were sleeping, heads hitting their desks in front of them. Nor did it matter that I lectured about research that showed conclusively that the *ability to remember information drops precipitously after the first fifteen minutes of talking and that at the end of an hour the ability to retain information virtually disappears.* The endless facts and inconsequential information kept pouring out even though I knew that half would be forgotten within a day, 60 to 75% in a week and 90% in a year. So, why bother? Because I was being paid to *lecture* and not to be effective. After all, I was a rather interesting speaker and that is what professors do. And remember, no one teaches professors about teaching, learning, remembering, change or personal impact. They are *content* experts, often linear thinkers paid to organize information, to transmit it and test for immediate rote retention without accountability for what students remember long term or, find useful.

Entering the World of Design

After some years, some professors become inured to dazed looks, pupils rolling back into heads, and people nodding off. For me that was impossible. It was embarrassing, no, humiliating, that I was carrying on the great learning charade that had been perpetrated on students for thousands of years. But, in order to change, I had to ask myself the most important teaching/learning question: What did I believe these students should actually take with them and never forget? Instead of thousands of pieces of irrelevant and often useless information, I would have to decide what was most essential and then create experiences which would be so memorable they wouldn't be forgotten even if they wished to do so. I would have to reframe my entire view of teaching. Of course, there would still be tests and the need to teach some forgettable material to satisfy certain course and/or university requirements. But, the difference was, I would now focus most of my energy on the facts, concepts and ideas which I hoped would be indelibly stamped into the minds of these students who were not such eager learners as a result of repeated unforgettable experiences that had been used to anchor their learnings up to this point.

The regurgitation of non-essential information has been a serious part of all our lives and continues to be even today. We talk about teaching students how to learn, but a test-crazed culture which values short-term cramming over long-term memory and application dominates our educational system from grade school through the most advanced graduate education. It is one of the central reasons why the education system is failing at all levels. Needless to say, the 600 page text on learning theory trivia and minutia I had used as an intellectual bludgeon over my early students gave way to more thoughtfully designed experiences which focused on essential concepts and applications. The dividends in motivation, interest and applied learning rose as "early memory loss" declined.

Design as the Key to Change

Learning is all about change, and about providing new choices based on new information and experiences. It is not about rote memorizing. It is about making a difference. Information is provided to promote new ideas, new ways of behaving, or clarifying, supporting and/or accentuating old views. Training (and learning), in organizations is, if anything, even more relevant, practical and applied.

The lines between information and action, between ideas and behavior are even closer. Using creative designs as part of the educational process enables people to internalize information in a usable form. The increasingly strong relationship between teaching and application has resulted in many training programs that are more creative and practical than the traditional high school or university education.

Recently, as part of an executive development course, I tried to impress a group of rather overweight, out of shape candidates for early coronaries that the quality of their lives and leadership could be enhanced dramatically if they were willing to commit themselves to regular exercise. Most of these "successful" people quite sincerely believed that they were too busy, that they didn't have twenty to thirty minutes a day for themselves and their rapidly deteriorating bodies. I could easily have talked for hours on the subject and knew that it would be to little avail. They would probably sit stone-faced, guilty, defensive and, above all, resistant (to change). My goal was for them to hear the information, to somehow internalize it and, hopefully, to give them a real opportunity to change and become healthier and more energized in their work and with their families after work. But, they had heard ad nauseam that exercise prolongs life and increases the quality of life for regular users. Any additional lecturing was bound to turn them off.

The challenge became what could we "design" which would motivate them to change. Without further talk, in a mere fifteen minutes, seven out of the eighteen people in the room had committed themselves to some form of regular exercise—and others were vacillating. In this context, "design" was a series of developmental activities aimed at moving the participants systematically toward the desired outcomes.

We asked them to come to the session in comfortable clothes for sitting on the floor or taking part in some physical activities. This peaked their interest and suspicion. They were divided into groups of three, with people they had grown to trust and told they would take part in four activities, none of which would take more than three minutes. They would be asked to compare themselves to others in their age group (national norms would be provided), and they would have the opportunity to measure their own performance in each of the exercise activities. The air was suddenly electric. *In one sense they knew we had them.* It was virtually impossible to defy such a simple request for information, and they expected that they would fall short—perhaps in their own group—and most certainly compared to the national norms. *They could make all the excuses they liked, but, the data would be in.* Suddenly, the learning was in their hands and not imposed by the "teacher" or authority. Also, the willingness to consider change would relate to the degree there was a discrepancy between their own image of themselves and the reality of the information they had contributed. But, most powerful in all of this was the "experience" they had in discovering just how limited they had become, just how far they had let themselves go. Interestingly, our fear of embarrassing them in front of their peers, was never mentioned. In fact, they were embarrassed for themselves in light of their own data.

By the time they had completed their test in push-ups, sit-ups, step-ups and stretching, they were much more open to considering the issue of balance in their lives and the simple alternatives available to them which could help them get back what they had so obviously lost. In short, they could read books or articles, listen to lectures, see films, but, nothing else would have provided the information they needed in a way they could actually absorb and accept it.

This is the art of design. It would certainly be easier for the facilitator or teacher to lecture "at" them. It demands less preparation, less creativity and, to some degree, less risk. But, the outcomes are less rewarding and the goals are far less likely to be achieved.

Developing a Design Mentality

For the teacher, trainer, facilitator or even a meeting leader, the key to increasing one's impact is to increase the ability to diagnose the needs of a situation, translate these needs into meaningful goals and to create an event or activity which will drive home the learning in an unforgettable way. The resistance to such logical efforts is enormous. Years after we have learned what good education is, professors and trainers refuse to come out from behind the podiums and "get creative." Years after we have learned how to run more engaging, productive and stimulating meetings, the great majority of leaders still plod through boring unproductive agendas wasting huge amounts of time and money. Taking the time to learn and practice the art of design pays huge dividends for those leaders and learners fortunate enough to experience the product of such efforts.

The Essence of Design

One reason why professors, teachers, trainers, and organizational leaders are unwilling to do more than impart information is that they are unskilled in "doing designs." You can read about baking a cake, have a hundred recipes at your beckoned call, yet, until you have gathered the ingredients, followed the recipe, risked failure and sometimes failed, you will never know how to actually bake that cake. People don't like to take risks, and certainly never choose to fail or to feel inadequate. They therefore remain in the comfort zone of low-risk mediocrity.

Even after experiencing a wonderfully creative, productive and successful problem solving design which has fully engaged a group, it is not uncommon for the leader and the participants to return to "business as usual." Not only does this keep them from having to be creative risk takers in their own leader roles, but it returns them to the high control, easy preparation and low contribution model which is acceptable. The cry from the "old boys" in the back of the room, "Hey, we're not going to do any of that small group junk are we?" is a cry for the status quo, and a cry for keeping the control of the meeting in the hands of the few loud voiced intimidators. After all, it is much easier to be a passive learner, a passive "participant" and a critic than to be involved in a process in which we are forced to include not only ourselves but others in the meeting or the learning experience.

Thus, leaders themselves and the participants often collude to insure that most teaching, training and meetings fall miserably short of their potential. At one great university, the president sets the tone for all management meetings. He refuses to utilize small groups, is disdainful of anything other than formalized meeting procedures and is unwilling to attend meetings of over two hours, since he is convinced that nothing useful could possibly be accomplished.

The concern is even greater since he runs the least productive meetings conceivable, receives no feedback and sets the standard for everyone else. The man is an extraordinary fund raiser, gives wonderful motivational speeches and has a fair share of wisdom. But, his ineffective design skills and limited expectations of meetings cost the university dearly in productivity, morale and candor. The irony is that he has been part of some thoroughly provocative, challenging and productive meetings which have been most effectively designed. But, they are not comfortable for him, for his style and presence and therefore, they are unacceptable. This example can be multiplied tens of thousands of times in all types of organizations.

The essence of design is helping to create an emotional connection to an intellectual problem or idea. It is the creation of an experience that engages us, moves us into action or new ideas, provokes a response, or, as suggested earlier, helps to internalize ideas or methods in a way that we won't easily forget. In organizations which are averse to risk or conflict and minimize fun, play and celebration, you will likely find little in the way of creative design. Effective designs depend on a climate of openness where the unpredictable is acceptable, where routine can be broken and where the needs of the moment can, on occasion, drive the agenda.

Finally, there is the need to recognize that the task or outcome goals of the organization are balanced with a concern for how work gets done. Thus, the "process" side of the work equation is, in most situations, as important as the product side.

To gain a greater understanding of the benefits of design, I will explore in depth a program where dynamic designs create a predictable outcome without becoming routine or stale. Enough possibilities remain at any point in time during the program to insure that those participating receive an experience that is spontaneous and, at the same time, consistent in reaching predetermined goals. Thus, this particular training program models the essential characteristics of any useful design.

How to Train Facilitators in the Art of Design

It is difficult to read about how to "design" a meeting or learning experience and then apply that knowledge. Then, how can we design a significant learning experience to train people in the art of design? Some years ago, we undertook this challenge and developed an intensive, total immersion training program called SGFIP (Small Group Facilitators Internship Program). During almost two decades, the workshop design has been tested again and again with consistent results. In a relatively short period of time, students walk away with the ability and the motivation to build creative and meaningful designs which can be used in their roles as managers and executives, classroom teachers, workshop leaders and therapists.

It was clear from the outset that the design of this program had to provide an intellectual understanding of small group behavior and create a trusting environment where people could test their skills and not be concerned with failure. In addition, the process had to enable participants to experience a wide range of "real" situations which would demand creative design interventions and allow them to actually practice using their new skills in these situations. This also meant that we would have to overcome the natural inclination of a group of facilitators, psychologists, educators and business leaders to perform for each other and to limit their willingness to be vulnerable in front of their professional peers. We were aware that many of the participants would translate their own need to avoid vulnerability into avoiding risks and the potential of failure. Thus, we predicted that many would revert to tried and true designs from their familiar "bag of facilitator tricks" which had somehow worked in the past. Such reliance on "canned" interventions is a sure road to mediocre meetings, workshops and classroom experiences.

Thus, the experience would have to stimulate the participants intellectually, challenge them diagnostically and test their design and intervention skills. In addition, it would have to provide specific feedback on their facilitation skills as well as their effectiveness as a member during the training period. In order to satisfy this tall order, we began the development of our program with a number of assumptions:

- The program itself had to be "real" and not composed of artificial role plays, simulations or other canned situations to which the participants would respond.

- Because the participants would normally represent a wide range of professional backgrounds and different levels of preparedness, we would have to create a level playing field in terms of certain baseline information if they were to succeed in such a challenging program.

- In addition to being "real," the program would have to be dynamic and intense so that the kinds of issues present in any group would surface and have to be dealt with by the facilitators.

- Finally, the program "design" would have to insure less dependency on the trainers and more responsibility on the participants than would be true in most classroom or corporate training situations.

A five day, off-site, total immersion experience was developed for sixteen participants. The first eight hours focus on a real problem solving experience that enables participants to develop a common language and some basic skills in relation to group process. They also learn about the fundamentals of "design" based on their experiences during the first five hours of the program.

By this point, individuals in the group have amassed an enormous amount of "unfinished business" that is waiting to be resolved and undoubtedly will have been avoided during the early stages of the new group formation. This is due, in part, to unresolved conflicts generated in the previous activities, differences in style (euphemistically called personality conflicts in most group settings), lack of clear goals and any number of other annoying realities which now influence the fledgling community. Since they have previously identified their personal and organizational goals for the five days together, they are now in a position to proceed with the critical design element of the program.

The names of the sixteen participants are placed in a hat: two names are drawn. These two individuals are asked to develop the most appropriate "design" possible for the group given its goals and current needs. The design itself must be original and reflect the reality of what has transpired during the previous eight hours. While the rest of the group takes a thirty minute break (or has dinner), the two erstwhile facilitators undertake a quick assessment (diagnosis) of the group, and, in the limited time available, design the most creative and effective intervention possible. They are told that at the end of 2½ hours their design will be critiqued by the rest of the community in relation to:

- appropriateness of their goals given where the group started
- perceived strengths and limitations of the intervention itself
- effectiveness of the facilitators' behavior
- kinds of problems and support experienced during the design period

After the thirty minute critique period which also focuses on group and individual learnings, two new names are drawn from the now infamous hat, and these two individuals have the opportunity to design the next 2½ hour session based on the standing goals of the group, the unfinished business and current needs of the group at this point in time. Again, they have thirty minutes.

This format continues until midnight approximately 24 hours later. By that time, every participant will have designed at least one 2½ hour session. During that period, it is predictable that nearly every issue that has ever faced a group will have been explored as a result of the diagnostic and intervention efforts of the various facilitators. Issues surrounding power and authority, control, trust, interpersonal conflict, diversity (racism, sexism, etc.), group goals, intimacy and a variety of other problems are typically addressed. The deprivation of sleep tends to shorten patience and increases the willingness of the group to "deal" with the issues which are acting to reduce the group's effectiveness. During the process, groups tend to develop a natural closeness resulting from shared risk taking, mutual support, and their newly realized ability to resolve issues that are usually avoided in most organizations.

The most compelling feature of this approach is that group members are actually able to take part in a wide range of creative designs derived from the needs of widely differing situations in a short period of time. At the end of the marathon, the group still has three full days to experience a number of other challenging designs which can be transferred to a wide variety of back home situations. As the group continues to develop as a community, new opportunities present themselves for additional designs, theory and discussion.

The final day of the program is devoted to a single activity which incorporates all the elements of effective design (diagnosis, design activity, intervention/presentation). The sixteen participants are divided into four groups. The four members of Group A are asked to consider each of the individuals in Group B and develop a thumb nail sketch of each person's strengths and opportunities for development as a trainer/facilitator/leader, based on how they have been perceived during the past week. In light of this assessment, they are to "design" an unforgettable event for each individual in Group B in a manner they believe will provide each with significant learning. Each event, which can take from five to fifteen minutes, must be perceived as a gift of insight and experience. Groups C and D are also creating design interventions for each other.

In most cases, the designing group creates an event for the person which must be responded to rather spontaneously. At the end of the experience, the four designers share their predicted "recipient" response to the challenge of the event itself. In the meantime, the four members in Group B are designing their unforgettable events for each of the members in Group A. The underlying assumption is that the success of any design is influenced tremendously by the leadership exhibited by the facilitator. If leaders are willing to ask people to experience the designs they create, they should be open to understanding their own impact and learning how to improve their own behavior in these roles. The trust and support which has evolved during the week long workshop enables these personal interventions to be extraordinarily free-wheeling, candid, dramatic and humorous. The entire design requires almost eight hours and demands in microcosm, the same skills and sensitivities that are present in any design situation.

Basic Rules of Design

The example of the training program in "design" incorporates several basic principles applicable to many carefully choreographed design initiatives whether in the classroom, training workshop or business meeting. While the following are not meant to be all inclusive, most will help insure greater success and can be a guide in a variety of situations.

1. *Taking a system view*: Every design situation should be looked at from the perspective of what has preceded the event, what is to follow and what developmental steps need to occur in the design itself to help move the participants toward the goal. It is rare that even thirty minutes is taken to design most meetings or that "tough" questions are asked to frame the meeting being planned. For example, most agenda-based meetings give little attention to how ready people are to deal with a particular topic, whether the level of trust is present to overcome differences, whether unresolved conflict will prohibit candor and honesty or to effective utilization of information, knowledge or skills. The success of the above marathon demands that the facilitators develop a diagnostic view and consider the consequences of past actions before designing the next period of time.

2. *The critical nature of the initial event:* In the training event explored above, it was essential to create a climate of shared risk while on a *level* playing field. Initial resistances, defenses and projections must be factored into the initial event so that fears, inhibitions and past history and routines do not set the stage for the predictable participation that hinders so many groups.

3. ***The rule of disorientation:*** A wise old Turk once said, "When in doubt, disorient, disorient, disorient." People become victims of predictable and often boring routines which can influence attitudes and behaviors in virtually any meeting or group. It takes some courage and a bit of creativity to design an event so that such patterns are minimized. Predictable examples include physical set up of the meeting room, participants sitting in the same places, discussion dominated by the same few, or standard agenda regardless of the needs of the group.

   It is the leader's role to disrupt non-productive patterns, to change existing norms, to be unpredictable so people are less able to anticipate and thus, manipulate events to serve their own purposes. The simple introduction of the marathon changed everything that would occur after that point. One does not have to be as severe as this, but, creating a climate of unpredictability forces people out of old ways of thinking and acting.

4. ***Designing for process as well as task goals:*** We are a society obsessed with getting things done, with quick responses, with action and moving ahead. Often this is done with little consideration of the factors which might be getting in our way and inhibiting our success. Thus, designs are created for task/product outcomes, for getting things done with little worry about the process or the means. It is the process of a current situation—the feelings and attitudes generated from how people work together—which will be carried into the next event or job. The quality of participation and involvement, the ability to resolve tactical as well as interpersonal conflicts, and being concerned with peoples' feelings about how business is being conducted, extend beyond task/product needs. Some of the design goals must focus on this critical process domain.

   With time virtually always limited, the first thing to go is anything having to do with building relationships. The price paid for the unfinished business residing in most groups shows up in issues surrounding morale, productivity, trust and efficiency. Designing for and dealing with here and now issues before they fester and undermine group effectiveness, is a key aspect to achieving a successful outcome.

5. ***Building in time for celebration, ritual and fun:*** As the design mentality develops, consideration is given to factors which unify a group, stimulate participation, and build a sense of team spirit. While fun and play can often evolve spontaneously as a group works together, celebration and rituals must be designed into the life of a group. Some organizations have developed norms which support the building of humor and fun into meetings as a change-of-pace, to revitalize the group and allow natural fun and play to have a positive outlet. During the marathon, the participant trainers had to maintain interest and the ability to perform under severe conditions. At times this demanded creative activities which could motivate, stimulate and challenge the group. Under normal conditions, some of these same needs are present and should be addressed through inspirational events or creative activities.

6. ***Endings as Beginnings:*** Just as beginnings set the tone and can influence the outcome of a meeting or workshop, so too, endings are often critical. All too often the deterioration of time and energy come together and result in mediocre endings without proper consideration of next steps, follow-through, the celebration of success or the nature of relationships at the end of the session. Unfinished business can have a lasting influence on morale, motivation and the willingness of participants to honor commitments.

Conclusion: The Tough Questions of Design

Leaders who are concerned with creating effective meetings, educational experiences, workshops or activities must take the time and effort to ask a series of tough questions. Then they must devote additional time to design the appropriate response to the information they have gathered. Finally, they must implement the design effectively. This is a far cry from fixed agendas, lectures and artificial simulations or case studies.

It demands time, skill and patience and the courage to move beyond what is easy and comfortable. But, done well, the payoffs in morale, productivity and overall performance will be worth the effort. Following are some of the tough questions which should be considered by those willing to undertake the discipline and planning required for an effective design:

1. Who's coming and what are the agendas they bring?
2. What unfinished business exists which should be addressed before the group can move ahead?
3. What are the task and process goals?
4. Does the group need to have additional information or education?
5. What level of involvement needs to be addressed in order to best utilize those present and to maximize interest as well as the ownership of eventual outcomes?
6. How can time be used as a critical tool in the event being designed?
7. What creative design strategies can be used to challenge and engage the group fully in the process?
8. Are there norms, attitudes or even individuals which could hinder the ability to achieve the goals? What designs can be used to solve these hindrances?
9. What is the best way to use the available physical space?
10. What predictable patterns or expectations could limit the ability of the group to achieve its goals?

EFFECTIVE FACILITATORS

RITA MILLER AND MARY TEETER

A Philosophy for Guide/Facilitators

You may have heard the expression "You can't just talk the talk, you've got to walk the walk" (source unknown), and an old Sufi adage, "Between saying and doing lies the ocean." Good experiential trainers have "walked the walk" and navigated the ocean.

A guide invites others to share in the walk while knowing that the oceans have depths they have not yet explored. They need not complete their journeys, yet they can point the way and witness their progress, and the progress of others. They encourage the effort and celebrate its existence. Facilitators provide safety and encourage participation. They have a good sense of identity and a working knowledge of the experiences at hand, the activities, participants and methodology. Two questions are always in mind: (1) Is this experience good for the individual and (2) Is it good for the group? Good facilitators require good faith, good sense, humility and flexibility; and above all, they must respect the trust placed in them and "proceed with the process" accordingly.

Boundaries for the Guide

The guide's experience is markedly different from that of the participants, and must not be forgotten. The boundaries that define roles and responsibilities include:

1. The contract between the guide and participants: a set of expectations and rules regarding guide and participant behaviors. It sets up exclusive tasks that belong to the guide, the participants, and defines shared tasks. For example, the guide presents the activity, sets up the guidelines, and defines the goal. The participants take the risks and provide the means to the goal. The guide provides safety elements, assesses and acknowledges and predicts.

    In a "design team" approach, the guide or facilitator meets with the client one or more times prior to the program to determine the group's readiness, the organization's needs and goals, and the relevance of the designed exercises as customized by the design team. Thus, the responsibility for these factors is shared by both the client and the guide.

2. Time: Participants are encouraged to be in the present, focusing on the task at hand and each other. The guide's sense of time includes an understanding of the group's history (via a needs assessment), the application to the present, and the anticipation of the future (Is the group ready? Are the roadblocks useful and manageable? Will the journey be safe?). These questions are the exclusive territory of the guide and will determine much of the guide's input in the experience.

3. Appreciation and awareness that the journey belongs to the participants: The guide's emotional connection to the participants should be one of encouragement; that is, if the group does "well" they receive the credit. If they don't do well, the guide and the client together bear the responsibility. This is a partnership approach to training and development.

Elements of the Journey

The facilitator, with client's input, has to establish "why we're doing what we're doing." There has to be a reason why people are to scale an eight foot wall, do a role-play, rappel a forty foot cliff or walk blindfolded through the woods. Many times, in the beginning design stages, these reasons or goals may be broadly defined, such as "team building" or "boosting confidence." The facilitator must clarify the specific behaviors desired (goals) and match the activities to these goals, while considering the physical, emotional and intellectual risks for the participants. For example, it may not be a good idea to take a group on a five mile trek through the woods in ninety-eight degree weather. We actually did this in one of our early forays into adventure-based experiences. Thankfully, there were no injuries or casualties, but even the facilitator ended up sitting in a creek to fend off sun stroke! So when it is time to "get the show on the road," the facilitator should mentally pack:

1. The *direction* (goal) of the journey.
2. The *activities* that are compatible with the goal.
3. The participants' *potential to attain* the goal.

Participant Perceptions and Reactions

Regardless of the activity taking place, it is the perception of the participants and their reactions that are the most valuable parts of the experience. Periodically, the facilitator must check the perceptions of the group, encouraging the sharing of ideas, feedback and respect for the differences that are expressed. Individuals need to be acknowledged for their efforts, both physical and intellectual, and celebrated for their participation.

The facilitator must keep in mind that it is natural for people to feel anxious in any new situation, and every experiential training program is a new situation. The facilitator can help people take charge of their anxiety by providing opportunities for participants to reach out to each other, master a skill, and/or use humor to relieve tension. One way to accomplish this is through the "Partner Introduction" exercise: Each participant chooses a partner not well known to one another and they talk together for a few minutes. Then each person is asked to introduce his or her partner to the rest of the group. Not only is this a good ice-breaker, it also gives each person a way release some personal anxiety and self consciousness by focusing on another person.

Another exercise which relieves tension is "Do a Favor." Each participant name is written on a small piece of paper and thrown into a hat. Each person then draws a name from the hat and keeps it a secret. The challenge is to do a favor for that person sometime during the day's experience without letting that person know it. At the end of the day, people can either try to guess who the secret partners were or the partners can reveal themselves. Again this allows people to channel anxiety in a positive direction with uplifting outcomes. And through these exercises and opportunities for feedback, the facilitator can stay in touch with the internal perceptions and reactions of the group.

The Guide's Development

A good facilitator needs to know the difference between content and process, similarities and crucial differences between people. Facilitators must be objective, acknowledging personal roadblocks in order to make unbiased, non-judgemental observations.

Facilitators should be skilled in listening beyond the words. Sometimes what people say and what they do are totally different. The facilitator needs to take note of how people behave. A verbal "That's okay, I'm fine," with a facial expression or voice tone that shows fear or anger should be apparent to the facilitator. The discrepancy must be addressed in order to maximize the learning potential of the activity. However, the facilitator might decide to make a mental note of the non-verbal response, continue to observe that person throughout the day and check in and on that participant later. The facilitator engages the participants in a process and helps them learn to trust the process to be useful to each individual as well as to the group.

The Responsibilities of the Guide

The responsibilities of the CEL guide range from the ordinary to the extraordinary. The emotional, physical and intellectual safety will affect the success of the experience for the group and each individual.

Physical safety

For those CEL endeavors involving a moderate degree of physical activity, instruction, demonstration, and modeling of physical safety procedures must be in place immediately, at the group's first gathering. Physical safety is based on the activity, the condition of participants and the goals of the program.

Intellectual safety

The participants need to feel that they can discuss information and knowledge without being judged. The transfer of learning, such as negotiating win-win situations, is a key program objective. Ideas are actively solicited and encouraged with a group ethos of exploration rather than censure. How the experiences and material will relate to business issues, and how to transfer that knowledge back to the work-place are primary goals.

Emotional safety

How people *feel* about the experience determines much of the outcome and affects retention. If people dislike or feel threatened by the experience, the skills learned will not be transferred back to the work-place. The following are the basic emotional safety guidelines for group training.

Emotional Safety Rules

1. No personal insults, name-calling, labeling or "put-downs."

2. If negative feelings arise, each person is responsible for "owning" their feelings and expressing them in the best interest of the group's welfare. The guide is responsible for determining the place and time for this.

3. The group is to be "confidential"; that is, people may share their *own* experience outside the group but other group members have the right to privacy.

4. All group members have equal (emotional) status. This is a monitoring function of the guide who is to structure and model inclusion behaviors.

5. No alcohol, drugs, or assaultive behavior.

6. Physical contact between members is by *mutual consensus* for *cooperation* and *camaraderie*, i.e., slapping hands (or "high fives") for congratulations or support.

Establishing the goals

The guide is responsible for articulating the established (attainable), goals for each experience. These goals and methods are determined by client and facilitators before the program and must be clear to everyone involved. It's the guide's responsibility to match the goals to the experiential program journey.

Characteristics of Effective Facilitators

1. Quality program design
2. Initiative
3. Sense of Humor
4. Reaches out to people
5. Uses highly participatory style rather than lecturing
6. Self-disclosing
7. Respects Differences
8. Non-judgmental
9. Direct communicator
10. Enthusiastic
11. Flexible
12. Good processing/debriefing skills

Defining the emotional climate—or up-up and away

The emotional safety of participants is extremely important. The emotional climate is the responsibility of the group itself, including the guide. The guide must be positive in approach by identifying and supporting each individual's participation and effort. This is "building on the positives". Criticism is absent with emphasis on the efforts rather than the "problems." (Pollyanna, of children's literature, was probably the first experience-based facilitator.) Participants are "invited" to try and "invited" to join and are included at whatever rate or level of involvement they can manage. The group in essence becomes the "I think I can" model of effort and mastery.

On the track—parceling and pacing the journey

Now that the guide has taken great strides to have everyone "buy-in" to the process, the experience has to proceed. The guide needs to match the goals to the time allotted and the ability of the group. Juggling these elements affects the choice of activities and the pace of accomplishment.

Each group evolves its own unique pace and style. The guide must support and modify this so the pace remains constructive. As the group gains in confidence and experience, increased control of the tasks and pace can be assumed by the participants. The guide supports the goals of inclusion, cooperation, physical safety and the positive emotional climate, responding to the group's readiness to increase shared responsibility. This enhances participant confidence and mastery individually, and as a team. Each new activity builds on skills learned and adds new levels (of skill), for the group and the guide. The guide needs to support, modify skill requirements, monitor time constraints and group size, in order to maximize the intended effects of the experience.

Nearing the end of the journey

Wrapping up or saying good-bye (as in a "one-shot" program or at the end of each session in a training series) is one of the most important aspects of the group experience. Depending on program design, one of the guide's tasks is to place the experience in a framework based on reflection and review. Participants can share whatever part of the experience will be useful for them. Feedback is requested, given and received in a supportive fashion. Each participant is acknowledged for their place in the experience.

Responses to past experiences also need to be addressed by the guide. Physical reactions such as fatigue, emotional reactions such as euphoria and "letdown" should be included in the "framework." It is what the participants feel that determine the usefulness of the training. It is vital that people leave with specifics regarding the application of their knowledge and experience to their jobs. Part of the debriefing should also involve discussions around how to implement learnings on the job and how to reinforce commitments to change behavior in the work-place.

The Providers of Experiential Training:
A Customer Perspective

Rosanne Ryba

Will experiential training meet your company's developmental needs? Even though accepted professional standards require a needs analysis as the basis for training and development programs, anecdotal evidence suggests that most experiential learning providers do not conduct them. As the following story illustrates, the decision is often based on a significant personal experience, rather than on a professional analysis of the organization's needs and goals:

> Tom Burns, the Marketing Vice President for a division of a Fortune 500 company, returns from a personal development program full of enthusiasm and insight. This experiential program was recommended by a friend; and now Tom, with the zeal of a convert, is recommending it for his company. Tom's enthusiasm is contagious. Soon the company is buzzing about his experience and how it has changed him, both personally and professionally. Suddenly, he's more participative in his management style and more sensitive to people's personal needs. He is bursting with creative ideas and encouraging everyone to "think out of the box" and to "go for it" by taking more risks.
>
> Tom eagerly assumes the role of champion for the program. He taps into his own budget and takes a small group of executives and managers, including the President, to the program. Upon their return, they report the same sense of personal accomplishment and growth and something more: a strong bond between one another. Everyone can see that this group has undergone a transformation. What was once a group of co-workers now appears to be a cohesive and committed team. With the President's support, a program involving all employees is launched.

No doubt, the company and the employees will benefit from the program.

Though no company wants to stifle the enthusiasm of a Tom Burns, a more rational, well-planned approach would not only help "sell" the program to the few (often vocal) skeptics, but would also maximize the return on investment in experiential training by ensuring that the program's design meets the company's specific needs. In most companies, the Training Department can identify training needs and evaluate the appropriateness of experiential training. If a company is too small to have such resources or lacks the expertise, an external consultant can conduct a needs analysis. A less costly approach is to form a task force, including HR, Training and line representatives; and charge them with identifying, evaluating and selecting the best approach, provider and program to meet company objectives.

If the company does not have existing data on training needs, the task force may decide to conduct a formal needs assessment, but there are other less costly alternatives. For example, a series of focus groups, including potential participants as members, will help identify training needs. Key executives' and decision-makers' opinions regarding the company's developmental needs are crucial and will also serve as a means to gain their buy-in.

The company's vision, mission statement and strategic plan can also provide valuable information about where the company wants to be and may suggest training needs.

Assessing the Experiential Training Option

What type of input, information and data would support the decision to conduct an experiential program? If the training needs cannot be met by traditional classroom training methods, experiential training may be appropriate. If attitude and behavioral change are primary goals, nothing works better than practicing those new behaviors and examining attitudes through experiential exercises. If building cohesive teams, team-based experiential exercises give participants a psychologically safe opportunity to work in groups and examine appropriate group behaviors. What better way to enhance creativity than by experiencing creative thinking and problem solving first-hand, with your team?

Research and personal experience as learners indicate that adults learn best by *doing*. Experiential learning is thought to be something avant-garde, but actually, it's quite commonplace. Some everyday examples include cooking classes, high school keyboarding classes, tennis lessons, and driver's education. While reading and lectures may enhance such training, most of the learning takes place through actual practice.

Learning the behaviors, skills and processes we use in business should be no different. Experiential training programs generally provide a psychologically safe environment for learning, the opportunity to shorten the learning curve through practice and facilitation, and promotes a deeper level of learning which transcends the purely cognitive processes of typical training programs.

Considering Corporate Culture, Norms and Values

Most experiential training programs are founded on a core set of values which include: respecting and valuing the individual, valuing diversity, believing in the power of teams and personal empowerment, creating trust and open communications, and facilitative leadership. If corporate culture is not aligned with these values, an experiential training approach may not be appropriate. However, if attempting to change the existing culture to one more closely aligned with these values, an experiential program can jump start and help sustain the change effort.

Today, many companies are facing competitive challenges which require a new way of doing business. That new way includes working in team-based, as opposed to hierarchical, organizations and pushing decisions down to the lowest, most effective level; making decisions through consensus; creating an environment which fosters empowerment and risk-taking; and partnering with the company's stakeholders (i.e., suppliers, unions, employees, and customers). If a company is facing such challenges, experiential programs can help to create the commitment to change, launch the change process, and build the muscle which will sustain the change.

A word of warning: do not undertake a major experience-based change effort if leadership is not seriously committed to change. If people open up to the possibilities of empowerment, teamwork and trust, and don't "walk the talk," the results will be disillusionment, anger and frustration. With a new sense of personal empowerment, an employee may even choose to leave the company.

Finding the Right Provider

One of the best sources of information about providers may be the corporate library, local college or university library. A literature search service can also conduct a search on experiential training. A brief review of the literature will provide the names of companies who have undertaken experiential programs and potential providers for your program.

Begin by contacting companies in your industry or related industries. Most people are more than happy to share their experiences and their endorsement of a provider is invaluable. Once a contact is made, ask for the names of colleagues within their company or in other companies who might be willing to talk with you. Before you know it, you'll have a substantial list of contacts. Follow-up and keep notes including their comments and recommendations for later analysis. There are also organizations such as local chapters of the Society for Human Resource Management and the Organizational Development Network that might provide additional information.

In order to narrow down the choices, assess the compiled contact comments and select three to five providers who appear to have good references. Contact each provider and request literature about their services, approach, philosophy and programs. Also, if outdoor adventure components are being considered, ask them to provide a list of clients and their safety record. Follow up with any additional references they have provided and review their safety record (you may want to check with their insurer as well). Most importantly, their philosophy and approach must be aligned with your organization's needs and culture.

Provider track record, experience with clients in a particular industry or geographic region and the cost of services are all considerations which may help narrow the choices. Arrangements should then be made to meet with representatives of each provider.

Ensuring the Right Match

How do you ensure that the provider selected is right for your company? First, analyze your face-to-face meeting. Did they inquire about and listen to your needs? Or, did they try to sell a packaged program? Did you feel that this was a collaborative meeting where your desired outcome was explored, or a sales pitch? Assuming that you are considering a long-term relationship with substantial investment of time and money, you want a collaborative relationship and a product that is tailored to fit your specific needs. If a provider is resistant to either, they're not for you!

Before making a final commitment, be sure to meet the person who will be responsible for designing and delivering the program. It is critical that your staff and the provider's key staff are able to work well together. One company coordinator recalled her relationship with the provider's project manager. From the beginning, "Henry" built a relationship of trust with her. He listened to the needs and desires of the company's project team. He worked to incorporate their ideas into the program and to ensure their needs were met. He shared his experience and skills with her and showed interest in her professional development.

Years later, she still considers Henry a mentor. This mentoring relationship may be somewhat unusual, but strong relationships between provider and project team often develop. At the very least, the provider must be a good listener and teacher. The provider and the project team must also share the same vision for the experiential program. They must be committed to the achievement of that vision within the company's broader vision. In summary, the key to ensuring the "right match" is a shared vision and a collaborative relationship.

Cost Considerations

Hopefully, you will find more than one provider who at least initially appears to be a good match for your company and your needs. However, there are other, more practical considerations you must address. No one has an unlimited budget; so, of course, cost is a consideration. It should be balanced against the quality of the provider's work, which can be judged on the basis of feedback from former clients, and the quality of the proposal. Cost will vary with the scope and length of your program and remember to include other cost factors, including location (travel requirements), lodging, food and related expenses. Be sure all the cost factors are fully disclosed before making a final decision.

If the provider is coming to your location or a conference facility, request an estimate of their expenses including materials, cost of diagnostic instruments, preliminary research or data gathering costs and charges for design or preparation work. How are the charges presented: flat fee for the training project, per day charge, or per attendee rate? Clarify all of the incidental costs so that you will be making a logical and fair assessment of the bottom line cost. There should be no surprises.

If the cost is outside the range of your budget, be open with the provider. Together, you may be able to find ways to cut costs without significantly impacting the program. For example, consider moving the location or shifting some of the administrative work to your company. Often, providers are willing to negotiate fees if, in return, there is a strong potential of a long-term relationship.

Experiential training providers' fees vary widely, but generally are comparable to sending a manager to a conference or outside seminar, and, if designed correctly, there is a much greater return on the dollar. In considering cost, remember that it is not just an expenditure, it is an investment in the company's future and employee development.

Finding "Common Ground"

It is critical that the selected provider understands and supports your company's goals and values. If you are in the midst of a change process and/or are using the program to promote change, it is essential that the provider believes in and supports that change process and your company's vision.

In many cases, the provider will help the top management team develop a vision and will design the program to introduce and communicate it. The provider should partner with you to achieve that vision. The story of one company is a good illustration of just how this can happen:

> The company, a start-up firm, had been working with an outside consultant to develop its vision, strategy and organizational structure. Their vision had been communicated and was fully supported by the employees. The company requested that the provider's project team meet with a team of employees and their consultant to identify the company's needs and co-design the program. Without hesitation, the provider agreed. During the meeting, the provider's project manager listened carefully and showed enthusiasm and excitement about the vision. They committed to make the vision a central

theme of the program and were willing to tailor the language, models and metaphors of both the program and printed materials to the vision. They also tailored the evaluation form to meet the company's needs and even used the company's colors on posters and other printed material. These willing concessions (though inconvenient for the provider), clearly showed support and "buy-in" of the company's vision.

Perhaps even more importantly, the company's vision, which stressed employee empowerment, facilitative leadership and a customer focus, was congruent with the provider's values. This common ground was used to develop an excellent experiential program and forge a lasting partnership.

Creating a Win-Win Contract with a Shared Vision

True partnerships require that both parties approach their relationship with what Stephen Covey calls a "win-win" attitude (Covey, 1993). The relationship with a provider is no exception. Creating a win-win contract with a shared vision should be the foundation of your partnership.

But, how to create a win-win contract? Again, as Stephen Covey suggests, start with the end in mind. What do you want to achieve? What is your vision of how things will be once the experiential training program and appropriate follow-up is completed? How will things be different? The two parties must be of the same mind in answering these important questions. There must be a shared vision or work together to create one.

A win-win contract must also benefit both parties. The client must define what benefit, or value, is desired. It may be a behavioral change, perhaps increased cooperation and teamwork, more creativity or risk taking, a renewed commitment to the customer. That behavioral change may also translate into bottom line savings, increased sales, improved customer satisfaction, and other measurable results. Part of the win-win contract should include a clear statement of your expectations, the results and how they will be measured.

The provider has expectations, too, including payment for their work within a certain time frame. (Don't forget that, though many providers are committed to very humanistic values, they still need to make a living!) It may include co-owning any materials or exercises created together with the right to use them with other clients. The provider's expectations may also include safety requirements, relationships with other consultants or subcontractors, use of the provider's facilities, and other practical matters.

The contract should also include expectations concerning level of participation, commitment to attending the program from beginning to end, level of involvement from top management, and commitment of human resources from both parties. Administration of the program(s) must also be clarified. Who will do what? Who selects and notifies participants? Who administers any inventories or follow-up evaluations? Who handles travel, housing and other living arrangements? And, what are the costs if the provider handles some of these administrative tasks or provides facilities, materials and housing? There should be no surprises.

The essence of a win-win contract is a shared vision, clear expectations, and no surprises.

Who are Your Partners?

Especially if the experiential training program is part of a major change effort, it will truly be a team effort. The first step is identifying who should be on the team. The organization's internal organizational development or training and development group bring a unique understanding of the company's culture, values and norms to the table and can provide valuable skills in organizational diagnosis, program design, and facilitation to the team. In the case of one large division of a major corporation who used classroom-based experiential training in a major change effort, the internal staff worked with the provider from the very beginning, from program conception and design through delivery and follow-up. The faculty of the program consisted of equal numbers of provider facilitators and internal facilitators. Their involvement was clearly a factor in the program's success.

Outside consultants with special knowledge and understanding of the organization's culture, values and norms, may also be valuable members of the team. In the start-up company case cited above, the consulting firm participated on the design team with considerable success. Such a team member brings not only valuable skills but also a more objective view of the company and their needs.

Ideally, the provider should staff the project team with professionals who have an understanding of your industry as well as significant experience and skills in experiential training. A key team member should serve as project manager for the provider and should bring expertise in both program design and delivery to the team. A team leader from the client company should be selected to provide needed coordination between all the partners.

A "champion" from top company management should provide leadership to the team. While they may not be involved in the nitty-gritty of program design, they should provide direction and insight. They should be involved in delivery, perhaps opening up the program with an inspirational introduction to the vision.

One consideration about program team composition should be diversity—diversity of experience, background, gender and race. This is especially relevant when the company has undergone, or is planning to introduce, a change program to increase awareness and appreciation of racial, cultural and gender diversity.

Numerous providers and clients report that one of the by-products of this type of training experience is a greater appreciation and acceptance of diversity, even when such change is not part of the design. Faculty provide a positive model for the participants, a model of men and women with diverse backgrounds working together as an effective team.

Designing the Program Together

As a first step, the provider should visit the company and become familiar with its culture and business climate. Relevant information including your vision for the future should be shared. The project team should clearly define the current state of the organization (or the work unit) and the desired future state. The design should unfold around the question, "How do we use an experiential training program to get where we want to go?"

There are a number of ways to approach the answer. First, review the provider's existing training materials and programs. With some tailoring, they may meet your needs and, thus, keep design costs down. With a thorough familiarity with the company and its change needs, the team should be able to select appropriate exercises or modules. For example, if the company is moving from one which traditionally rewarded internal competition among sales representatives to "team selling" which requires cooperation, an exercise which focuses on competition versus cooperation (and teamwork), would provide a metaphor for the desired sales team behavioral changes. Events such as a "low or high V," where two people must work together to successfully cross cables (a ropes course element) might also be appropriate. Though less dramatic, a simple ball toss exercise which first sets teams up as competitors, then shifts the paradigm by making "winning" dependent on cooperation can succeed very nicely in meeting program objectives.

Of course, experiential exercises can be designed that specifically fit your organization's needs. One approach used by many companies is the simple skit, created by the participants, reflecting the issues facing them through dramatic role playing. One firm facing a problem of communication across major offices, created a "newspaper" for a regional retreat in which all the offices contributed. They followed-up with skits, modeled after news shows, that dramatized where each office would like to be in three years.

The design team should list the existing options and brainstorm new ones; evaluate the applicability of each option and select exercises which address their needs. Then consider the flow of activities, how the exercises "fit" and compliment one another, and the mix of discussion, in-classroom activities and outdoor exercises. For example, for a three to four day retreat, it is helpful to do some work early in the program focusing on the vision, norms and values of the group. If using an outdoor ropes course and going for impact (the big "unfreezing") designed to increase risk taking, you may want to do the course early on, perhaps the second day.

The most important aspect of any program or exercise is how it is "framed", or put in a context that is meaningful for the participants and applicable to their corporate reality.

Creating this context may take only a few minutes or hours depending upon the complexity of the exercise and context. This must be carefully planned by the design team. The facilitators should have a clear understanding of the exercise's relevance to the company, the participants and the behavioral change (or "ah ha!"), they are trying to stimulate. A key concept should be presented which is easily grasped and remembered by the participants and reinforced in the "debrief."

After the exercise, the facilitator should conduct a debriefing with the participants. The success of the debrief is critical to the success of the program and participants' learning. It takes a skilled facilitator to draw out the participants reactions and feelings about the exercise. The facilitator's job is to observe the activity and note behaviors which reflect "old" behavior and desirable behaviors which reflect the new values and norms adopted by the company. During the debrief, the facilitator poses questions which encourage reflection upon their own and team mates' behavior during the exercise and sharing observations and responses to the exercise with the group.

Much of the learning in experiential programs takes place during the debrief. Therefore, it must be planned as carefully as the exercises themselves. How do you plan something which depends on the participants' spontaneous behavior? First, be clear on the objectives of the exercise. Fashion your questions around the behavior you are trying to model. Second, anticipate the behavior of the participants. How will they behave and what questions should you ask to provide insight into their behavior? Finally, how have other groups behaved in similar exercises? How did the facilitator successfully draw out discussion around their behavior? The team can then provide the facilitators with a good understanding of what behavior to expect and how to facilitate it. Keep in mind that flexibility must be built into every exercise, including debriefing.

Sometimes there are surprises in CEL, no matter how carefully planned. Sometimes from those surprises comes the most profound learning. When the design team has selected the exercises they wish to use, designed the "frames", scripted the debriefs and planned the classroom activity, they need to step back and look at the program as a whole. Does it fit the time allotted? Does it flow? Does it allow time for reflection for the participants? Is there some fun built in? Most importantly, does the program meet the objectives? If the team can answer these questions in the affirmative, the program is ready to go!

Collaborating on Delivery . . . Tweaking as You Go

At this stage, the design team often becomes the delivery team, or faculty. The design team must decide how company (design) team members will participate. Are they part of the faculty, or are they participants? It is difficult to do both.

This decision should be based on the company team members' relationship to the participants, their own training needs and desires, their skills, and what is best for the participants overall. Especially when a program is designed to increase commitment to a new vision and teamwork, the company team members should participate if they are part of that particular section of the organization. If they are in-house consultants, such as members of the internal HR or Organizational Development Group, it may be better for them to be part of the faculty.

Their participation as faculty provides a number of benefits: they hone their facilitation skills; offer broader and deeper insights into the company; and enhance organizational learning through the transferred knowledge of the provider facilitators. If the program is to be rolled out to numerous groups over time, the company may benefit from design team members and other key employees attending as participants and later becoming members of the faculty for future sessions. These same benefits will accrue from such an approach.

The "champion" or leader of the organization also has a role in the delivery. The leader can be key in introducing the program. His or her vision for the future, and encouragement of the program's success as a catalyst in achieving that vision, should be communicated. There may be opportunities throughout the program when it is appropriate for the leader speak to an issue or provide strategic insight. The leader's role in closing the program is also important and should provide a transition back to work and home. From the outset, the leader should work closely with the design team to script his or her role and respond spontaneously to the participants' issues and behaviors.

Throughout the program, the faculty (including the design team members), should meet frequently to evaluate the progress of the program and be ready and willing to "tweak" the design. These brief meetings provide the opportunity to learn from experience with the particular group and use that learning to refine how events are framed and debriefed. It may also become necessary to make adjustments to time allocations for subsequent activities. This flexibility is crucial and can make or break a program. In one actual half-day program, the design team decided on some short exercises that demonstrate this flexibility:

The first was a *Birthday Line-up*. In this event, participants are instructed to line up in order of birth month and day, without speaking. This is generally a simple exercise after which the debrief focuses on the difficulties of non-verbal communication. Two major twists in this exercise resulted in a considerably longer and more complicated debrief: the group's inability to assimilate three latecomers into the exercise without intervention by the facilitator, and a "quality check" spontaneously performed at the end of the exercise to make sure they had lined up correctly.

The first incident sparked conversation around what it was like to be a new employee in this company and the difficulty of assimilating and feeling part of the group. The second resulted in a discussion around levels. Usually "quality assurance" was done by experienced, high-level managers. In the exercise, a junior manager stepped forward and took the initiative. He received total cooperation from the participants and made some last minute changes which made their efforts successful. The discussion centered around what it was like to feel empowered, as if level didn't matter, and one could do whatever was thought to be the right thing. If the faculty had been committed to sticking to the original design and schedule, this valuable discussion would have been cut off. Instead, they allowed the discussion to continue and, after closure, called a brief break, came together and decided to cut one exercise which had focused on empowerment and levels. As a result of this flexibility, the program was a big success.

At another program, the facilitators noticed some joking among the men about the women in the group—good natured but somewhat annoying to the women. The facilitator responded to the group dynamics and opened up a discussion on the women's achievements throughout the program and how they had broken down stereotypes about their ability and courage during the ropes course. A number of the male participants noted that they would never think a woman was unfit for a job back at work just because she was a woman. He noted the real bravery he had observed in the women on his team who had pushed beyond their limits both on the ropes and in the classroom. While the discussion lasted longer than scheduled, it was valuable in that it resulted in both meaningful learning and a closer bond among team members.

The closing of an experiential program requires a good deal of spontaneous facilitation and last minute adjustment. Before the closing, the faculty should meet with the organization's leader to discuss the high points and the significant learnings that occurred during the program and plan to recognize these points in the closing. Any rituals that had been planned, such as a group wave or bestowing of a symbolic gift, should be examined to ensure its appropriateness. The leader's role in the closing the meeting should be evaluated for its timeliness and meaningful content.

The flexibility we have discussed does not mean a loose or ill-planned program. On the contrary, a well-planned program should be open to change and allow for flexibility. Such an approach creates a challenge for the faculty which can be fun and exciting, and maximizes the chances that the program will be meaningful to participants and successfully meet its goals.

Evaluating the Results

Most providers conduct a participant evaluation immediately following an experiential program. This often consists of a generic evaluation form requesting feedback on the program's effectiveness and impact, along with suggestions for improvement. These evaluations are often sufficient for a one-time, short program. However, if the program is repeated for other groups, or if the program is of significant duration (with the hopes of effecting major change), a program-specific evaluation form may be more appropriate and revealing. The design team can work with the provider to develop one. A drawback of a unique evaluation is that it cannot be compared to other groups participating in the same or similar programs. If such a comparison is important, the provider's standard evaluation form may be useful.

Conducting a subsequent follow-up evaluation, perhaps in three to six months, is also an important tool. While evaluations immediately following programs are generally favorable, longer term follow-up can provide valuable information about the long-term impact of the training.

One company found that their immediate results were highly favorable. Participants reported a significant personal impact as well as increased commitment to the company. Six months later, while the personal impact was still significant, the commitment to the company had decreased. This was further reinforced by the number of people who had left the company. On a closer look, the company concluded that the employees, newly "empowered" by the experiential program, had indeed received lasting personal benefit. They were more willing to take risks, more confident in their abilities to meet challenges, more open to new ideas and possibilities. However, the culture of the company did not change as rapidly as some of the participants. As a result, there was greater dissatisfaction with the company and in some cases, participants chose to leave. This is meaningful information for the company to consider when designing future programs.

Experience shows that long-term positive evaluations result when the company offers follow-up programs and undergoes significant cultural change which is in line with the program objectives. If the program is designed to support the company's vision and the company is serious about achieving that vision through cultural change and employee empowerment, the probability of positive long-term impact is increased.

The Importance of Follow-Up

Christopher Roland
Mario Kölblinger
Leonard Diamond

Studies on transfer of training programs to the work place indicate that all learning outcomes of a training course are in vain, unless the company is prepared and willing to apply the newly learned skills and behavior of the participants (Gist, Baretta, Stevens & Kay, 1990; Baldwin & Ford, 1988; Roland, 1981). If training programs are relevant, then these transfer factors are taken into account and the connection is made between experience-based training and follow-up activities.

Concentrating the majority of resources and efforts on the preparation (e.g., needs analysis; design) and implementation of CEL, with little regard to follow-up or maintenance, compromises the opportunity to optimize outcomes at the target of all training: improvement in the workplace.

Many training and development programs need to be journeys, i.e., processes rather than programs. The process begins with a needs analysis, proceeds to a review where all team members agree on specific needs, and then continues with a design for a relevant and meaningful program. Once all of the preparation is completed, the experiential program begins. If the program has been well-designed, including a specific follow-up strategy, then the stage is set for the transfer to the work setting.

A number of effective strategies can be directly tied to the outcomes desired by the client. Ideally, the first follow-up should take place within one month following the initial program.

Before discussing follow-up strategies, it is necessary to understand how an initial program can set the tone for follow-up. One type of initial program design utilizes *learning partnerships* (McCauley, 1994). The formation of these partnerships provide an "anchoring" mechanism back at work. An "anchor" can be a colleague at work, one in whom trust and confidence can be placed, and who understands what is needed to become more effective in the workplace. The anchor reminds the employee to routinely practice new behaviors at the workplace.

These dyads can be created randomly through an activity, or in the event that the client desires specific pairings, the partnerships can be preassigned. The objective of the learning partnership centers around developing levels of trust which will enable each partner to share with the other, and through their experience, have a frame of reference from which to rely on each other, i.e., to become that crucial anchor for one another.

The strength of each partnership can be enhanced through careful sequencing of the activities where partners are given time together for sharing thoughts on specific issues or questions. Examples of activities and focus areas which are commonly used to reinforce the learning partnership are presented below:

The Partner Walk:

Partners are asked to take a ten minute walk and interview each other for five minutes. Focus questions given by the facilitators can include: a little known fact about oneself, a personal and/or professional goal or a statement about expectations of the training program.

At times, the partnership may be given an assignment for which it must develop a single viewpoint. For example, they may be asked to bring back or create an object which represents their organization today. This information would be shared with the group during the report back. This type of activity would be used early in the program to help participants get to know each other on a different level, and to build the dyad relationship.

Trust/Support

In preparation for a trust or support-building segment of a particular program, partners are asked to discuss a work-related and/or personal trust or support issue with each other. They are told that each will have an opportunity to share their thoughts in a subsequent activity if they so choose. Following the partnership discussion, a variety of trust exercises can be facilitated, with each person sharing some work-related thoughts regarding this topic. The goals of these activities are to create a safe environment for participants to share pertinent business-related issues. Often an ancillary benefit is increased trust and support within the group.

Action Planning: Commitments and Accountability

Near the end of a program, in preparation for the follow-up step in the learning process, partners are asked to take a fifteen minute walk to begin developing an action plan that may begin with:

- ◆ Something that each will do differently when they return to work in support of a training program goal or team discovery.

◆ What each partner will do to hold the other accountable for honoring this commitment.

◆ Help needed by the individual from the group in carrying out the commitment.

Following the walk, the group is taken to an activity where each partnership discusses its commitment, the process of holding each other accountable and the group support needed for this to take place. This type of activity provides powerful metaphors for the individual, partnerships and group. Consideration should be given to documenting each commitment on a flip chart and/or on film for use by the client during follow up.

Teaming partnerships continue into the follow-up phase of the program in several ways, including:

1. Follow-up workshops, an essential link between the initial CEL training program and application to the work place, connecting elements of looking back with elements of looking forward. These workshops provide a good indication of how the group is working together and offer opportunities to address new areas of importance or concern. Often, the workshops are helpful in recalling the experiential, challenging atmosphere during the initial program while addressing skills, knowledge and behavior.

2. If a new member joins the group (a frequent occurrence), further experiential exercises will acquaint the new member with the process as well as integrate the new member into the existing team. If outdoor exercises were a part of the original program, then the new member should have an opportunity to experience similar activities. This is an excellent opportunity to let the "novices" catch up with the "experts" while allowing the experts the chance to pass on their knowledge. This mutual process of empowerment is an obligation of the whole team and together they organize this learning process.

3. If action plans were developed during the initial program, they must be reviewed during follow-up. Did participants follow-through on their commitments? In other words, did they "walk the talk?" If not, why not? What are the obstacles, the rubs, the roadblocks, the show stoppers?

   Were learning partners successful in reinforcing commitments? Action plans are not easy—they require constant monitoring, revising and following-up; and in order for plans to become operational, participants often need to discuss additional personal, team and/or organizational requirements.

4. After the initial follow-up session, additional workshops can take place as needed. Off-site sessions involving a series of indoor/outdoor exercises help to experientially evaluate progress towards goals, commitments and action plans. The design for these sessions is developed from participant feedback and management review.

5. Videotaping of initial training is an excellent tool to use during one or more follow-up sessions. It can set the tone, getting participants in the right mood

(emotive framing), recalling memories, experiences, togetherness and success. This is especially pertinent for outdoor adventure CEL programs in order to focus on single key experiences, refreshing and demonstrating examples of success and avoidance, and reviving teaming contracts.

Playback of the videotape can be used during the opening and warm-up segments of the feedback session, and as refreshers for positive reinforcement of particular training and transfer subjects. These issues could be the focus of deeper insight and maintenance of newly learned skills and behavior.

6. If the initial program was evaluated by an external evaluator, using reliable instrumentation (in place of "smile sheets"), the quantitative data generated can be shared with the group, supplemented with anecdotal participant (and possibly subordinate and superior) reports. Ideally, the time between pre- and post-testing should be at least three months.

7. One area that is frequently identified in the initial program is creating more effective meetings. Consultants are asked to observe selected meetings and give feedback regarding the meeting process. In some cases, the consultant will co-facilitate one or more meetings.

An example of how a common CEL strategy is transferred to the work environment is the concept of "check-in." During experiential programs, participants often become accustomed to checking in with each other regarding their "mindset" at a particular moment. Involved/not involved, attending to the task at hand, "spacing out," allowing/not allowing outside situations to interfere with the thinking process, etc. are focus points that participants often utilize when checking in with each other. This type of check-in is uncommon in the corporate meeting room; however, when this new behavior is transferred to the meeting room, the response is often positive.

8. There are other areas that are often identified as areas needing attention such as time management, understanding and working with a variety of personality styles, teaming styles and negotiation. Specialized workshops can address these needs.

9. After attending the initial program, participants sometimes realize the need for additional feedback regarding individual leadership styles and methods. As part of follow-up, consultants are available to provide one-on-one coaching over a period of time.

10. Community projects: Executive work teams become involved with community projects that demand a great deal of teamwork, leadership, etc. Facilitators work closely with the team by facilitating discussions regarding progress with the community project as well as applications back at work.

11. Train-the-Trainer (TTT) programs are becoming popular for transferring CEL skills to the work place. The programs are offered by many CEL providers, and vary greatly in content and length. One model that has proven successful involves three phases.

Phase One: The training team participates in a one or two day CEL workshop in order to experience the activities and processes.

Phase Two: The actual five day Train-the-Trainer program including a full range of modules consisting of Theory & Models, Needs Analysis, Facilitation Process, Experiential Exercises (using equipment that can fit in a duffel bag), and follow-up strategy design. Additional time is allocated for each participant to practice a few experiential exercises while being videotaped; during evening sessions, the videos are reviewed and each person receives feedback from peers and facilitators.

Phase Three: Each participant co-facilitates with the CEL consultant in a stand-alone experiential program or an existing program (e.g., Creative Problem Solving) in which experiential exercises are integrated. Depending upon the success of this initial program and the trainee's comfort level of design and facilitation, other co-facilitation sessions may be required or, in some cases, the trainee can go "solo."

12. A simple follow-up strategy often used to maintain the momentum is the phone call. "How's it going?" "How are the action plans coming along?" "Can I be of any help?" are questions that take only a few minutes. Even when an organization does not contract for follow-up, a phone call one month after an initial program speaks highly of the provider. "These guys are really interested in the outcomes of that experiential program!" is a comment that can resonate throughout an organization.

13. Informal team support networks. Shared challenging experiences, successfully overcome obstacles, the emergence of a team spirit and growing awareness of mutual needs in a team are a good foundation to implement an informal support network. It builds on the development of a safe and comfortable environment in which to share sensitive business issues and could become a common ground on which to base further personal intentions and connections.

This is particularly advantageous for those teams whose members are widely dispersed throughout the corporation, in different departments and/or different locations. Under these circumstances, a well maintained network is an important link to the company and often a valuable link for consultation. Informal support team networks focus on pursuing private and professional intentions and objectives. They provide additional resources (mainly informational), across hierarchies, departments, locations and countries. Not all superiors take a favorable view of networks as they sometimes tend to elude formal structures and official channels.

Network activities can begin on the last day of an initial or follow-up program during the development or refinement of action plans. After a short introduction about the benefits and potential of networking, the participants are asked to draft an outline of their network, which is enriched and refined during the interval between the initial training and the follow-up workshop. This leads to a lot of interaction among team members and is part of the networking process. The new network is open to other networks and teams in the company, in particular to those groups that have been involved with experiential learning. Typical tasks of establishing a network are: Vision, mission, strategy and name of the team support network; establishing an inventory of material and non-material resources.

In order to bridge the gap between the classroom and the workplace, it is imperative that various customized follow-up and maintenance strategies are implemented. "Relapse Prevention" (Marx, 1992) should be a theme from the very beginning of the process; participants need to be keenly aware of the potential for relapse and to identify situations in which they may not be able to maintain their new learning (Gibson, 1994). Used wisely and frequently, follow-up methods will minimize relapse while maximizing transfer. Many decision-makers question whether sending employees to a one-, three- or five-day experiential program will really get the "biggest bang for their buck." Without follow-up there is a good chance that they won't. Participants, even though energized and committed to change at program's end, will relapse to old ways without the reinforcement of follow-up processes.

Chapter Four

New Applications

One day, multiple day and wilderness-based programs are considered the more popular experiential training applications. But, as Chris Clements pointed out in her "Indoor/Outdoor" article, CEL does not necessarily need to be a "stand alone" program. This chapter introduces examples of how experiential methods can be integrated into three popular training and development areas.

Chuck Wolfe explores how corporate culture change can be enhanced through experiential learning, using well-designed and facilitated experiential events. However, he points out that experiential training and development may not be helpful **by itself.** He agrees that CEL must be integrated with other, often traditional, training environments and training techniques.

Iris Randall discusses how experiential learning can be integrated into many traditional training techniques to influence and (perhaps), accelerate participant learning and awareness of cultural diversity. She points out that one of the key reasons for using experiential training is to increase participation and involvement. In other words, experiential learning is not expected to be **the reason** for changed attitudes and behaviors regarding diversity, but a means to increase attention and awareness, enabling more traditional techniques to be more effective.

Finally, Ron Lewis from Ottawa, Canada shares the Canadian Police College design of specific experiential activities as part of a five week leadership development curriculum. A train-the-trainer program using an outside consulting/training firm, enhanced and reinforced trainers' design and facilitation skills.

Corporate Culture Change Applications

Charles J. Wolfe

The most significant learning is profoundly simplistic, i.e., experiential learning, as part of an overall plan, can be an extremely powerful tool for facilitating a change in corporate culture. This paper reviews several definitions of corporate culture and then cites several real life applications where experiential training contributed successfully to a corporate culture change. The summary focuses on the lessons learned from these successful experiences.

There are many ways to describe corporate culture change. Deal and Kennedy (1982), describe culture change as behavioral changes throughout the entire organization. People identify new role models, tell different stories to explain what is occurring around them, and spend time differently on a day-to-day basis. This time might be spent calling on different accounts, asking different questions, and carrying out different work rituals. Examples of a change in culture might include becoming more customer or market focused or more cost effective.

Athos and Pascale (1981), describe corporate culture change using a "**Seven S**" model of management. At the heart of the organization—and the first "S"—is *Superordinate Values*. These are the values that represent the behaviors and actions that are rewarded in the organization. To change subordinate values, the organization must plan and implement strategies for each of the other six S's:

Superordinate Values

Strategy	Style
Structure	Skills
Systems	Staff

The first three are designated as "hard," while the last are "soft." The authors theorized that the reason for Japanese companies' competitive advantage was primarily due to their effectiveness in addressing the soft S's.

Bolman and Deal (1991), provide a set of frames for viewing and changing corporate culture: structural, human resource, political and symbolic. The *structural* frame represents the organization of the company. Effectiveness, i.e., accomplishment of the established goals, is achieved through coordination and control of authority, rules, policies, standard operating procedures, information systems, meetings, lateral relationships and a variety of informal techniques. The structural frame provides a business rationale for producing degrees of predictability and efficiency. This frame describes the segment of organizational life that Athos and Pascale call the hard S's, i.e., strategy, systems and structure.

The *human resource* frame adds the dimension of the interplay between organizations and people. This frame focuses on peoples' skills, insights, ideas, energy, and commitment as the most valuable resources of the organization. Ideally, organizational practices, policies and systems enable employees to maximize their individual potential while contributing to organizational goals. The unfortunate reality often is that organizations are so alienating, dehumanizing and frustrating that human talents are wasted and human lives are distorted. Often, experiential training can reinforce the positive aspects of an organization's culture as well as point out its deficiencies. The human resource frame appears to describe the soft S's in the Athos and Pascale model, i.e., skills, style and staff.

The *political* frame views organizations as political arenas that house a complex variety of individual and group interests. These interests are often defined as coalitions relating to various departments, hierarchies, professional groups, unions, gender and ethnic subgroups. Differences may be seen in values, preferences, beliefs, information, life philosophies and perceptions of reality. Important organizational decisions are often about the allocation of scarce resources. Goals, decisions and resource allocation are often achieved through bargaining and negotiation of different coalitions.

The *symbolic* frame is represented by the different stories people tell about how things happen and what appears to really matter to senior management. It is not what happens that seems important, but instead what it means. Given that the political frame describes coalitions and individuals as having different perceptions of reality, the same event may have very different meanings for different groups. During very uncertain and ambiguous times human beings create symbols to resolve confusion, increase predictability, and provide direction. Although events may actually be random and meaningless, people tend to give them meaning so that there is some semblance of rationale to their surroundings.

> "The symbolic frame sees the rush of organizational life as more *fluid* than linear. Organizations function like complex, constantly changing, organic pinball machines. Decisions, actors, plans, and issues continuously carom through an elastic and ever changing labyrinth of cushions, barriers, and traps. Managers who turn to Peter Drucker's *The Effective Executive* for guidance, might do better to study Lewis Carroll's *Through the Looking Glass.*" (Bolman & Deal, 1991, p. 245)

Together, the political and symbolic frames represent the first S in the Athos and Pascale model, *superordinate* values.

Application of Experiential Training to Change Management

The application of experiential training to meaningful organization change must occur within the broader context of an overall organizational plan.

> "Our finding that training programs, regardless of how personally powerful, do not change organizational behavior is reinforced by previous research that points to serious problems in the transfer of learning from management training to the job. These programs simply do not affect enough elements in the system-roles and responsibilities at work, the boss, rewards, and structure, for example to change organizational behavior." (Beer, Eisenstat & Spector, 1990, p. 33)

Beer, et. al., find that in order for experiential training to be successful, program design must recognize systematic changes. Those professionals conducting experiential training who request meaningful information regarding the context for such training beforehand, are at the high end of the quality continuum. When CEL is planned to help change a culture, the internal politics must support the proposed changes or, at least, be neutral. The organizational structure must support, or be in the process of changing, to support the changing behaviors. The human resource policies, practices and systems, along with symbolic events must be aligned to maximize the experiential training's contribution to corporate culture change. Several overviews of successful outdoor experiential programs as catalysts for changing corporate culture follow.

Example 1—Improving Customer Focus

In an insurance company undergoing a restructuring, based on improved customer-focus, senior management requested an experiential training component to facilitate a smooth transition. Internal and external consultants planned the program by considering what organizational information was necessary to ensure meaningful transfer of learning to the work place. Each participant was interviewed, as were senior managers, in order to understand the part played by each of the Seven S's in organizational change. Individually, participants were asked to describe their understanding of the coming change, its structural components and what politics might be at work. These questions helped to ascertain the roadblocks that might interfere with the success of the change efforts. The data was analyzed, summarized and presented to members of the design team which included the consultants and the senior members of the team who were to participate in the workshop. When the strategy, new structure and systems were aligned with the style and skills being addressed in the workshop, the training began.

The training generated rave reviews from the participants immediately following the workshop. And, more importantly, there was noticeable improvement in key working relationships. The re-structuring took place as planned, and the organization improved their customer-focus and its *bottom-line results!* The vice president of sales reported that customer survey results improved and employee morale was raised. Two years after the workshop, it has become part of the symbolic frame, i.e., one of the stories told in the organization symbolizing the meaningful change that occurred.

Example 2—From Competition to Collaboration

Two groups in the same company often found themselves competing for the same business in the marketplace. In the past, the groups were isolated by organizational structure, and the respective heads of each work group had made little effort to cooperate. Although the overall corporate strategy suggested that the organization would become more prosperous through collaborative efforts, the existing reward system and structure recognized only competitive behavior. At times, customers of both groups complained about being confused by having different representatives from the same company calling on them. For the company, the worst situation occurred when the two groups competed against each other for business with the result being lower returns than might otherwise have been expected!

The CEO announced a corporate cultural change effort encouraging cooperation as a means to achieve higher profitability and an increased return on equity. Although no plan was in place to address the structural or political issues that created the competitive behavior, the groups decided to focus on the symbolic frame; that creating more teamwork on their own might achieve some meaningful level of success. They worked with an external consultant designing a three day outdoor experiential workshop emphasizing the power and synergy that could be realized through teamwork and individual risk-taking. The results were immediate: the lessons transferred back to the work place and the teams achieved a level of cooperation not thought possible prior to the workshop. The results were not as dramatic as they might have been had there been a strategy in place to re-align the structure; but nevertheless, the workshop, like the one before, has become part of the company story telling and continues to be seen as a turning point in company culture.

Example 3—Plans Not Implemented

A very recent example took place with an intact management team responsible for one line of business. Like the others, this workshop was designed collaboratively with members of the management team and a group of consultants. The team from the line of business was very wary of any off-site experience. For the past two years they had held off-site meetings, producing many action plans that were never implemented. The concern was that whatever took place would not have any lasting impact. There were issues regarding major differences between the two leaders of the line of business, significant relationship issues between key members of the department and major concerns regarding raising expectations. The consultants were internal, with some knowledge of the department and its members. They offered several options:

1. an experience designed to directly confront issues that had been problems within the department for some time;

2. structured relationships skills workshop with some experiential elements customized to address internal issues indirectly; and

3. a relationships skills program without any customization to deal with internal issues.

The design team selected the second option; viewing the workshop as a beginning. If it was successful they were willing to move to a higher level of risk-taking.

The workshop dealt powerfully with interpersonal relationships. The consultants and design team decided that the workshop could be strengthened by conducting pre-workshop individual interviews with all workshop participants. The interviews related to relationship issues among the participants, all of whom were members of this line of business senior management team. The facilitators would build in experiential exercises to address the themes that emerged in the interview process. The workshop exceeded all expectations! Participants carried the new lessons learned back to the work place and demonstrated an ability to cooperate with one another in ways unthought of before.

Experiential training helped change the skills and styles of the individuals to be more supportive of one another and of corporate, rather than department goals. The symbolism associated with an off-site program in a campground environment broke with established patterns of training in hotels or in company headquarters. Typical office politics are difficult to continue in light of the experiences and learning that often result from outdoor experiential training. However, unless the context of the structural frame and business rationale is supportive, these events are usually doomed to failure. The individuals will gain useful knowledge from an experiential training experience, but the culture can not be changed by training alone, no matter how powerful.

Summary and Lessons Learned

In Example 1, the marketing area had an overall plan in place to change its culture to become more customer focused. The training was designed to give people additional skills and to create a bonding experience among affected departments. This marketing department has been highly successful in accomplishing its cultural change as evidenced by quantitative and qualitative evaluations by its customers.

In Example 2, the corporation had specific goals in mind but plans were the responsibility of the various market segments and business groups. The experiential training was one example of a planned event supporting the CEO's cultural change efforts. Its success was limited because the structural and political frames were not changed.

In Example 3, the culture change was never stated formally as a goal. The experiential training was conceived as a beginning effort to assess the possibilities. This group continues to work on additional plans for a more cooperative, customer-focused culture. Here, experiential training provided a vehicle for individuals to believe in themselves and one another, and an impetus to move forward.

With so many organizations changing their cultures, it is likely that carefully crafted experiential training will be used more extensively as a tool for cultural change. The ability to transfer learning from an experiential training experience to enhance cultural change efforts is tied to a quality design effort, highly talented consultants/facilitators and the readiness of the organization.

Cultural Diversity Training Applications

Iris Randall

Pioneers

Early entrants in the field of managing diversity spent most of their time educating upper management in how to think about diversity. This was especially true when it came to the new work force demographics and its impact on corporations. These were the facts behind the movement, the reason companies were willing to pay "big bucks" to have someone help them understand what the demographics meant. Although many companies listened, few were willing to make the commitment required to bring about change.

Upper management held meetings; officers and staff were enlightened and, although reticent to admit it, some were even frightened. The demographics indicated that soon they (white males) would be in the minority. After the initial manager awareness sessions, most companies opted to either use their own training department to bring awareness to the balance of the organization or did nothing, feeling that management enlightenment would be sufficient. It wasn't.

During the past six years, new technology has entered the work place and quality programs (e.g., TQM), have been initiated; but neither the technology nor quality initiatives have been able to address the "isms" that continue to plague the work place and undermine these programs. It is clear that something must be done.

The Solution

The solution is that not only must people be educated, they must also learn the skills required to manage differently. To do this they must first learn more about themselves, about others and how to enhance their interpersonal relationships. This is what makes *experiential* diversity training so important.

Experiential training is effective because learning environments are created. Structured experiences require high participation and interaction. In any seminar, at any given time, probably 1/3 of the participants are *tuned out*. However, in an experiential exercise, participants can't be passive. Everything, from the discussion to the debriefing, involves every participant both physically and emotionally. Each participant becomes both teacher and student.

For the first time those in power can begin to understand what it is like to feel unempowered. Those who have often felt disenfranchised now begin to understand what it means to be in a position of strength. Diversity training allows people to empathize. Although we can't fully experience someone else's situation, we can try to see from another's perspective. This effort is critical.

The Learning Cycle

Experience helps one move around the learning cycle: from concrete experience, to reflection, to testing, to theory. This accelerates the ability to allow another person to be different, to have a different set of values and goals, to react differently to same situations, to use different problem solving methods, to behave differently. The ideal is not to necessarily agree with everyone, but to have positive regard for one another.

Another reason experiential diversity training works is that it is fun and we learn more when we are enjoying ourselves. For some, standard seminar training can be a bore; make it enjoyable, and it will be memorable and welcome. It is also more likely to be put into action by participants.

How Does Experiential Learning Differ from Other Forms of Training? What is Included in Experiential Exercises?

Experiential learning is inductive learning and what is to be learned cannot be exactly specified beforehand. The objectives of the structured experience must relate to questions in each participant's mind. Therefore, it is best to state objectives in terms such as "to explore . . . ," "to examine . . . ," "to study . . . ," "to identify . . . ," etc. The goal of this first stage of the learning cycle is to develop a common data base for the discussion that follows. Whatever happens in the activity (expected or not) is part of the information to be processed in the next stage, critical analysis. Almost any activity that involves either self-assessment or interpersonal interaction can be used as the "doing" part of experiential learning.

When to Use Experiential Learning

Integrate experiential learning during different phases of training to facilitate learning. Short exercises like the *Birthday Line-Up* are very useful in creating understanding, taking no more than 7-10 minutes depending upon the design and group size. They are often best used early in the program or prior to a break so that conversations can continue informally.

> **Birthday Line-up**
>
> Participants must line up by birth month and birth day without talking or writing. The activity should be done in silence.

It is important to consider the mix of exercises needed to teach the skills required to manage diversity. A blend of low involvement and high involvement activities work best. The following chart details training initiatives relative to participant involvement. For example, reading is a low interactive activity while case studies (discussed in a small group), are a medium interactive activity and a structured experience such as the *Blind Partner Walk* enable high interaction and involvement. Some issues call for low involvement while others call for high involvement.

The Trainer's Tools

High Involvement

Intensive Growth Group
Structured Experience
Instrumentation
Role Playing
Case study
Participation Training
Discussion
Experiential Lecture
Lecture
Reading

Low Involvement

For example, experiential lecture is more involving than the traditional lecture because it incorporates activities on the part of the audience. Interspersed among the sections of content are brief interactions among participants. These are designed to personalize the points of the lecture and/or to generate readiness for the next topic. A survey on demographics, both of the nation and the organization, is an experiential activity: each person answers the questions individually and then as a team. The answers to the survey are presented on overheads or slides while all participants check their scores. This way, presenting demographic data becomes interactive.

A planning model helps customize training. First, determine the participants' learning needs. This is best accomplished during the needs analysis. Two good questions to ask are: what observed behavior would you like changed, and how will you know if the change has been accomplished? Answers to these questions and others, determine participant needs. Then the Learning Cycle and the Interactive Chart are used to create appropriate learning environments that focus on individual behavioral change.

Be aware that almost any activity involving either self-assessment or interpersonal interaction can be used as the "doing" part of experiential learning. The goal is actively involved participants, not as passive listeners.

Congruence and Flexibility

Both congruence and flexibility must be part of the program design, as well as the qualities of instructor and participants. A congruent person is aware of him/herself, aware of actions, feelings, and is able to communicate that self to another person in a straightforward manner. A flexible person is not dogmatic, opinionated, rigid or authoritarian. This awareness of instructor and participant actions enables the instructor to move the program along at the participants' pace.

To be successful in experiential diversity training (or build a learning environment), the facilitator must first understand his/her own personal prejudices. This is crucial in order to help others understand theirs. Everyone has biases and it is the responsibility of the facilitator to move participants from *judging* to *understanding*.

Adequate processing of all diversity training experiences is extremely important, so that participants can integrate learning without the stress generated by unresolved feelings and/or lack of understanding. Knowledge and comfort of the facilitator becomes crucial at this point, in order for the experience to be relevant to the learning and emotional needs of the participants. Facilitators must be confident in their ability to process emerging data. Participants' needs and the facilitators' competence are critical components of all experiential exercises.

Debriefing

After the activity, participants are ready to share what they experienced during the event. The purpose in sharing individual reactions is the benefit gained by the group from each individual's experience. During this step, main points are clarified. Simple methods often work well and include:

◆ Asking for observations and comments in a free-association go-around.

- Small group sharing; generating lists such as a double-entry: "What we saw/ How we felt."
- Posting and round-robin listing; total group input recorded on a flip chart.
- Interviewing each other and asking the "how" questions about the activity.

The debriefing process is critical to the success of experiential exercises. This step must be thoroughly designed and then processed before proceeding to the next activity. It cannot be ignored, must not be rushed and should evolve from the information being shared. Using the Blind Partner Walk as an example, a number of relevant questions can be asked:

- What did you learn about your partner while he/she was blindfolded?
- What did you learn about yourself while you were blindfolded?
- How did you take care of your partner during this exercise?
- What did you need to be effective as an individual, as a partnership?
- What were some examples of trusting each other during this activity?

Blind Partner Walk

A blindfolded participant is taken for a walk by a sighted partner, who has been instructed to provide a safe ten-minute experience. This activity is done in silence. Upon returning to starting area, participants switch roles.

The next critical step is the relevancy step; connecting the exercise to real life circumstances. Participants focus their awareness on situations in their personal or work lives that are similar to those in the activity just experienced. Their task is to abstract from the exercise some principles that could be applied "outside." This makes the structured experience practical, and if it is omitted or glossed over the learning is likely to be superficial. Some debriefing strategies for connecting experiential exercises to real life circumstances include:

1. Guiding participants to imagine realistic situations at work and to determine what is applicable from the experiential activity and debrief. How this relates to organizational culture, unwritten rules and new employee adjustment will give impetus to a very active discussion.

2. Writing statements from the debriefing discussion about what is "true" about the "real workday." This works well after a role play, fish bowl or structured improvisation of a real life situation. Each person enters that situation and takes responsibility for its outcome.

3. Using the 70/20/10 rule. This rule states that 70% of the information they glean from what they already know, 20% they learn from each other and 10% from the facilitator. They review in writing "What I already knew," "What I've learned from watching others" and "What I learned from the facilitator."

Particularly in diversity awareness/management training, it is important that topics such as "leadership," "communication," and "feelings," be discussed for potential positive generalizations. One helpful exercise calls for participants to complete the sentence "The effectiveness of our diversity program depends on . . . "

The facilitator must remain objective and non-evaluative about the learning that occurs, drawing out the reactions of others to generalizations that appear incomplete, undivided, or controversial. Participants need to focus on clarifying what was learned. The facilitator can bring in theoretical and research findings to augment the learning, providing a framework for the learning and a reality check of the process. This outside information is not "owned" by the participants and should be used carefully and selectively.

Having participants answer three questions is one of the briefest, yet most helpful activities. Now that they have completed the learning experience, what have they learned that they must start doing; stop doing; and continue doing? They should also note dates when they will evaluate their progress and share their plans with one other person.

As a final activity, each participant should have an opportunity to speak again on the personal impact of the day's program, recalling various exercises and interactions.

Making a Difference

The results of experiential diversity training can be very positive. Participants' awakening will be evident during the processing and their delight with the program will be evident in their attitude change. This is an excellent way to make a difference.

LEADERSHIP DEVELOPMENT APPLICATIONS

RON LEWIS

Sgt. Preston of the Royal Canadian Mounted Police exclaims, "You want me to drop an egg 12 feet to the floor without it breaking and the only protection is some masking tape and a few plastic straws? By the way, does this have any application to police work?" Well Sgt. Preston, I want you to learn up-to-date management practices, you'd better tie up the horse, listen and observe carefully. We will be instructing with the help of "Experiential Training."

Sgt. Preston could have been any one of many middle management police officers who attend the Canadian Police College located in Canada's national capital, Ottawa, in the Province of Ontario. The Canadian Police College, also known as the C.P.C., is a national training center operated by the Royal Canadian Mounted Police. The C.P.C. provides advanced training to all police services in Canada and is also available to foreign police agencies. The curriculum includes various courses in management, executive development, computer applications, explosives, forensic identification, communication skills, polygraph, and many areas of investigative techniques such as drugs, major crime, traffic collision reconstruction, hostage negotiation and intelligence analysis.

Sgt. Preston's "Experiential Training" was a portion of the Senior Police Administration Course (S.P.A.C.). This five week intensive management course has been offered to law enforcement personnel since 1968. It is designed for middle managers with supervisory responsibilities, usually holding the rank of Sergeant, Staff Sergeant or junior commissioned officer. The class consists of 28 students from various police agencies throughout Canada and, usually several foreign students. S.P.A.C. is a stay on campus course with a curriculum that includes adult learning; innovative problem solving; writing skills; stress management; functions of managements; human behavior; community policing; police in society; ethics; values and social responsibilities; managing diversity; interviewing and counselling; time management; oral presentations; organizational communication; leadership; risk taking; resistance to change; decision making; group dynamics and other selected subjects.

The Way It Was

Since 1968, S.P.A.C. has continually evolved to meet the changing needs of Canadian police managers. The training began as traditional classroom instruction covering the required management concepts. The subjects were taught mostly by theory with several sessions of hands-on skill exercises such as interviewing and counselling, conducting a problem solving meeting using brainstorming techniques and the delivery of an oral presentation. Periodic survey questionnaires were used to complete cumulative program evaluations along with formative evaluations during each course. The clientele seemed to be very satisfied with the end product.

The Future

Staff members of the Management Training Unit who delivered S.P.A.C., were searching for methods to enhance this training and to transform the theory of management concepts into practical application before the students finished the course. This would create a better comprehension of the material and demonstrate to the instructional staff that each student truly understood the theory.

The Search

Throughout the research phase, "Experiential Training" kept surfacing as a viable alternative and enhancement of cognitive learning. The task became locating and developing this method of training to support the existing curriculum. The first step began in late 1992 while reviewing the Canadian Department of National Defense's middle management course. A classroom session called "Exercise Enterprise" was observed where the students conducted a hands-on exercise of building paper airplanes using the newly learned skills of planning, organizing, controlling and directing. The exercise included the elements of communication, leadership and team work. Later in the exercise, the element of change was introduced. This created a resistance to change component which was developed through facilitation by the training staff. Each phase of the exercise was debriefed by the students with the assistance of a staff facilitator.

This exercise was adopted by S.P.A.C. and adapted to our course topics. The results were tremendously successful with the students' written evaluations and, more importantly, unsolicited verbal comments that this exercise pulled together many session topics and theories. According to the students, the theory was brought to reality in such a manner that the ideas were clearer and more understandable because they experienced the concepts personally.

The staff knew that they were using a very powerful training method. Suddenly, the skills taught in an academic course were immediately evident to the students even before they left the course. An additional benefit was that this training was *fun*. The significance of this cannot be understated when considering that these students are accustomed to plenty of stimulation, excitement and variety in their normal work day.

Suddenly, they are sitting in a classroom for eight hour days , five days a week for five weeks. It takes very skillful lecturers to motivate them to pay attention.

Since the training staff wanted to further enhance the course, the search continued like a dog searching for a bone (or a suspect). The caution lights were also flashing that the course not turn into one large *game* with many unrelated exercises and unconnected philosophies. We sought professional, academically qualified resource persons in the field of experiential training.

The Solution

The trail led to many companies specializing in experiential training, both in Canada and the U.S.A. Many of the training companies concentrated on the physical activity of the exercise and not on the facilitation process (debriefing). Many companies had staff whose background was developed from the physical activity more so than an educational or training perspective. Another major obstacle was that most companies were geared for training intact groups for developmental purposes. The C.P.C. would become just another client and the consulting company would be needed as a continual resource. Ideally, Management Training Unit staff wanted a company to "Train the Trainers" in experiential training methods. Not surprisingly, "We Got Our Man" or, should I say, we got our "Company".

Staff members of the Management Training Unit visited a U.S.A.-based organizational development firm in January, 1993 to meet and review our proposal to integrate experiential training into the S.P.A.C curriculum, and to determine if the firm's ideas on experiential training were compatible with the philosophies of the Canadian Police College. The initial meeting was very successful and a subsequent meeting was scheduled for June, 1993, in Ottawa.

From the outset, it was made clear that the C.P.C. staff wanted to be trained as *trainers* in the area of experiential learning.

Along the trail, we met a university professor who had conducted research world-wide on the effectiveness of experiential training. He had been evaluating this type of training for the past five years and had developed a methodology focusing on group and individual behaviors. This researcher also attended the June meeting to help design the training and to begin discussions about evaluation. Prior to the June meeting, the consulting firm conducted a curriculum review of the existing S.P.A.C. to determine the placement of experiential training in the syllabus.

Eventually, the complicated process of allowing non-Canadian citizens to work in Canada was solved through many telephones calls, contacts and a mountain of paper work. The June meeting was held in Ottawa resulting in the formation of a design team. The consultants' preliminary curriculum report was reviewed and revised by the design team until a consensus was reached. Certain factors such as winter weather conditions in Ottawa dictated the type of exercises selected.

The "Train the Trainers" (TTT), course was scheduled at the Canadian Police College during early September, 1993. Participants included C.P.C. staff involved in S.P.A.C., other staff members and three resource lecturers who had taken a special interest in this method of training. The course included exploring the various sessions which make up S.P.A.C and enhancing them with an experiential training segment. Additional sessions were developed which would introduce new topics or concepts. The TTT course included the process of developing a "Frontload" or frame, conducting the exercise and process facilitation (or debriefing). Many exercises were demonstrated utilizing all participants in order to experience the results. Upon conclusion of the course, selected exercises were chosen which could be implemented by S.P.A.C.

A pilot project included the integration of experiential exercises in S.P.A.C. based on the September, 1993, course. A one-half day session entitled "Applied Learning" was used to introduce new topics on the course. This included a session which was designed primarily to address decision making, with additional emphasis on team building, problem solving, leadership, and communication. A second session introduced risk taking and built upon the previously mentioned management topics. Additional minor enhancements were added to existing sessions: one was an "ice breaker" and an introduction to experiential training methods in the course orientation, and the other dealt with changing paradigms.

The Results

During the September S.P.A.C. the two outside consultants co-facilitated the one-half day sessions with the C.P.C. staff members. The initial verbal feedback from the students indicated a successful introduction of experiential training. Subsequent written session evaluations confirmed this assumption.

The Evaluation

The final stage of this project was an evaluation by the researcher. His findings indicated that the experiential activities group reported a much more positive attitude toward the program than did two non-experientially trained groups. In addition, there appeared to be a clear and consistent improvement in the behavioral variables throughout the program following each of the experiential activities. In general, participants in the S.P.A.C. enjoyed the program better with the experiential activities than without those activities.

Conclusion

At this time four courses (S.P.A.C.) have been conducted utilizing experiential training sessions. Even at this early stage, it is very apparent that the project has been successful. All feedback has been enthusiastic and positive. It is very obvious that the students find this method of instruction stimulating and interesting. The success of experiential training given to intact groups has usually been measured by the degree of positive change in individual's behavior and/or the group's productivity. This introduction of experiential training is somewhat different. The individuals are not a part of an intact group on a permanent basis. It is hoped that eventually, each student will feel the effects of this training, view it as being positive and pass it along to their fellow employees. It has been discovered that the most important aspect of introducing this method of training into an academic course is that the material taught is more comprehensible and learning becomes easier, more enjoyable, more effective, more efficient and longer lasting. With this kind of accomplishment, the winners are the students and ultimately, the most important client of all, *the community,* which receives the benefits of the final product.

CHAPTER FIVE

EVALUATING EXPERIENTIAL TRAINING PROGRAMS

DONALD L. KIRKPATRICK, PH.D. AND RICHARD J. WAGNER, PH.D.

When efforts to evaluate outdoor experiential training programs began in the Spring of 1988, almost no meaningful research could be found, despite the fact that an estimated $200 million had been spent annually on these programs.

Even after six years of evaluating a variety of experiential training programs around the world we are no longer surprised at this lack of rigorous evaluation. Organizations that do conduct serious evaluations of their training programs are the exceptions, rather than the rule. Donald Kirkpatrick, probably the best known person in the area of training evaluation, summarizes his 30+ years in the field of training evaluation, beginning with a general view of the current state of training evaluation. He then discusses important reasons for evaluating training programs. Following this, is a discussion of the four levels of the "Kirkpatrick Model of Training Evaluation" with some specific guidelines on the uses of each of the four levels.

Interwoven in Kirkpatrick's article are comments from Dick Wagner, a professor of management, and skilled program evaluator. These comments focus on specific issues related to Dick's work in evaluating Corporate Experiential Learning programs around the world.

How Is Training Evaluated?

Donald L. Kirkpatrick with comments by Richard J. Wagner

Mark Twain was quoted as saying, "Everybody talks about it but nobody does anything about it." He could have been referring to the evaluation of a typical corporate training program, but he was actually talking about the weather. It isn't exactly true that nobody does anything about evaluating training, but it pretty closely reflects what we have found. There is a growing interest among many trainers in the issue of evaluation. While they feel a need to do it, little or nothing is done. Several reasons are commonly given:

- ◆ Time: Trainers spend their time planning and implementing training in order to meet organizational needs. Traditionally in most organizations, there has been little pressure from top management to justify the existence of the company's training programs, so the trainers don't give evaluation a high priority.
- ◆ Knowledge: Trainers really don't know how to do it. Most programs limit "evaluations" to participants comments (often called a "smile" or "happiness" sheet). Anything beyond this exceeds their knowledge and experience.

The objective of this article is to highlight, and offer some explanation of the following issues:

1. Why evaluate training programs?
2. The four levels for evaluation
3. Guidelines for each level
4. Suggested methods and techniques
5. Where to (and how to) go for help.

Why Evaluate Training Programs?

Three primary reasons why trainers should evaluate their training programs are:

1. To justify the existence of the training department and their programs to management.

2. To decide whether to continue or drop an individual program.
3. To improve the effectiveness of an individual training program.

Trainers must earn the respect and acceptance of upper-level managers. And if they are going to keep their jobs and justify their programs in the case of corporate down-sizing, they must convince upper-level managers of the payback or value added by these programs. It may be prudent to look ahead and be prepared to justify training programs to top management, for it will probably be too late to try to develop an evaluation when this request is made.

The second reason for evaluating is to determine whether a specific program is cost effective. "Pilot" or experimental programs that may or may not be offered in the future should utilize evaluations to assist in weighing the benefits versus the cost.

The third reason for evaluating is to determine how an existing program can be improved. Evaluation should include content, instructor, techniques, aids, timing, location and the selection of participants.

The Four Levels of Evaluation

Evaluation is confusing and frustrating because meanings and interpretations vary among trainers. Some think only in terms of comment sheets while others want to measure changes in behavior. Still others think only in terms of results such as increased productivity, improved quality and even return on investment (ROI).

I developed a four-level approach, "The Kirkpatrick Model" for evaluating training programs. It is a simple and practical way to clarify the *meaning* of evaluation. Organizations such as Motorola, Intel, and Arthur Andersen use this model as the basis for evaluating all of their training programs. Evaluation is so important to these organizations that they have created separate Departments of Evaluation.

The four levels of the Kirkpatrick Model are:

Reaction: How the participants feel about the program. It is really a measure of "customer satisfaction."

Learning: To what extent did participants change their attitudes, improve their knowledge and increase their skills?

Behavior: To what extent did the participants change their on-the-job behavior?

Results: What final results occurred? This would include such factors as increased sales, improved quantity of production, improved quality, reduced costs, reduction of accidents, education in turnover, increased profits and return on investments.

Organizations have training departments and training programs in order to improve operating results. In order to accomplish this, trainers must determine what kind of behaviors are needed to bring about those results. Then they need to determine what kind of a program promotes the needed behavior. Training programs often focus on changing participant attitudes, increasing their knowledge, and improving their job-related skills. These desired objectives then determine the program content, training aids and specific training methods. Finally, trainers must determine how they can conduct the program in such a way that the "customers" (e.g., participants, corporate management), are happy. Trainers should be evaluating at all four levels, beginning with reaction and ending with results.

Given the enormity of this task, many trainers find it necessary to start at evaluating "reaction." As time and knowledge of evaluation methods permit, trainers should then move on to the higher, more sophisticated, levels of evaluation.

Guidelines

Evaluating Reactions

1. Clarify objectives.
2. Design a form that will *quantify* reactions.
3. Encourage written comments and suggestions in addition to the quantifiable responses.
4. Get 100% *immediate* responses, usually right at the end of the program.
5. Encourage complete and honest responses.
6. Develop acceptable standards for the participant reactions.

Evaluating Learning

1. Use an untrained "control group" if practical.
2. Evaluate knowledge, skills, and/or attitudes on a pre- and post-program basis.
   a. Use a "paper and pencil" test to quantify measurable changes in knowledge and attitudes.
   b. Use a performance test to measure increase in skills.
3. Get 100% response.

Evaluating Behavior

1. Use an untrained "control group" if practical.

2. Allow time for changes in behavior to take place.
3. If practical, evaluate on a pre- and post-program basis.
4. Survey and/or interview one or more of the following:
    a. The trainees.
    b. The immediate supervisors.
    c. The subordinates.
    d. Others who frequently interact with the trainees.
5. Use a 100% response or a sampling of the participants.
6. Repeat the evaluation at planned, regular intervals.

Evaluating Results

1. Use an untrained "control group" if practical.
2. Determine results criteria to be measured.
3. Allow time for the results to be achieved.
4. Measure on a pre- and post-program basis.
5. Repeat at appropriate times.
6. Consider the cost of the evaluation versus possible benefits.
7. Be satisfied with inferential evidence if absolute "proof" is not possible.

The guidelines are structured so that each level becomes increasingly complicated, time-consuming, and difficult. For example, "control groups" are suggested at the last three levels. A control group consists of persons who do not attend the training program but are essentially the same as the "experimental group" that attends the training program. Using a control group allows for comparisons of changes within each group over time, and of differences between groups. If the control group and the trained group are truly comparable, then any differences in the groups can be attributed to the effects of the training program. The concept is sound, but the words "if practical" are necessary because of the difficulty (and sometimes the impossibility) of establishing a control group.

Wagner: The use of a control group is very important if we are to make inferences based on any changes found in the trained group. The measure of interest is the "change score," the post score minus the pre-score (the score after training minus the score before training). If the trained group had a change of +1.14 from the pre- to the post-test we might be tempted to say that this suggests that the training was very effective. However, this could be an erroneous conclusion based only on the information given, since some "external condition," such as a new manager, a change in policy or procedure, could have caused a change for the entire company, with or without training. However, if a control group is used, and the trained group shows an increase, but the untrained (control group) does not, we have a much better case for saying the training program was effective.

From a pure research perspective, people should be assigned to the control group and the trained group on a totally random basis. Obviously, when working with corporate work teams, this type of assignment is impossible. An alternative to random assignment is the concept of a "stratified group," in which the members of the control group are "matched" to the members of the trained team on the basis of potentially important differences. For example, if the trained group contains 6 females and 12 males, the control group should consist of approximately the same mix of males and females. Other factors which may be important to match groups include: age, educational level, type of position or responsibility with the company (management, clerical, sales, etc.).

The last three levels of evaluation (learning, behavior & results) suggest the use of pre-program and post-program measurement in order to determine the impact of the training program. This means measuring each level at least twice, and creates some additional problems for the trainer.

Wagner: Using a pre- and a post-training measurement is essential for effective evaluation. The pre-measure establishes the baseline from which participants start. The post-measure(s) then allow a determination of the amount of change from the baseline. One issue to consider is the timing of the post measure. If the post measure is too soon after the training program, this measure can contain a great deal of "post-training euphoria." This means that rather than measure any changes in behaviors or results, we might be measuring a *halo* effect based on how well participants liked the program. On the other hand, the longer we wait to collect the post-training evaluation, the greater the chance for other (non-training) factors to influence the measurement, thus invalidating any inference that it was the training program that caused the changes found.

For example, Sales Reps attended a 5-day experiential training program in March. A post-training evaluation ten months later indicates January sales 28% above the March level. As trainers we would like to "infer" that the sales increase is the result the improved customer focus due to our wonderful training program. However, the Sales Manager points out that a new product was introduced in November, and that it is this new product has dramatically increased sales. Because of the time span from the training program to the post-training evaluation, other factors

besides the training program have influenced the outcomes and no con-
clusive answer is possible.

Many of our program evaluations employ multiple post-evaluations, most
commonly at approximately four weeks after the program, and about
four months after the training program. The four week post gives the
organization some "quick feedback" on the program, and gives us a
"point" to begin to look at the learning curve for the program. The second post-questionnaire examines the long-term effects of the program,
and provides a further picture of the learning curve for the program.

Suggested Methods and Techniques

There are numerous practical forms which can be used to evaluate an applicant's *reaction* to a training program. Figures 5-1 and 5-2 use slightly different approaches to
evaluate reactions. In both cases, the reactions can be quantified for easy evaluation,
while encouraging written comments and suggestions for improving future programs.

Wagner: Self report questionnaires using five or seven-point "Likert"
scales (i.e., 1=disagree strongly and 5=agree strongly), are the most common type of evaluation questionnaires. They are quantifiable and subject to easy interpretation. For example, if the pre-value was 3.11 and
the post-value is 3.82, an increase of .71 occurred. A t-test can be used
to determine the statistical significance of this increase.

Gathering additional comments and suggestions in an "open ended"
question format can be very beneficial in interpreting the data from the
questionnaires. For example, a quantifiable increase in team-work can
often be amplified by responses such as "the group gets more done,
since we no longer argue over petty items such as who should take the
notes at the meeting." This information not only tells us what happened,
but why it happened.

Other methods used to collect this type of information include individual
interviews, focus group interviews and participant journals. However, the
open-ended response item on the questionnaire is undoubtedly the simplest and most cost effective to administer, as well as easiest to use.

The evaluation of *learning* can also be accomplished in a number of different ways.
Figure 5-3 is an example of a learning evaluation for a training program called "Improving Communication Effectiveness." An eighty item "Supervisory Inventory On

Figure 5-1   Reaction Sheet

Please give us your frank reactions and comments to help us evaluate this program and offer suggestions to improve future programs.

LEADER _____   SUBJECT _____

1. How do you rate the subject? (Interest, benefit, etc.)

    _____ EXCELLENT   Comments and suggestions:

    _____ VERY GOOD

    _____ GOOD

    _____ FAIR

    _____ POOR

2. How do you rate the conference leader? (Subject knowledge, ability to communicate, etc.)

    _____ EXCELLENT   Comments and suggestions:

    _____ VERY GOOD

    _____ GOOD

    _____ FAIR

    _____ POOR

3. How do you rate the facilities? (Comfort, convenience, etc.)

    _____ EXCELLENT   Comments and suggestions:

    _____ VERY GOOD

    _____ GOOD

    _____ FAIR

    _____ POOR

4. What would have improved the program?

Figure 5-2   Reaction Sheet

LEADER _____   SUBJECT _____

1. How pertinent was the subject to your needs and interests?

    _____ Not at all   _____ To some extent   _____ Very much

2. How was the ratio of presentation to discussion?

    _____ Too much presentation   _____ OK   _____ Too much discussion

3. How do you rate the instructor?

	Excellent	Very Good	Good	Fair	Poor
a. In stating objectives					
b. In keeping the session alive and interesting					
c. In communicating					
d. In using aids					
e. In maintaining a friendly and helpful attitude					
f. Overall rating of leader					

Comments and suggestions:

4. What would have made the session more effective?

5. List one or two things that were new for you.

6. List one or two things that will help you in your job.

Figure 5-3   Learning Evaluation Method

Name of Test _____   Date _____

Please circle the questions you answered incorrectly according to the scoring key:

1	2	3	4	5	6	7	8	9	10	11	12
13	14	15	16	17	18	19	20	21	22	23	24
25	26	27	28	29	30	31	32	33	34	35	36
37	38	39	40	41	42	43	44	45	46	47	48
49	50	51	52	53	54	55	56	57	58	59	60
61	62	63	64	65	66	67	68	69	70	71	72
73	74	75	76	77	78	79	80				

RAW SCORE: 80 - _____ = ☐
                         (# incorrect)

Your Title:

_____ Production Foreman, Supervisor

_____ Office Supervisor

_____ Middle Level Manager

_____ Other _____

Communication" is administered to the participants as a pre-test before the program, and again as a post-test after the program. Each participant scores his/her own test and completes the form illustrated in Figure 5-3. The tests are kept by the participants and become the basis for practical discussion of communication concepts, principles, and techniques. The completed form in Figure 5-3 is turned in to the trainer and becomes the pre-test, while the post-test is given at some time after the training program.

Figure 5-4 illustrates a method for comparing *total* pre-test scores with *total* post-test scores. This evaluates the *overall* gain or improvement score. Figure 5-5 compares pre and post-test responses for *each item* on the test. This second evaluation provides specifics on the degree of success achieved in changing attitudes and increasing knowledge. This is helpful in planning future sessions with different groups and/or follow-up programs with the same group.

Figure 5-4   Comparison of Pre-Test and Post-Test Total Scores

Number of participants: _____

	Average Score
Pre-test score	
Post-test score	
Gain score	

NOTE: These figures can be analyzed statistically to determine the level of significance or confidence level.

If, for example, the training program involves teaching speaking or writing skills, then a pre-test and post-test on these skills would be conducted. The scores from both tests would be evaluated by a competent instructor to determine the level of improvement in these skills. If the training program involves a less tangible skill, such as presentation skills, videotape can be used before and after to determine the effectiveness of the program. The table in Figure 5-5 could be used to evaluate the gain score for either of the examples discussed above.

The best approach to measuring *changes in behavior* is to observe the behavior before the training program is offered and after the program, to determine what changes occurred. This is easy to say but is often very difficult to do because behavioral observation is a highly skilled, often subjective, time consuming technique which is expensive

Figure 5-5   Comparison of Pre-Test and Post-Test Individual Items

Number of participants: _____

Item # 1	Number of responses that were:		
	Correct	Incorrect	
			Pretest
			Post test
			Gain

Item # 2	Number of responses that were:		
	Correct	Incorrect	
			Pretest
			Post test
			Gain

(Each item has a similar table)

NOTE: The figures for each of the items can be analyzed statistically to determine the level of significance or confidence level for each item.

to implement, and can cause self consciousness on the part of participants, possibly changing their behavior. An alternative approach is to measure behavior after the program and try to determine how it differs from the behavior of people who did *not* attend the program. Then, the question is how to measure the success of the program in changing behaviors, and compare pre- and post-program behaviors between the groups. The more people (who interact with the trainees), surveyed or interviewed, the more reliable the data. Supervisors often do not observe behavior, but expect results and rely on third-party feedback for information regarding behavior. Therefore their input in evaluating program success by behavioral change is limited.

When evaluating workshops attended by an intact work team, immediate subordinates see behavior through the perspective of receiving direction and/or supervision, and respond accordingly. Perhaps the subordinate cannot recall previous behavior. Even so, subordinates of the participant are probably the best sources of data regarding behavioral change. However, many participants may not want subordinates to be questioned about supervisory behavior. Or, subordinates may give subjectively-biased responses, perhaps to raise self-esteem, protect personal image, or due to lack of adequate observation and recall skills. Some other sources of information are peers, customers, and others having regular contact with the participant. However, their responses present the same problem of subjectivity and a lack of expertise in evaluating the behavior of others. Given these difficulties, the more sources tapped, the better the results.

In an evaluation of the behavioral change in supervisors who attended a University of Wisconsin Management Institute, patterned interviews were conducted with the participants as well as their immediate supervisors, three months after the program. In nearly all cases, both sources reported positive behavior changes as well as improved financial results. However, participants indicated a much higher degree of behavior change than reported by immediate supervisors. The data was convincing that positive changes took place, both in behavior and results, since both sources reported the positive changes. However, the magnitude of the changes could not be established.

In evaluating *results*, before and after data is usually available. For example, if an increase in number and amount of sales is the training objective, then pre- and post-program figures are readily available. The same is true for any number of areas of the business with measurable output (e.g., output of piecework, number of accidents, turnover, scrap). The real challenge is to verify that the positive results occurred *because* of the program and not because of other factors. For example, it was determined by training professionals that the high turnover among new employees was caused by poor orientation and on-the-job training by the immediate supervisor. Therefore, a training program was conducted to teach supervisors how to orient and train new employees. Immediately after the program, the turnover rate was reduced and continued at a lower rate for six months. Trainers were proud that their objective was accomplished. But, can these results be proven; that the reduction in turnover was a direct result of the training program? Other factors related to hiring, salary adjustments, changes in jobs, the economic climate in the community and a new involvement program might have caused the same reduction in turnover. This is an example of "evidence instead of proof." Sometimes trainers and upper-level managers must be satisfied with this. If the program design incorporates the acceptable measurement of results and management agrees to accept evidence of improvement rather than proof, then the success of the program will not be compromised.

Where to Go for Help

The information in this chapter provides an introduction to training program evaluation. It has provided some basic concepts, principles and techniques, describing the four levels of evaluation (reaction, learning, behavior, results), guidelines for each, and some suggested forms and procedures. The key point is that program evaluation can be effective in three ways: 1) to justify the existence of training programs; 2) to help determine training curriculum courses and 3) to help improve programs offered.

Measuring *reaction* is simplest and most helpful provided that accurate, objective forms and procedures are used. Evaluating *learning* and *results* can be achieved by clarifying learning objectives and measuring the levels on a before and after basis. Evaluating *behavior* change is more difficult, but if evidence rather than proof is acceptable, then it is more easily achieved.

The following resources can aid the evaluation of training programs:

1. Basarab, David J. Sr. and Darrell K. Root. *The Training Evaluation Process*, Boston, MA, Kluwer Academic Publishers, 1992.

    This book contains case studies of actual evaluations as well as philosophy and principles. It is based on the "Kirkpatrick Model" of four levels and was written by Basarab, Manager of Evaluation, Motorola University and Root, Professor of Program Evaluation, University of Dayton.

2. Holcomb, Jane. *Make Training Work Every Penny*, Del Mar, CA: Wharton Publishing, 1993.

    Holcomb also uses Kirkpatrick's four-level model as the basis for this basic and easy to read book, including principles as well as suggested forms and techniques. In addition, one section deals with pre- and post-program counseling to help participants get maximum benefit from a program.

3. Kirkpatrick, Donald L. *Evaluating Training Programs: The Four Levels*, San Francisco, CA, Barrett-Koehler Publishers, 1994.

    This book provides many principles, forms and techniques for evaluating at each of the four levels. It also contains case studies of evaluations done at Motorola, St. Luke's Hospital, Kemper Insurance, First Union National Bank of North Carolina, Arthur Andersen, Intel, IBM and other organizations.

4. Kirkpatrick, Donald L. *How To Train and Develop Supervisors*, AMACOM, New York: NY, American Management Association, 1993.

    This book describes principles, specific methods and techniques for determining needs, setting objectives, implementing effective training programs and evaluation, including examples of effective training programs at Deere & Company, St. Joseph's Hospital, General Electric, Dana Corporation, DuPont and ServiceMaster.

5. Phillips, Jack J. *Training Evaluation and Measurement Methods,* 2nd edition, Houston, TX, Gulf Publishing Company, 1991.

    This reference handbook emphasizes the need and process for evaluating results, including sections on determining program cost, evaluating return on investment and communicating evaluation information.

CEL Evaluation Today

Richard Wagner, Ph.D.

An evaluation team of Dick Wagner and Tim Baldwin (Indiana University), and Chris Roland (Roland/Diamond Associates, Inc.), was contracted to evaluate a major team building program conducted by the U.S. Navy in the Spring of 1988. This two year evaluation began with a review of evaluation processes for outdoor based CEL programs world-wide. Extensive and exhaustive research yielded almost no quality evaluations of these programs.

The few evaluations found generally fit into one of two categories: qualitative evaluations based on the anecdotal evidence of one or two people; and quantitative (empirical) evaluation based on samplings of three to seven participants.

The U.S. Navy evaluation employed Kirkpatrick's Four Level Model described above. Based on the goals of the specific program, the evaluation concentrated on levels 1 (reaction), and 3 (behaviors). Reactions are a measure of motivation; behavior changes were the basic organizational goals of the program—improved group interactions leading to improved team performance.

Several issues made evaluating results difficult to assess. These issues are common in many organizations: the goals of the training programs did not include specific, measurable results, but focused on team behaviors and interactions; results were not easy to identify because the group being trained did not produce any specific outcome *on their own*. Rather, their outcome was part of a larger group, most of which did not attend the training program, or were not scheduled to attend for at least one year.

One pre- and two post-training questionnaires were developed and given to each participant. The results were analyzed using a t-test to evaluate the statistical significance of any changes in the six behaviors evaluated. The initial evaluation did not use a control group, but because each group was evaluated in turn (twenty-five groups were evaluated during the first year), a baseline was established using the pre-training measures from each group.

Behaviors evaluated

The number of behaviors evaluated has increased over the years as the number of (primarily corporate) programs with different goals and objectives are evaluated. Currently, more than fifteen behaviors can be evaluated based on the objectives of specific programs. All of the behavioral measures contain from four to twelve questions, and many use "reverse-coded" questions as a response validity check. A list and description of the more commonly evaluated behaviors follows. Each of these behaviors has been evaluated in experiential training programs throughout the world. Data on these behaviors have indicated high statistical reliability, and have confirmed the initial face validity of the behaviors. Our data base includes as many as 20,000 individual responses from a variety of organizations. A sample portion of the questionnaire can be found in Appendix B.

Behaviors Measured in Outdoor CEL Evaluations

Attitude towards training. Participant's general impression of, and willingness to participate in the training program. As a post-training measure, general satisfaction with the training program.

Locus of control. Rewards and outcomes of work are controlled by one's own actions (internal), or by other forces, or people not within one's own control (external).

Self-esteem. Measured on a continuum from a positive view of oneself at work (high self-esteem), to a negative view of ones ability to get the job done (low self-esteem).

Trust in fellow workers. The extent to which one is willing to assign good intentions to, and have confidence in the words and actions of one's co-workers. Measured in two ways: *faith in peers*, and *confidence in peers*.

Interpersonal relations/communication. A measure of the degree to which people effectively communicate with each other including relations with others, receptivity to others, openness to others and the ability to accurately/correctly interpret meaning and messages of others.

Acceptance of change. Openness to new ideas and methods.

Organizational commitment. A measure of desire to continue as a member of the organization.

Group awareness. A variety of functional characteristics including: *group homogeneity*—the feeling among group members that each member of the work group recognizes the differences in abilities between the individual members of the group; *group clarity*—the feeling among group members that each member of the work group shares the same understanding of the group's common goal; and *group cohesiveness*—the feeling among group members that each member of the work group is committed to working together to achieve the overall goals.

Group effectiveness. A measure of the overall functioning of the work group, by level of cooperation, group competence, and motivation to accomplish the group's tasks.

Bonding with the group. The quality and depth of the relationship and commitment of each person to the other members of the group.

Problem solving and decision making. One's ability to consider all aspects of the problem, to reach a best possible solution including the ability to involve other people in reaching the best solution (consensus).

Risk-taking propensity. The degree to which one is willing to explore new directions and take calculated risks, both personal and corporate, in the work setting.

Methodology Used in Questionnaires

A pre/post methodology is used to evaluate the CEL programs. The pre-training questionnaires are administered at the start of programs to establish a baseline measurement. Many programs use two post-training questionnaires: four to six weeks after the program, and then four and six months after the program.

The second post-questionnaire generally eliminates almost all post-training euphoria. Unfortunately, as Kirkpatrick discussed, it becomes very difficult to attribute behavior changes to the program only, after four to six months have passed. During this time, many other changes have occurred in an organization which could effect behavior changes. One way to avoid this problem is using a "control group" with similar characteristics and experience, except for the training program. This type of evaluation is highly recommended, and more than half of the organizations we evaluate do so.

Multiple Groups and Demographic Issues

Another level of analysis becomes possible when evaluating a program with multiple groups going through a similar training program over a period of time. For example, ten groups from the Sales Department are trained over a three month period. When evaluating this type of program we can statistically evaluate both the *individual* groups on a pre/post/post training basis, and the *overall* program, also on a pre/post/post basis. Conclusions about the overall program, and comparisons with each of the individual groups to the overall program results can then be developed and analyzed. Inferences regarding other group characteristics can often be analyzed. For example, if five of the groups are from the Western Region, and five of the groups are from the Eastern Region, regional comparisons can be attempted.

A variety of demographic data can also be collected via the questionnaires including age, gender, educational level, etc. This information enables other statistical analyses and comparisons on the basis of male/female participants, college graduate/non-college graduate, etc. The actual demographic data collected and analyzed is very specific to the individual organization.

SAMPLE PRE/POST QUANTITATIVE ANALYSIS

BEHAVIOR	Pre (Mean/S.D*.)	Post 1 (Mean/S.D.*)	T-value	Probability
Attitude toward the program	3.80 (.708)	4.00 (.644)	1.55	.123
Trust in peers	3.51 (.836)	3.62 (.760)	0.74	.460
Group awareness	3.53 (.624)	3.78 (.575)	2.23	.028**
Self esteem	2.08 (.622)	2.19 (.658)	0.91	.365
Group problem solving	3.64 (.441)	3.72 (.383)	0.98	.332
Interpersonal communications	3.29 (.612)	3.54 (.607)	2.21	.029**
* Standard Deviation ** Statistically significant change				

Standard deviation is a measure of the "dispersion" or variation in the responses. A small standard deviation indicates that the responses fall within a small range (all are 2, 3 or 4). A large standard deviation indicates that the range of responses is very large (responses vary from 1 to 5). A statistically significant change means that the probability of finding a change of the magnitude from the pre- to post- test is very small. For example, the probability of finding a change of .25 in Interpersonal Communications (3.54-3.29) is .029. This means that the probability of finding this change "by chance" is slightly under 3%.

Beyond Quantitative Analysis

The statistical analysis of the pre/post training data is very appealing to many organizations. It produces charts (and graphs) of measured results (see the PRE/POST ANALYSIS above). However, this type of analysis may present several problems. Managers often become overly reliant on the "statistics," and ignore the analysis, or message. Another problem may rest with the validity of the data collected and/or the analysis itself. Relying on participant self-report questionnaires is often questionable if it is the only data collected for analysis. Some participants do not take the questionnaire seriously, or try to respond in *ways in which they think* they are supposed to respond.

While our original evaluations relied heavily on quantitative analysis, these evaluations have evolved over the years to include qualitative methods which *enhance* the statistical analysis from the pre/post-training questionnaires. These methods range from easier to quite complex. One method, as suggested by Kirkpatrick, the expanded questionnaire administered to peers, supervisors and subordinates of the trainees, provides new insights into the effectiveness of CEL programs. The statistical analysis is similar to that of the participant questionnaires.

Participant interviews, including both individual and focus group have been refined over the last few years. Initial efforts were limited to a few interviews with willing participants while collecting the final post-training questionnaire. These initial interviews were unstructured and followed no particular format. In order to improve the quality of data collected during the interview, the following model was developed.

Post-Training Interviews

1. Conduct interviews *after* the final post questionnaire analysis. This gives the interviewer some insight into areas that seemed to change, and those which did not. Phrasing of the questions can be adjusted from these "leads." If the questionnaires indicated a significant change in trust, for example, the interviewer might ask, "In what way did the CEL program give you more trust in your fellow workers?" This provides a focus for the interviews based on the indicated results of the program, and will informally "validate" those results.

2. Prepare the interview questions in advance (i.e., a structured interview), taking careful notes following a prepared format. Interviewing provides a great deal of "rich" information, often a lot more information than needed or sought. The less structured the format, the more likely this additional information will appear. Selected interview questions used to evaluate CEL programs is found in Appendix C.

3. Use a "stratified" method to select *who* will be interviewed. Try to interview 25% of the participants reflecting the same proportions of participant demographic characteristics as found in the larger training groups (age, gender, education, job tenure, etc.).

4. When unable to conduct interviews in person, due to time and distance considerations, we have used "open-ended" questionnaires as a final post evaluation, six to eight months after the program. These questionnaires give the participants an opportunity to express their thoughts. The questionnaires are

not as effective as interviews, because they are not interactive, but sometimes they are the only option available. Alternatively, a telephone interview can be used *after* the questionnaires have been returned.

5. When using a focus group interview, follow the above guidelines, and have an assistant take notes, videotape, or record the interview with permission from the group. With a focus group interview involving eight to ten participants, advance planning is very important. This interview technique works best when evaluating team-building programs.

6. When evaluating programs focusing on individual issues such as leadership and self esteem, observational techniques can enhance the evaluation process. They are very time consuming, but yield valuable data. Observational methodologies have been used by other researchers including Darl Kolb of New Zealand, 1991.

7. "The question of involvement is critical to human functioning. The degree to which people commit their attention, interest and labor, determines the ultimate success of the venture at hand" (Cheffers, Brunelle & Von Kelsch, 1978, p. 1). Other structured observer systems are available that can assist with determining the level of involvement (Roland, 1992) as well as interaction between trainer and trainee (Roland, 1993). Observations can take place prior, during and after a particular training program/process.

8. Participant journals have been used to successfully evaluate participant behavioral changes resulting from wilderness adventure programs. Participants write in their journals several times during each day of the program. A "semi-structured" journal methodology has been developed, which allows the gathering of open-ended information from the participants, while guiding them into areas of interest for the organization.

9. The Critical Incident Technique (Flanagan, 1954) is a method that records and analyzes individuals' thoughts of why there is perceived change in a particular team, department or organization. After a certain period of time, participants are asked to answer a specifically worded question. For example: *During the past ten months you have experienced a number of changes in your department. As a result, we have seen an increase in productivity. In a few sentences, please share one or two "critical incidents" during this time period that you felt were important to this productivity increase.*

CHAPTER SIX

INTERNATIONAL AND MULTI-CULTURAL PERSPECTIVES

JOHN CAMPBELL, RICHARD J. WAGNER, HEATHER BROWN,
MARIO KÖLBLINGER, TOCK KENG LIM, MIKE MAIN*

Experiential training is used in various forms in many countries around the world. In order to design and facilitate effective programs, trainers face a web of cultural issues. This chapter explores some specific cultural issues, and relate these issues to designing and facilitating experiential programs both on a multi-cultural basis, and in different parts of the world. We acknowledge that the authors of this chapter are products of their own cultures, and therefore, the chapter has a distinctly Anglo-American flavor.

A recent article in a British paper reported, " . . . multinational companies are invincible. I know this because of a recent chat with a British man employed in selling Japanese film . . . the stateless corporation was a fact of life. It had no country, no loyalty . . . " (The Guardian, April 1994). While this article was written partly tongue in cheek, it contains a great deal of truth regarding today's world economy. The consequences are bleak for countries continuing only "inward investment" and is far outweighed by the efforts of multinationals to protect their investments by creating effective multi-national organizations. Effectiveness must account for and accept the cultural background and birthright of local employees. This is true even in considering the substantial economic and political power of the multinational corporations. Research suggests that, under pressure, people revert to their cultural roots even if they have learned to adjust to new ways in "foreign" countries (Laurent, 1986).

Thus, there is an increasing need for organizations and managers to understand the dynamics of mixed culture work forces. This is true for organizations functioning in one country or in several countries.

The work of Andre Laurent at INSEAD, the European Institute of Business Administration (the European equivalent of the Harvard Business School), concludes that multi-cultural work forces have the potential to become exceptional performers if they can learn to capture the diverse talents, creativity and viewpoints of its members, and overcome communication difficulties, prejudices and ignorance. His research examined team performance and could produce a normal distribution curve as illustrated in Figure 6-1.

* Special thanks to Ann Hilgendorf, Julie Nason and Gail Ryan for their significant assistance in the preparation of this chapter. Heather Brown acknowledges the significant contributions of the late Barry Young.

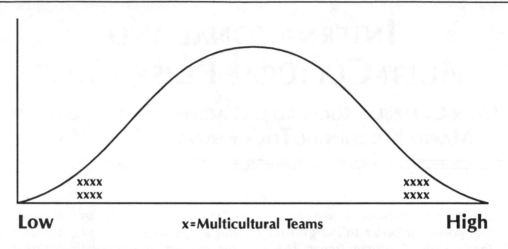

Figure 6-1   Team Performance

Multi-cultural teams tend to cluster at both extremes of the performance distribution curve, suggesting that a higher proportion of multi-cultural teams do get bogged down in communication difficulties and therefore become ineffective. But at the top of the performance curve there is a higher proportion of top performing multi-cultural teams than that shown for all teams taken together. While it is probably more difficult to train and develop multi-cultural teams because of language, values and prejudice, the payoff is worth the effort and can generate superior performance.

This finding has significant implications for training, particularly experiential training, since experiential training tends to tap all the resources of the learner: physical, mental, psychological, emotional and sometimes spiritual. These aspects are significant cultural elements to acknowledge and accommodate during the training process. Before these elements can be managed, they need to be understood.

Examples of cultural issues

All people are products of socialization; each culture with its own characteristics and idiosyncrasies. Since experiential training relies heavily on social interaction and on social experimentation, it is important for the experiential trainer to be aware of and sensitive to the kind of cultural issues that may emerge in running experiential events for participants from different societies and cultural backgrounds.

> *Heather Brown, a trainer with Telecom Australia in Melbourne, Australia, amplifies the importance of cultural background in designing experiential training programs where a number of key cultural differences can have a critical impact on the design, implementation and facilitation of the experiential process when working with Australians:*

It is theoretically possible that an Australian alive in the 1990s could have had great grand-parents on the first fleet that landed in Australia in 1788; Australia's history since coloniza-tion is very short, even by American standards. Australia is often spoken of as a young country; one observer (Mackay, 1993) compares Australians in the 1990s to adolescents trying to establish their personality in relation to the outside world, whose behaviour is characterised by mood swings, the feeling of wanting it all and an identity crisis.

This identity crisis shows itself in the love-hate relationship many Australians have with things imported; the "Buy Australian" campaign is strongly advertised, but the wording of other adverts implies quite clearly that imported (particularly European) is better. Australia takes much of its architecture and TV from the U.S., but attempts to import U.S. management theories and practices have been greeted by many with accusations of U.S. hype and the assertion that Australians need to be treated differently.

For many Australian migrants, pioneering history is still very recent; the sealing of the road that links the east and west coasts of Australia was only completed in the 1970s Much of the country is still hard to cross, difficult to work and unforgiving in a crisis. One character who has therefore become highly valued in Australian culture is "the Aussie battler, with an infinite capacity to overcome hardships" (Mackay, 1993). In the harsh climate of the outback, far from rescue services, the men creating the sheep farms and putting up the telephone poles had only each other, their mates, to rely on. The concept of mateship united men who were "thrown together by some emergency in an unfriendly environ-ment and have become of one blood in facing it" or provided simply "comradeship within a male fraternity" (Horne, 1964). Mates shared "a belief in equality and the habit of judging a man by his performance rather than his inheritance (Manning, 1963) but were also "mor-bidly suspicious of the newcomer or the intruder who might . . . disturb their way of life" (ibid.). This fierce loyalty, built on common experiences and problems solved together, rarely included verbal communication or the expression of feelings; there was no time for that when the job had to be done. In Australia today there is still little room for anyone who is not "fair dinkum" (straight, fair, honest), who uses high flown language for effect, or who puts themselves above others (the proverbial "tall poppy").

Since the end of World War II, Australia has become a much more multi-cultural soci-ety, although the prevailing cultural influence is still largely from the U.K. New mi-grants from Southern Europe, and increasingly Asia, tend to adapt quickly to the estab-lished behaviour of "getting the task done" rather than talking about interpersonal rela-tions, as they strive to become accepted in the new country. At work, the traditional divide between male and female roles was maintained as the most practical way of getting all the work done, and this was often echoed socially. However, similar to men in other countries, Australian men are now facing the need to come to terms with the redefinition of gender roles brought about by working women and by the reduction in work force numbers in many traditionally male jobs.

Although, and perhaps because, Australia is one of the most urbanised countries in the world, the sense that "real life" (and perhaps true self-fulfillment) is to be found out in the bush still survives strongly for many Australians. The ideal of buying a plot of bushland

and building a house on it is still a real and realisable goal for many. A holiday ambition for many Australian families is to "get right away from each other, to some little place where the house faces only the open sea or the silent grandeur of wooded mountains . . . there is a clear ethic of travelling to somewhere where you can legitimately feel right off the map" (Knight, 1990).

These formative experiences have led to the following deeply held values for many Australians:

- the outdoors, either as a romantic vision of self-fulfillment, or as the scene of honest toil to create the desired lifestyle
- physical prowess and getting the job done; Australia is still largely a primary producing nation
- preparedness to have a laugh, and tendency to create bonds by making fun of each other's mateship, with the attendant reluctance to reveal or discuss feelings, and the loyalty that hesitates to give feedback for fear of "dobbing someone in" (telling tales on someone)
- until recently, clearly divided male and female roles, with women's views and contribution to decision-making often not considered because they were not the ones who did the physical work

When organisations were stable, employment levels high and a "she'll be right" (it'll be all right on the night), attitude was sufficient to produce the required level of results, there was little urgency for workers and managers to examine their personal style and the effect it had on team work and productivity. However, growing competition and the increasing pace of change in the mid 1980s led to the need for training to achieve culture change in organisations which had until then relied on the legacy of the "lucky country" to see them through. Telecom Australia, for example, mounted a large scale experiential program using team-building, problem-solving and personal challenge exercises to underpin and accelerate change to a TQM, customer-oriented approach focusing on competition.

Providers began to tackle participants' reticence to examine personal feelings and issues by allying themselves with management consultants with a background in psychology, rather than relying on instinct and personal experience. They began to use psychological models and theories to improve their understanding of how people learn from experiential activities, which enabled them to review activities in much greater depth. In order to take account of Australian reticence when talking about emotions, they adapted reviewing techniques to challenge participants gradually, for example by asking people to imagine their behaviours in a given situation rather than asking for information about emotions or attitudes. "Where an Australian manager might resist answering a question such as . . . 'How do you feel when that happens?' the answer may be more readily forthcoming if you instead ask 'What would you sometimes like to be able to do (or feel like doing) when that happens?' (Dick, 1991)."

These days, the need to challenge and examine personal behaviour is becoming more widely accepted in Australia. However, because of the importance Australians attach to relationships "treat me as if I belong here; acknowledge me as a person; let's act as if this commercial relationship is a personal relationship" (Mackay, 1993), they prefer to take a more gentle approach to examining and changing behaviour, recognising and valuing the already existing positive features, and building on them to bring about improvements.

The renewed interest in personal responsibility and values coincide with a growing awareness of the need to understand and recognise the rights of other peoples' cultures, both inside and outside Australia. Until recently, the culture and rights of Australia's indigenous Aboriginal peoples have been little valued by Australians of migrant stock, but the 1990s are seeing a change in this situation, as Aboriginal peoples claim back the rights to their ancestral lands. One of the roadblocks to navigate around when negotiating is the difference in values and negotiating procedures between the cultures involved. Many social agencies are working to establish cultural bridges in this area and at least one provider has for some time been using outdoor experiential programs, with Aboriginal facilitators, to help government agencies and Aboriginal communities to build a common negotiating language (Adamson, 1993).

Some of the values which have been part of Aboriginal life for thousands of years bear a striking similarity to those mentioned above as emerging corporate concerns; Aboriginal cultures place great emphasis on community living and interdependence, on living lightly on the land and on being aware of the effect of one's actions on others.

Interest in Asian cultures is also high, as Australian businesses are keen to make the most of Australia's crucial geographical and trading position on the Pacific Rim. Some companies are asking providers to develop cross cultural training programs to build teams with members from different countries. Others are working with providers to develop activities which use the icons of Asian societies (Samurai, the Tao of War, Zen, etc.) to inspire Australian business people (Young, 1993).

> *Dr. Tock Keng Lim of the National Institute of Education at the Nanyang Technological University of Singapore describes some of the cultural issues found in the unique culture of Singapore:*

Singapore consists of three main racial groups: Chinese (78%), Malays (14%) and Indians (7%). While there is a general underlying Asian culture, there is also an ethnic culture peculiar to each of the three Asian races, including religious differences. These differences are more characteristic of older Singaporeans than of younger Singaporeans.

Western influence in Singapore is strong because of the education, the language, and mass communication technology. English is the medium of instruction in schools, and the main language of commerce, technology and administration. Despite this fluency in English, and their western way of life, they still preserve their Asian cultures.

The Asian culture respects the virtues of humility, reserve, modesty and consensus, and is uncomfortable with Westerners who are bold, aggressive, frank and familiar.

Singaporean participants in experiential programs express their discomfort in "strange" ways. Some participants might laugh out of context at the "misfortune" of other team members in order to hide their own feelings of embarrassment or nervousness. Most Asians are not fond of touching each other, and would find any training activity involving close body contact to be very difficult. In addition, few Asian participants are able to "open up" and share their feelings on a deep personal level.

The Chinese are mainly Buddhists or Christians, the Malays are Muslims, and the Indians are mainly Hindus or Christians. Even issues such as eating can be difficult. Buddhists and Hindus do not eat beef, Indians like mutton, but Chinese hate mutton, considering it "smelly". The Chinese main meat staple is pork, which is forbidden for Malays. In most training programs in Singapore, chicken becomes the main meat staple.

As Muslims, many Malay women wear veils and clothing that covers the whole body, even for outdoor and indoor experiential training programs. Malays also fast during the month of Ramadan. Experiential programs require problem solving skills and trust in fellow participants, in which females often do as well as, or better than, males. This is perceived as a threat to the traditional Asian concept of "male domination" which is a factor in many experiential training programs.

> *Dr. Mario Kölblinger, an experiential trainer based in Germany, with training experience throughout Europe, gives some insight into the cultural issues which can affect training in Germany:*

In Germany, as in much of the industrialized world, there is a critical need to find more effective training methods. This training must offer more opportunities for active learning; personal and meaningful involvement of the participants; direct and immediate control of learning success; more group learning and an increased transfer of learning. While many of these essential elements are inherent in outdoor-based training, German executives are rather reluctant to engage in this, and other more novel forms, of experiential learning.

This hesitation seems to stem from several sources:

1. There appears to be some confusion about how these programs could fit harmoniously into the existing body of corporate education. How does this type of (experiential) training successfully mix with other forms of learning and traditional indoor workshops? Besides the lack of information on this type of training, German managers tend to be skeptical towards everything new and unusual.

2. Our economic and industrial approach, in general, is characterized by a (natural) conservatism, which does not allow for much non-conformism, experimentation, or risk-taking. There seems to be an unspoken agreement about what is learning and what is fun, with a strict separation between work and play. Children are taught to clearly differentiate between the two. Serious activities should not look like leisure activities. It is no wonder that enjoyable

experiential learning activities are not easily accepted by German managers.

This impression of fun and leisure is regularly reinforced by the press and television, with a tendency to emphasize these aspects of experiential training to attract interest and attention. Their presentation of these programs ignore learning needs and objectives, progression of the activities, and any attempts to transfer the learning to the work setting. For an uninitiated observer this makes it very difficult to see a valid connection between experiential learning and performance in the work setting.

3. German managers tend to reject new and novel ideas without first asking for the justification and theory. Anglo-American cultures allow managers to experience novel issues in a more unbiased way. If they believe that it could serve a purpose, British and American managers seem to be more ready to use it without requiring the theory behind it. German managers tend to question new training methods thoroughly. They are interested in the reasons behind it, research data, underlying scientific explanation, and proof of efficacy. To meet these demands, it is often best to approach German managers with an analytical presentation of new training programs. For programs emphasizing "soft skills" this can be difficult or impossible.

4. Conformity to culturally acceptable norms plays a major role in management's view of experiential training concepts. German companies and their managers do mind what other companies, their managers, customers and the public might think (of them) if they used programs like outdoor adventure training. There is concern for their reputation; whether their training programs will match their corporate credibility, image and standing. Some departments and their managers are afraid that they will look "silly" when they suggest using experiential programs, or are assigned to attend one as a pilot project ("Why must we be the first in the company to do adventure training?"). The decision to use outdoor development programs is often very dependent on who else is using these programs in their business and industry. There seems to be a "hidden benchmarking" attitude between German corporations that "Me too" works!

Sometimes clients ask to de-emphasize the outdoor approach in the written program information, or even "disguise" the emotive words "outdoor workshop" and replace them with "action learning workshop." This concept of substituting labels works for other terms, such as "peak experience" or other more militaristic idioms and metaphors like "electric fence", "mine field", "the wall" or "one shot solution activity." When these phrases are avoided and the outdoor profile kept low, it helps overcome fears and harmonize expectations within and outside the company. Then the training results can speak for themselves.

5. Other reasons for hesitation and doubts about experiential training programs are found in Germany as well as other cultures. These reasons include:

◆   "Distance" to the work place.

◆   Preference for cognitive forms of training.

◆ Fear of getting too "informal" between employees (addressing each other with the informal "Du" instead of "Sie," which is often an unwritten habit in the outdoors, and sometimes raises serious concerns).

◆ Fear of personal disclosure.

◆ Fear of physical strain.

◆ Fear of looking silly in front of others.

◆ Fear of the military or macho climate.

◆ Gender issues.

◆ Safety and risk issues.

◆ Fear that this looks like recreation, not work.

◆ Fear of a different incentive atmosphere (rewarding rather than challenging).

Mike Main, a trainer in the African country of Botswana, looks at one culture in Africa, and how that culture can affect the design and use of experiential learning.

Botswana is a large, land-locked country located in central southern Africa with a population of a little over a million people. A former British Protectorate (not a colony), it became independent in 1966 and discovered fabulous diamond wealth at the end of that decade. As a result in the short space of twenty-eight years, one of the poorest and least developed nations in the world has hauled itself into the twentieth century from the leisurely and uncomplicated existence of a largely pastoral society.

Although generalizations are misleading and often inaccurate it is true to say that many Batswana (the country is Botswana, its people are the Batswana and an individual is a Motswana) find themselves with one foot lingering in a deeply traditional way of life and the other, less confidently, seeking an uncertain path through the labyrinth of Western capitalism's commercial values, practices and norms.

Successive tribes that arrived in the country over the centuries are seen as "waves" of settlement. Each wave dominated its predecessors, sometimes by force or threat of arms. A social "pecking order" is also apparent in Botswana, based on the dominance of each "wave" over the preceding "waves." The effect of this, while not marked in an overt sense, especially in urban societies and among the better educated, still persists in a covert sense. Thus a Mokgalakgadi will be looked down upon by a Mopedi who will, in turn, be considered inferior by a Mongwato. All of them consider the earliest arrivals, the San, to be infinitely inferior.

Generally, subordinated peoples (especially the San, who were subordinate to all) were incorporated into the wards (administrative units) of the dominant group, sometimes as *Batlhanka bagaKgosi*, (the Chief's servants) or as *Malata* (essentially, serfs). *Batlhanka* did not receive any status and were not recognized as members of any group. Nor were *Malata*, who were unable to represent themselves. They were not accepted as belonging or being part of the dominant tribe and were not allowed to attend the tribal court (Campbell & Main, 1991).

In traditional Botswana, tribal hierarchies are a marked component of social interaction. The modern manager finds it hard to escape being touched, however lightly, by the social consequences of this legacy.

In the past and to a certain extent today, tribes are administered by a tribal authority headed by a chief. Contact with the tribe and tribal opinion is maintained through the traditional court or *Kgotla*, where all members of the tribe may speak their mind and where issues affecting the tribe are discussed. The *Kgotla* is the root of Botswana's modern democratic tradition, the existence of which suggests an egalitarian and democratic value system. This is only partly true and highlights another discordant aspect of the modern manager's dilemma.

Research conducted by the Botswana Society (1988) suggests that traditional democracy in Botswana is much more a process of consultation than one of participation. Traditionally, the Chief is the father of the people, the leader, and is responsible for the welfare of his people. If there is war he must defend them; if there is drought, he must feed them. His word is law and is not to be questioned. This paternalistic, autocratic society encourages an abrogation of individual responsibility to central authority.

Open disagreement is not a tradition in Botswana. Historically, when serious dissension within a tribe grew, it would be covertly discussed but little would appear on the surface until, quite suddenly, a new leader would emerge and the group would fragment. Only then would the existence of an open breach be acknowledged. Traditionally, tolerance in the modern democratic sense, was not as widespread as institutions such as the *Kgotla* might suggest. These traditions of paternalistic, autocratic leadership, and lack of open discussion of areas of dissension stalk the business manager of today.

A further issue from tribal culture, one that is pervasive and a very real factor in management situations, is that women are subordinate to men. Men dominate management and business and, in the commercial world, women are regarded by many, especially the older generations, as being less than equal. To some extent this effect is beginning to dissipate today as a result of the women's rights movement.

Botswana is a multi-party democracy which follows the British model. While Parliament is the sole law-making authority, there exists a constitutional body that meets regularly, called the House of Chiefs, whose purpose is to act in an advisory capacity. There has, over past decades, been a steady diminution of the power of the Chiefs, the decline of which may be shown by future researchers as closely parallel to a shift in the demographic profile as older, more traditional people are slowly replaced by the young. This shift is often reflected in managerial cadres, especially when the old and young are working in the same organization. As elsewhere in the world, age is strongly deferred to in a traditional society. In Botswana today, the old expect to be obeyed and respected, simply because they are old. Increasingly, however, younger generations are beginning to challenge this right, generating a conflict that provides another factor influencing the way managers manage.

When the economic growth that accompanied the mining and diamond boom occurred, the country was found to be woefully short of professional and management resources. Necessarily, ex-patriate staff were employed, creating in the eyes of the Batswana, a resentment that jobs were being "taken away from them."

In the three decades since independence, a time span that has seen pervasive conflict in the sub-region (Rhodesia, Mozambique, Angola, Namibia and South Africa), Botswana's wealth and political stability have acted as a magnet for the displaced and the poor. This, plus the influx of ex-patriates, has helped exacerbate a (perhaps) incipient xenophobia. Resentment of foreigners is a theme that often emerges in training situations.

While generalizations are risky, the trainer of Batswana managers today can expect, especially in the middle to senior management range, to encounter strongly traditional males; accustomed to an autocratic and paternalistic management style; given to consultation, not participation and, therefore, often overly directive; reverence for age and seniority; inability to see women in equal terms; xenophobic; tribe and status conscious; probably under-trained and weak in some essential skills for the positions they currently hold. These factors combine in interesting ways to create issues in management which trainers need to address. Some examples are:

Decision-Making: There is more than ordinary reluctance to make decisions inside structured organizations. While individuals, acting in their own interests and on their own account, are perfectly capable of making decisions, the same does not hold within paternalistically structured organizations. Here the shadow of tradition is long. Decisions are seen as the responsibility of the "Chief." There is a tendency to find out "what the boss thinks is right" (regardless of what may actually be right). Ideas of delegation, responsibility and authority have yet to take a firm hold.

As managers enter upon, and climb the ladder of management promotion, they are taught, by example, how to manage, and tend to use that same style later on in their careers, as senior management. In this way a management ethos is created and perpetuated.

Correcting Others: Closely allied with decision making issues is a marked reluctance to correct other individuals. Supervisors are willing to tell subordinates what they want them to do but are unwilling to do what is necessary to see that subordinates actually carry out specified tasks. This tendency pervades the management ladder.

Hierarchy: Position is highly valued and sought after, not necessarily for the responsibility, reward or satisfaction it gives but for the status that is assumed by the incumbent. Position is power, power is influence (and money). It is very important to "be" somebody.

Communication: This is markedly one-way. Communication as a modern issue in Botswana's commercial world is the child of the autocratic tradition. People are accustomed to being told what to do and to tell others. Listening skills are underdeveloped.

Language and Literacy: The country has two official languages: Setswana and English. All Batswana speak the former, many the latter. The degree of fluency, however, varies widely. The language of the business world is predominantly English. Because the level of education is quite low for many, considerable communication barriers exist. Trainers need to be alert to this complex problem area.

Misunderstandings are endemic both in the giving and receiving of instructions. Trainers must either match their language level to the lowest common denominator or instruct in Setswana. Unfortunately, few managers or trainers are able to instruct in Setswana.

Feedback Sessions: Batswana are unusually sensitive to criticism. Feedback sessions are eagerly greeted in principle but must be carefully structured and handled so as to avoid appearing critical. It is more important *how* something is said than *what* is said.

Traditionally, an individual's thinking was largely done for him, and as a result people are not accustomed to being introspective. For this reason, personal questions and questions such as "How do you feel?", "What do you think?" are often met with uncomprehending silence.

The Black/White Mix: For many, this is a problem area. Whites largely control the commercial sector and fill all the top positions. Invariably the CEO and the accounting/financial positions are white. Technical posts are also filled by whites, reflecting the paucity of local skills.

Most whites are employed on ex-patriate terms—given remuneration that approximates what they might have earned in their home countries and compensates them for the "hardships" of working in a Third World country. As a result, the resentment with which some Batswana view ex-patriates is quite understandable; "They take all the top positions and pay themselves huge salaries, getting two or three times what they pay us." Periodically, in local newspapers, an outcry flares up over the way in which "expats" are "ripping off" the country.

Expectations: The so-called "crisis of expectations" which so often accompanies the emergence of newly independent states in Africa is not now an issue in Botswana. When the country became independent, there was nothing to "expect." Now that the economic booms have passed (for the moment), those who were going to become "Haves" have reached their goal.

Some traces of unrealistic expectations linger. Many people still fervently believe that length of service equates with "promotability." Promotion is a function of time on the job, not of performance in the job. In Botswana it links strongly back to the tribal system where the Chief relied for support upon village elders, men who reached their position simply by staying alive.

A second expectation, closely linked to the first, that if the job is (merely) held, it must have been held satisfactorily. Accordingly, it is expected, appropriate reward should be forthcoming (usually in the shape of at least a double increment!). Attitude towards work also impacts severely upon issues such as time-keeping and absences from work for personal or family/community reasons (funerals, weddings, births, etc.). It has been said that no one is more creative than a Mostwana when it comes to giving reasons not to be at work! Many of these characteristics can be found in other cultures and certainly to a greater or lesser degree in many American sub-cultures, reinforcing the necessity to train and accommodate culturally diverse work forces even within a single country.

> *These excerpts were selected to give the reader a "feel" for the importance and diversity of the cultural issues involved in experiential training in multi-cultural situations. A few more brief examples further illustrate this issue.*

◆ The French, whose Descartian system of education institutionalizes starting any exploration with an hypothesis to test, in other words, starting at the abstract conceptualization stage rather than at the experience stage.

◆ The Japanese, whose lives are generally highly ordered, with everything and everyone having a place. Any change to this pre-ordination will require permission from those above, so that experiential training can only be effective if it is conducted in "free time" where non-conformist behavior is acceptable.

◆ In Buddhist countries confrontation or conflict is seen as counterproductive, reflecting badly on those involved, and a misuse or abuse of energy that could otherwise have been put to productive use.

◆ Many cultures consider personal and open feedback to be difficult and/or outright insulting.

These examples are stereotypical, which can be dangerous in specific situations and are changing rapidly in many parts of the world. Nevertheless, they provide a starting point for multi-cultural experiential learning, and help to emphasize that the cultural heritage of the participants is critical to the design and facilitation of experiential programs.

Cultural concerns can be categorized into two general areas: socialization issues and language topics. The remainder of this chapter analyzes these areas in depth, and presents specific examples from around the world. These categorizations are broadly based on the work of Trompenaars (1993).

Socialization

Socialization is the sum of values acquired as people mature. A number of specific aspects of a person's cultural background have a direct impact on the experiential learning process, including:

Relationship-oriented versus Rules-oriented: Cultures with a rules orientation are frequently found where the dominant religion places a high value on obedience to written laws. Rules-oriented cultures are more likely to use the courts to solve their problems, whereas the relationship-oriented cultures will look for ways of resolving matters through the use of their relationships. In fact, the whole purpose of the relationship, and the time devoted to develop it diminishes the prospects of mistakes and errors later on. Each of these orientations tends to view the other with mistrust!

How do experiential trainers design a program to meet the needs of the relationship-oriented and the rules-oriented participants? Even the description of an activity could have entirely different meanings depending on one's cultural background. Asking participants to perform a task shortly after the start of a program, and then review it by providing meaningful feedback, may be entirely appropriate for some participants and bewildering or offensive to others. Conducting programs in a multi-cultural environment must have a balance between establishing relationships and moving forward with the active elements of the program.

Cultural background also influences how issues are addressed in the observation (feedback) phase of the experiential process. Behaviors that do not conform to the rules will be frowned upon by rules-oriented cultures, whereas there is likely to be a far higher level of tolerance from relationship-based cultures. What may be anathema to one may be entirely appropriate for another!

Group or individual orientation: In the western world this differentiation correlates with religion. The Protestant work ethic rewards the individual for hard work. Roman Catholics perceive themselves as a community of the faithful. Catholics score higher on group choices than do Protestants (Hofstede, 1984). This difference can significantly affect the way in which business is conducted. For instance, a single Anglo-Saxon might participate in a negotiation and be prepared to make decisions on behalf of his/her organization. However, unaccompanied people from group-oriented cultures are assumed to lack status. Hence it would be rare to find a sole Japanese, Frenchman or Nigerian negotiating; they would either arrive as a delegation, or require time to confer, preferably face to face, with their colleagues at home. In group-oriented cultures, decision-making typically takes much longer often with sustained efforts to win people over to a consensus point of view. In the case of the Japanese it might mean providing enough time for apparent dissenters to change at their own pace, which might take months. In Anglo-Saxon cultures issues might be put to a vote, and assertive behavior is valued as a strategy to convince others.

For the experiential trainer, group or individual orientation can impact the way decision making strategies are encouraged. Individual accountability, and the choice of appropriate programs are affected. For example, there is little or no need for team-building programs in Japan, since the educational system is based on a collective approach, and the highest level of achievement is to be in harmonious relationship with oneself and the environment. These issues influence both the design and facilitation process: what is right for a group from one culture may not be right for a group from a different cultural background.

"Diffuse" culture versus "specific" culture

This difference is based on the work of Kurt Lewin, and his theory of the amount of private and public space individuals require (Lewin, 1936). Public space refers to that part of their lives that people are willing to share with others, while private space is that part of their lives that they will not readily share. Those from a diffuse culture will have a large amount of private space, while those from a specific culture typically will have a small amount of private space and segment their public space into many small parts. Americans are typical of a specific culture, with a small amount of private space, and segmented public space. Americans can seem very friendly to other cultures because they readily allow others to share one segment of their public space, since this is not a very big commitment. However, being welcome in one area of public space does not mean one is welcome in all of these segments, or that one is welcome into the small private space.

On the other hand, Germans are said to be typical of diffuse cultures where there is a very large private space. Once a person is admitted into a German's private space, then admittance expands into almost all the private spaces. Many Germans see Americans as noisy and superficial and Americans often perceive Germans to be remote and difficult to get to know. A major problem with interactions between these two cultures is defining the impersonal or the highly personal issues because each is perceived so differently by diffuse and specific cultures.

This complex area, and potential minefield for trainers, can only be traversed by careful design and sensitive facilitation. The amount and content of disclosure, and sharing, of thoughts and feelings which is acceptable in one culture may be totally unacceptable in another.

Achievement of Status Through Doing or Being

In Scandinavian, Dutch, British and American cultures, status accrues through achievement. Success is identified with achievement, and people tend to be promoted based on accomplishment rather than social stature. In other cultures, status is often considered a birthright. In Botswana, managers are not respected for their track record but for the position they hold. It is generally assumed (often incorrectly), that they were given this position because of seniority and tribal origin, which would indicate to their subordinates a higher quality of life experience.

Generally, ascriptive (being) cultures tend to respect such things as age, education, profession and social connections rather than task achievement. Andre Laurent (1986) found that French and Italian managers were much more emphatic about needing to know all the answers than were managers from "doing" cultures.

This has significant repercussions in the business world and in particular, the training environment. For example, the function of delegation in an "achieving" society frees the manager's time to work on more important tasks. It could also mean that the boss does not know the answers to subordinates' questions. In a "being" society, delegating work sends an entirely different message and could be very confusing. For subordinates in France and Italy, it might translate into a loss of respect for the boss. In Botswana it could mean a loss of initiative since it is expected that the boss makes all decisions.

Corporate experiential learning program design must be based on the cultural orientation of the participants as well as the desired corporate goals. Is the purpose of the program to help people be more aware of each other or is it to try to change their work behaviors? This is especially significant in many emerging Third-World countries. In many parts of Africa much of the industrial and commercial capital comes from Europe and America. Thus, many of the corporate cultures are basically Anglo-Saxon, and "achieving" in orientation. This senior management orientation often leads to frustration with more junior African managers who demonstrate little desire to take the initiative or to be accountable for their work teams because of the culturally valued decision-making process. The African managers are also frustrated and uncomfortable since they are being asked to act "out of culture." Interestingly, there is no evidence that "doing" cultures are more economically successful than "being" cultures. The real potential for organizational success lies in the potential fusion of the two cultures. The real challenge and benefit in the experiential event is that these differences can be discussed openly, and dealt with in a safe environment.

Time Management

There seem to be two distinctly different approaches to managing time. One views time as a commodity in short supply and sequential in nature. Cultures using this approach insist on using time management, plan in a series (or stages) needing careful description and check points, and also have extreme difficulty trying to do two things simultaneously. The other approach views time as cyclical and repetitive, in which the goal is tracking many things in parallel and doing several things at the same time. In a sequential society you may walk into someone's office and find them on the telephone; you are waved to a chair, the conversation finished and then you are greeted. In a synchronic society it is considered rude not to be greeted immediately and spontaneously, even while on the phone. Time management is not a critical element in a synchronic society. This has a dramatic effect on the way business is conducted. Meeting times in these societies are approximate, and can range from 15 minutes late in Latin Europe and Latin America, to part or all of a day late in the Middle East or Africa.

This has an interesting effect on the approach to planning. Sequential cultures use intermediate check points to reach a destination, and it is as important for them to reach each of the intermediate points as it is to achieve the final goal (i.e., measuring progress). In synchronous cultures the ultimate objective is far more important than the specific route taken to reach it, thus, people spend more time producing alternative paths, thereby increasing the likelihood of getting there.

For the experiential trainer these different views of time are important considerations in the selection of appropriate experiential activities and the conduct of reviewing these activities (including the debrief, feedback and evaluation). Not only will different cultures experience the activities differently, but they will also have different approaches to accomplishment. The orientation of the trainer, and the predominant culture of the organization may well determine which approach is deemed to be correct. This reliance on a single, most effective approach to planning, is unfortunate, since there is evidence that a more holistic approach to planning is more effective in times of rapid and unpredictable change.

Language

Language differences are crucial in multi-cultural training. While the corporate management world uses English as the primary language, the majority of employees in many other countries consider English a second language or a foreign (unknown) language.

Experiential programs around the world often have participants from a number of different countries attending at the same time. The participants grasp of English will vary from superb to tenuous. The commitment and energy (physical & emotional) required for some experiential programs is often substantial. The added difficulty of working and expressing feelings in a foreign language requires considerable empathy on the part of both facilitators and those who speak English as a native language. The speakers of English as a second language often revert to their native language both during and after exercises even though it can cause concern among first language English speakers who may wonder if this is some deliberate exclusion tactic!

To facilitate conversation and dealings with other nationalities, speakers of English as a second language often resort to a sort of "off-shore" English (Guy and Mattock, 1991), which is a stripped-down version of English with its ambiguities removed. People can be extremely fluent in this version of English, but not familiar with the innuendoes, inflections and idioms used by those who speak English as a first language. This can be confusing and frustrating to the team, and possibly, to the facilitator. This environment highlights the need for clear communication in a way that is assumed (rightly or wrongly) in a mono-cultural situation.

We should not overlook the potential for mis-communication among peoples whose languages are all "English." Many examples of confusion and embarrassment illustrate this point: the "fanny pack," a commonly used term in the U.S. for a small bag belted at the waist. In Britain the word "fanny" refers to a part of the female anatomy and is not used in polite company. In the business environment to "table an item" in Britain means to add it to the agenda for immediate discussion, whereas in America, it means to defer discussion to another time!

This creates challenges for the corporate experiential trainer in the description and presentation of exercises. They need to be simple, clear and avoid idiomatic expressions whenever possible, and yet not be patronizing. The same concerns must influence the nature and communication style of the review sessions as well.

Experiential Training Around the World

This chapter is based on a comprehensive collection of material provided by many experiential trainers. The authors wish to thank and recognize the many contributors from around the world whose information has been woven into this chapter. Their contributions are outlined in the table below. The examples shed more light on some of the socialization issues peculiar to each country, which may be found in multi-cultural training environments.

EXAMPLES OF INTERNATIONAL CULTURAL ISSUES	
Australia **(Steve Colman)**	Many of the providers come from a military background & some carry this military training a little too rigorously. In the "new Australian Management style", self directed work teams and participative management are replacing traditional "positional power." For most Australians, outdoor experiential activities are fun, but bear no relationship to the work environment.
Australia **(Jan Stevens)**	Physical contact is not the norm in the work place, and there is usually some initial wariness about touching in mixed gender groups.
Belgium **(Dr. Luc Lefebvre)**	Moving from a relatively fixed economic environment into the unknown period of global competition, managers must now make decisions rapidly and correctly the first time in order for their business to survive. Activity/metaphor example: Manager steps into a kayak just before the curve in a wild water river. He/she can hear the rapids, but not see them, and must listen to quickly sense the speed and direction, and paddle accordingly.
United Kingdom **(John Campbell)**	A mix of models has been found—from the "overactive" wilderness programs, to interactive outdoor models such as "virtual reality" training. (Wagner & Campbell, 1994)

EXAMPLES OF INTERNATIONAL CULTURAL ISSUES	
United Kingdom (cont'd.)	Having to deal with multi-cultural issues is becoming common. The U.K. is not a single entity. Wales and Scotland and Ireland exhibit fierce nationalistic tendencies, which require careful programming.
Indonesia (Shinta Suliswayati)	Uses a broad-based approach with most providers concentrating on the activities rather than the process. A predominately Muslim community which, nevertheless, takes quite well to the concept of experiential training. They have no culturally acceptable way of dealing with conflict, and this requires sensitive handling.
Japan (Munehiro Mitsuzuka)	Collectivism is a way of life, and begins in the early grades of school. Team work and cooperation is taught from the earliest years. Thus, team building is not necessary for corporate training, since it is ingrained in workers since childhood. Honest or open discussion is a function of whether the participants are on "free time" (non-work, or personal time) or company time.
The Netherlands (Dr. Ton Duindan)	Basic concept of learning is through the "collective" or group. One belief—the "best headmaster" at a school is the one that does nothing—forcing the student to learn by doing (thus, experiential learning). Dutch word for experiential learning is "ervaringsleren"—and is considered a "value free" experience.
New Zealand (Dr. Darl Kolb)	From bungee jumping to heli-skiing, heli-rafting or heli-just-about-anything, "Kiwis," (New Zealanders) love adventure and the outdoors. There is a historic self-sufficiency required to live in this small nation of islands. Although changing rapidly, rates of formal education in New Zealand are low in comparison to other developed nations. Cradle-to-grave social programs and very low unemployment until the past decade meant that many Kiwis developed skills through apprenticeships, on-the-job training and the school-of-hard-knocks. In sum, historically, formal (passive)

EXAMPLES OF INTERNATIONAL CULTURAL ISSUES	
New Zealand (cont'd.)	Paths to education and development have been eschewed by many Kiwis in exchange for learning by doing. There have been few lawsuits for accidents and injury on adventure or challenge courses. Indeed, most education and training companies carry little or no liability insurance.
New Zealand (Trevor Laurance)	Outdoor adventure activities are used to "test" relationships under stress. Team programs have also evolved from similar outdoor leadership training, and military leadership training tasks. Outdoor Management Development (OMD) is based on the British model, and uses "Indoor Workshops/Debriefing of Exercises" and "Management Simulations" to achieve long term attitudinal and behavioral changes.
Scotland (Roger Greenaway)	Primary focus is on team building programs. Most of the cultural issues are the same as in Britain (see John Campbell above). The concept of "rugged individualism" seems to favor the more adventure-oriented program.
Singapore (Dr. Victor C.H. Lim)	Raising and discussing personal issues is quite difficult. Managers tend to start out with a task-orientation. A number of religious taboos (e.g., touching in some instances) need to be dealt with. A key in most experiential programs is individual choice to attend, or not attend a program.
South Africa (Dr. Willie Marais)	A culture going through a massive upheaval. Cross cultural training is a way of life, and the "work organization" has been the only source of stability for many people for the last several years.

These examples enumerate some of the more difficult cultural issues which corporate experiential learning must address. In Japan, orientation is a lengthy process (six months or longer) and incorporates experiential activities as part of the "get-acquainted" process to help new employees understand what is required of them. Corporate experiential training is not well developed in France, although Outward Bound, Inc. and other providers use experiential methods. This appears related to the learning styles of the population (Mumford & Honey, 1986). French participants can be broken down into three distinct groups. The first group thinks they are on a holiday in which they can do fun activities; the second group wants to prove they know more than the facilitators, and the third want to try out this new and perhaps strange methodology. This means a struggle for the facilitator to influence the behaviors within any diverse group incorporating all three types. These styles often appear in experiential learning programs in the United States, as well.

Experiential learning is not a substantial part of the training process in Arab countries. Schooling in the Arabian culture is focused on the formal classroom, where the teacher is the prime mover and expert; so the idea of the learner-centered process is foreign.

Applications for Experiential Learning

This varies around the world, yet, with some common themes:

Team building is probably the most common issue addressed by experiential training programs throughout the world. As mentioned, this has no relevance in Japan, but is a very common in Indonesia, Australia, New Zealand, the U.K., much of Europe and the U.S. Evidence suggests that intact work teams benefit the most from this type of training (Wagner & Roland, 1992).

Leadership and management skills training: Although not necessarily the same, these two issues are frequently combined in the same experiential program. In Great Britain this is probably as common as team building (see John Campbell & Roger Greenaway above).

In Botswana (Main) this is the prime use for experiential training, just as it is in South Africa (Marais). The primary area of concern is which leadership or management model is appropriate for a particular organization. Most practitioners in English speaking countries or trainers working with multi-cultural groups will use American or British models.

Based on the cultural issues discussed earlier, just how appropriate are these models to the participants? Batswana managers have had to adjust to the dramatic economic improvement of the country in the last twenty-five years and come to terms with the effects of this new wealth. In addition, foreign industrial investment has changed the nature of work, managerial prospects, diminished traditional tribal status, and is gradually changing the role of women in society and business. Yet, the Government encourages business to employ Batswana in senior posts for which they are unlikely qualified, in the eyes of the investor. What is appropriate? How to achieve a delicate balance between old and new? All of these issues influence the way in which management skills are developed (Main and Campbell).

Issues such as delegation, accountability (of the individual), empowerment, the need to be the expert as well as the manager, and the power/distance relationship (Hofstede, 1984) all vary in different cultures and affect the way in which experiential programs are developed and administered.

Feedback: Generally, conflict-adverse cultures find the notion of giving feedback a difficult proposition, as it could involve humiliation (losing face). In these cultures, a safe methodology needs to be developed so that giving feedback is seen as a helpful process, and not a threat to the individuals or the group. A free and open discussion of issues would not work in conflict-adverse cultures like that of Japan. There, appraisals are a private judgment of the subordinate by the superior and are not communicated openly. Feedback in a Japanese experiential program would have to be legitimized first, by casting the program in "free time," not in work time.

In Indonesia, a predominantly Moslem, and conflict-adverse culture, experiential programs are on the increase. While there may be an acknowledgment that conflict exists, the participants need to develop their own, non-threatening plan, for dealing with this conflict with the assistance of a skilled facilitator (Shinta Suliswayati).

In Australia, the concept of "mates" can be seen to have a major impact on the experiential training process. Mates will accept any challenge, but will not willingly share their thoughts and feelings. A skilled facilitator is needed to get the most value from an experiential training program (Brown).

Style of experiential training: There are many forms of experiential training programs used around the world. Americans favor ropes courses (either high or low), although wilderness programs are also quite popular (Wagner & Roland, 1992). New approaches are being developed all the time. There are programs where the activities are real-life situations with a real problem to solve and where the payoff for both parties is also real. (Caudron, 1994; Johnson, 1994; Wagner & Campbell, 1994)

New Zealand (Laurence) and the U.K. (Campbell) seem to be moving away from this activity-based approach, and into a more structured and outcome driven approach in which the real emphasis is on review, participant theory building and internalization of the training (Kolb). Evidence from a number of countries suggests the use of experiential training for culture change issues (Britain and South Africa).

Experiential training programs are very effective in multi-culture and diversity issues training. As the multinational organization continues to gain importance in the world economy, the importance of these training programs can be expected to grow as well.

Programs are generally designed to address a particular topic with the design and facilitation inevitably couched in the culture and language of the facilitator and the sponsoring organization. There is some legitimacy in this approach, since employees will have to survive in the prevailing corporate culture, and both employer and employee will benefit if training programs emphasize the working culture of the organization. However, the appreciation of cultural strengths and taboos woven into the fabric of the program maximizes the success of the program and benefits all concerned.

As Laurent has shown, the potential for a multi-cultural team is great, but so are the problems in training this type of team to be a top performer. Multi-cultural teams tend to be either at the top of the performance group, or at the bottom. The sensitive design and implementation of experiential training programs can guide these groups to the top of the performance curve.

CHAPTER SEVEN

ISSUES AND CONCERNS

While the popularity of many experiential learning models is growing, there are some serious issues and concerns that, if ignored, will cause the corporate experiential learning movement to deteriorate to a fad, or as controversy and skepticism continue, to be rejected by many organizations.

After a tongue-in-cheek vignette by Bob Weigand featuring some currently popular activities that are often viewed as "experiential learning," this chapter continues with a comparison of experiential learning and the encounter-group movement of the sixties and seventies. "Parallel Revolutions: 1970 and 1990" by Tom Smith and Chris Roland suggests that Experiential Learning evokes similar reactions and concerns as did the earlier Encounter Group movement. CEL can also be viewed as a refinement of the encounter group movement; evolutionary, in that it has taken some of the encounter group objectives, focused them on specific organizational settings and particular behavioral, personal and interactive goals, in order to improve the quality of personal and organizational life.

*One specific concern focuses on the providers and facilitators who are charged with making experiential programs and processes relevant to the business setting. Who are they? What are their credentials, philosophies and perspectives? Todd Miner addresses these questions in "The Providers of Outdoor-based Training." However, it is important to note that Todd's research is focused on providers of **outdoor-based** programs. Not included are the many providers who utilize experiential methods (primarily indoors) in an effort to reinforce particular learning points.*

A second concern, involving facilitators, is addressed by Tom Smith in "Crossing the Line: Psychological Considerations." Though many CEL activities and exercises are designed and facilitated to focus on business issues, participants sometimes find themselves discussing very sensitive and private emotional issues. How qualified are the trainers to handle the significant responsibility of carefully and professionally guiding the personal growth of participants?

A number of issues deal with "Experiential Learning: Outdoor Adventure" (OA) models. These models require participants to leave the indoor environment for team development, leadership development, etc. Outdoor Adventure activities typically involve high levels of physical ability, including strength, balance and coordination. These experiences, where participants find themselves balancing on cables, climbing over twelve foot walls and speeding down "zip lines" has evoked much controversy. Jackson (1992) commented, "As a vehicle for [training], experience indicates that ropes courses . . . are virtually worthless—marginal parallels with military training notwithstanding. Derisively referred to as "tree therapy" by some senior executives, many ropes courses are big on style, but exceedingly short on substance."

Warren Cohen discusses this perception in "Ropes Courses: Misconceptions and Applications." Then Camille Bunting presents research on physiological concerns in Outdoor Adventure activities. This information is critical to any organization considering Outdoor Adventure models; Ryan (1991) noted there have been at least four deaths from cardiac arrest associated with ropes course programs from 1986 through 1991.

Among professional concerns for the welfare and well-being of clients and participants, these scary facts also point to legal liability concerns. Kezman and Connors (1993) discussed areas of potential legal pitfalls for companies using physically and emotionally demanding team-building and risk-taking exercises including negligence claims for personal injury, intentional infliction of emotional distress, invasion of privacy, false imprisonment and wrongful discharge. The recent Americans with Disabilities Act (ADA) raises questions about training providing equal access and fair treatment of employees based on ability.

Betty van der Smissen, a foremost authority on legal liability in the Outdoor Adventure area, discusses these issues in "Legal Implications of Corporate Outdoor Adventure programs."

Is THIS Corporate Experiential Learning?

Robert Weigand

"Congratulations," the letter read, "You've won an all expenses paid trip to some training sites around the country, and even in Europe. Your mission, if you decide to accept it, is to resolve this question: *'Is THIS Corporate Experiential Learning?'* "

First stop: New England. In the midst of a sales training session: "Group, today you will be doing something unique, something different. Today you will be fire walking! That's right, in front of you appears a fourteen foot long bed of 1,200 degree coals. No need to worry, once you learn the technique, it's a piece of cake."

A woman attempting to walk across, finds her toenails on fire. Luckily, the firefighter, hired as part of the program, extinguishes the flames quickly. Reminded of last summer's near singe at my neighbor's cookout, I opt to leave early and continue my search for Corporate Experiential Learning.

Next stop: Arizona. For the "experience" that would have cost $4,000, I receive Aroma Therapy, Herbal Wraps, Mud Treatments called "total body fangos", all in the name of finding my inner self. Feeling aromafied, and massaged to the max, I continue my journey.

By now, certain words are beginning to creep into everyday conversation. Almost unconsciously, I find myself saying things like, "end state vision," "internal resource," "metanoic" and "structural integrity." This new vocabulary keeps me in good company at my next stop.

New Mexico: Searching for a less expensive experiential program, I find myself at a wine and cheese reception on the eve of a one day seminar on team building. It is advertised as "most unique"—and so it is—our team will be headed *underground to a "maze cave."* There, our team will need to collectively determine the correct path out (and up). But first, after the wine and cheese, we learn about "synergism," "pareto optimality," and "contribution vs. domination." After a night's sleep we embark on our day of adventure. At the entrance to the cave, I don my gear, listen to my instructor's safety reminders, followed by, "Turn your head lamps on, folks. It's time to go below . . . "

Not yet convinced that I had found experiential learning, I returned home to Pennsylvania. I called a few friends to let them know of my quest and ask them to let me know if they hear of anything that might fit into my search.

The following night I received a call. "Bob, this is Paul, I came across a videotape that highlights an experiential learning program in Europe." "Great, come on over, let's look at it."

Paul arrived and we plugged in the tape. The director of the program explains that the aim of the course is the improvement of teamwork, communication, and leadership. A group is asked to strip to their underwear and swim in frigid water up to a rocky coast with their belongings in tow. Then they set up their own tents while blindfolded. That same night a storm hits the campground collapsing one of the tents on its inhabitants. They climb a summit in 80 mile per hour wind gusts. Again, I hear the words, teamwork, communication, and leadership . . .

Final segments of the tape show the group instructed to abandon ship because it's "sinking." They have minimal time to make the decision. Instead, they opt to throw the group leader overboard.

Since water activity really isn't my thing, I find myself in Florida ready to embark on a team building adventure in the sky! As I strap myself in a single engine high performance aircraft, I keep thinking about those words: teamwork, communication and leadership. As we (whew—there *is* an experienced pilot on board!) reach speeds of 200 miles per hour and begin dogfighting with another aircraft, I am not thinking about how this experience will help me back at work—I am thinking about simple things, like my family. Our aircraft is screaming towards the "enemy" aircraft on a head-on course: we're getting closer, closer . . .

I am being shaken. "Bob! Bob!, wake up. You've been dreaming". "Huh, what?"

My wife, Susan, is peering over me. I'm in a sweat from head to toe. "Whoa, Suz, you're not going to believe the dream I just had."

"Yeah", she said," you were shouting something about corporate . . . experiential . . . learning . . . and asking, "Is this it? Is this it?"

"Yes," I consciously wonder, "Are these methods and activities (that actually *do* take place in corporate training) experiential learning?" Many corporate managers and professional providers are wondering, too . . .

This vignette highlights several concerns and issues regarding CEL:

♦ Does the public equate these activities and only these activities with experiential learning?

♦ After an organization tries one of these programs and does not achieve the goals it had hoped for, is the organization likely to try other models or applications of experiential learning?

◆   Do these aforementioned programs, program leaders and clients consider:

Need analyses

Customized program design

Quality facilitation

Customer-provider partnerships

Follow-up transfer of learning

1970 AND 1990: PARALLEL REVOLUTIONS

THOMAS E. SMITH, PH.D.
CHRISTOPHER C. ROLAND, ED.D.

Psychological, physiological, legal issues

The corporate experiential training and development movement continues to expand throughout the United States. Other experiential movements (e.g., "Challenge/Adventure Education" in schools, "Challenge Therapy" in hospitals) also continue to expand. To many professionals in these fields, these movements have become revolutions.

The movements have generated a fascinating continuum of reaction—from extremely positive to extremely negative and similar to many "revolutions," have been the subjects of debate and concern. "Fad," "non-business related," "trendy," "dangerous" are some of the comments heard. The experiential/challenge/adventure movements parallel the popular "Encounter Group" movement of the 1960s and 1970s. Over time, in many business circles, this movement has developed a negative reputation due to the abuse by some practitioners. Today, the words "Encounter Group" are often met with a degree of cynicism.

There are still some training organizations that use encounter group methodologies, but it is no where near the popularity it had in the 1970s. The following excerpts from "Human Potential: A Revolution in Feeling" published in *Time Magazine*, November 9, 1970[1] and the authors' rewrite[2] illustrates the distinct and somewhat chilly parallel between Encounter Groups and the experiential/challenge/adventure movements. What can be learned from history in order to avoid the same fate?

[1]Copyright 1970 Time Inc. Reprinted by permission.
[2]An * indicates a fictitious name and/or place.

ENCOUNTER GROUP MOVEMENT, NOVEMBER 9, 1970:

" . . . In an Evanston, Illinois high school, students of English Teacher Thomas Klein shrouded themselves in bed sheets and crawled wildly about the floor. At a body-movement session in Beverly Hills, CA, participants took turns pummeling a sofa pillow with feral ferocity. From a four-story midtown Manhattan brownstone, the sound of screaming can be heard all day long. It comes from the patients of Psychiatrist Daniel Casriel, who believes that such release is therapeutic. In Escondido, CA, a group of naked men and women, utter strangers, step into what their leader calls a "womb pool . . . "

" . . . To many Americans, these activities typify a leaderless, formless and wildly eclectic movement that is variously called "sensitivity training," "encounter," "therapy for normals," "the body biz," or the "acidless trip." Such terms merely describe the more sensational parts of a whole that is coming to be known as the human potential movement—a quest conducted in hundreds of ways and places to redefine and enrich the spirit of social man."

EXPERIENTIAL/CHALLENGE/ ADVENTURE MOVEMENT, JANUARY 9, 1990:

At an Evanston, Illinois high school, students of English Teacher Garret Jackson* cover their eyes with blindfolds and walk through an obstacle course in the hallway. At a therapeutic recreation session at the Rehabilitation Center of Greater Boulder,* the group lifts members high above their heads and rocks them to and fro. From the loft of the gymnasium at Brandon High School* in Brandon, Massachusetts, come the cries of "on belay" and "belay on" as students scramble up wooden blocks bolted to the wall. Cheers, congratulations, and hugs are the order of the day at a Kalamazoo, Michigan* outdoor program, as a group of teachers in training help each other conquer the "two line bridge."

To many Americans, these activities are difficult to understand. They are part of an eclectic movement that is variously called "adventure counseling," "challenge education," "experiential adventure," or "outdoor challenge." Some of the programs have slogans such as "go for it," "search for excellence," "bounding upward," and "natural highs."

Such phrases describe the purported journey to self-discovery, improved social relationships, and released inner potentials—a journey conducted in hundreds of ways and places, by a vast array of "professionals," to redefine and enrich the spirit of man.

ENCOUNTER, 1970:

" . . . To reach man's unawakened re-sources, the movement focuses on the actions and interaction of individuals in a group. In this it has borrowed freely from psychology's past, from such extenders of Freudian theory as Karen Horney and Harry Stack Sullivan, who realized that no individual can be defined, and no emotional disorder healed, without an examination of the interchange between one man and all the others in his life. Society itself is defined by the group. The movement's exponents argue that by expanding the individual's self-awareness and well-being within the group, a new feeling of community develops that strengthens both the individual and the group . . . "

" . . . The human potential movement has already touched the major social institutions: church, factory, school, and state. In a study for the Carnegie Corporation, Donald H. Clark, associate professor of education at New York's City University, reports that the movement has permeated every level of education from kindergarten to graduate school and beyond. Encounter sessions or T- (for training) groups have been held, sometimes as parts of the curriculum, in dozens of colleges and universities, among them Harvard, Columbia, Boston University, and the New School of Social Research. Big business has enlisted its employees in human potential centers in ever increasing numbers, and many companies now operate programs on their own . . . "

EXPERIENTIAL, 1990:

To reach man's unawakened potentials and guide him to understand self and others, the movement focuses on activities and adventures for small groups. In this they borrow from psychology's past, from the extenders of Freudian theory, Karen Horney and Harry Stack Sullivan towards group definition of self. The movement owes much to the social psychology theories of Kurt Lewin, and his emphasis on group dynamics.

There is also indebtedness to English educator Kurt Hahn, who believed in steering students to risk-taking and personal challenge. The movement's exponents argue that by expanding the individual's self-awareness and sense of well-being within the group, a new feeling of community develops that strengthens both the individual and the group.

The adventure/challenge movement has already touched major social institutions: church, factory, school, and state. Although research data is lacking, many professionals believe that challenge education has the potential to impact at every level of education, from kindergarten to graduate school, and on to advanced professional training. Adventure programs for training executives have been developing rapidly, and offers of "executive challenge" come from colleges, private consultation and training companies, and the companies themselves. Big business has enlisted its employees in challenge programs across the country, and many companies now operate their own adventure courses.

ENCOUNTER, 1970:

" . . . Aided by widespread publicity, including the movie *Bob and Carol and Ted and Alice* and Jan Howard's best-seller, *Please Touch*, the movement is spreading explosively. Two years ago, when California's Esalen Institute first sought to export its own brand of the new gospel east, 90 curious New Yorkers showed up for a five-day encounter group in Manhattan. A similar event last year drew 850; and in April, 6000. Since January 1969, when Donald Clark counted 37 "growth centers" about the country, the census has risen past 100 . . . "

" . . . To Esalen in San Francisco and Big Sur, come 25,000 people a year, and if the pilgrim is turned away there, he can find similar sanctuaries in San Diego, New York, Chicago, Houston, and scores of other communities. The groups can vary in size from half-a-dozen to hundreds and even thousands of complete strangers at a psychological convention. The gamut is as wide as the cost, which can run anywhere from $30 or less for a weekend marathon encounter session in a church basement, to $2100 for a seven week training program at the National Training Laboratories . . . "

EXPERIENTIAL, 1990:

Aided by widespread publicity, including documentaries on public television, the movement is spreading explosively. For example, the well-known Outward Bound, Inc. organization has expanded from one Colorado-based program ten years ago to over a dozen sites nationwide and around the world. An east coast adventure program now boasts graduates of their program working in all fifty states and several foreign countries. A corporate training center near Chicago brings in executives from across the country and around the world. Conferences for these new wave educators draw near 1000 professionals wherever hosted in the country. To the Colorado programs alone, hundreds of people come each year, to lift, be lifted, climb, raft, and solo journey in the wilderness. If there is no room at the inn, then the adventure seeker can find programs in Santa Fe, Portland, Minneapolis, Boston, or Cazenovia, Wisconsin. And if you don't reach out for the programs, then they will reach out for you—in resort/centers, colleges, training programs, and conferences. The groups vary in size from half-a-dozen to hundreds at large conference trainings.

The gamut is as wide as the cost, which runs anywhere from $25-$250 per person at a "ropes course," to $20-$30 from a weekend outing of caving and group interaction that spins out of a church basement, and on to $2000-$3000 for one week or more of corporate adventure training.

ENCOUNTER, 1970:

" . . . Even though the movement's advocates deny that it is therapy, many people visit the new growth centers or attend informal group sessions in quest of precisely that. The American Psychiatric Association estimates that in California more troubled individuals already seek help from the human potentials movement than from "traditional sources of psychotherapy." Yet the human potentials group sessions are largely valueless, and even dangerous, for the severely disturbed. Psychologist Carl Rogers, one of the movement's charter members, and many others consider it a learning experience for "normals" rather than a therapeutic experience for the sick, who are too engrossed in their own emotions to fully feel another's . . . "

" . . . Psychologist Rogers calls the new group movement "the most significant social invention of this century . . . " It may not be quite that, but even the American Psychiatric Association has bestowed guarded approval in a 27 page task-force report: "The intensive group experience is intrinsically neither good nor bad . . . if properly harnessed, however, the experience may be a valuable adjunct to psychotherapy . . . "

" . . . Critics have accused the movement of everything from Communist-style brain washing to sedition. Dr. Joseph T. English, formerly head of the Health Services and Mental Health Administration of the U.S. Department of Health, Education, and Welfare, thinks that it has been 'oversold to an unaware public.' U.S. Representative John R. Rarick of Louisiana, its most voluble enemy, has filled pages of the CONGRESSIONAL RECORD with unre-

EXPERIENTIAL, 1990:

Even though many of the movement's advocates deny that it is therapy, many people feel that the adventure/challenge sequence is indeed a personal growth journey. One psychology association estimates that more troubled individuals are seeking and receiving help from the adventure/challenge programs than all of the traditional psychotherapies combined. Some experts have warned that the group "debriefing" or "processing" sessions, and the whole challenge sequence, are quite valueless, and even dangerous for many emotionally distressed people. Project Adventure, one of the charter members of the movement, has accepted the therapeutic impact of challenge activities, and has published the overview text, *Islands of Healing: A Guide to Adventure Based Counseling* (1988). In the forward to that text, it is suggested that the whole challenge/adventure sequence is "an important process tool, and a landmark of healing in the sea of human experience." Professional educators have considered the movement as "a most significant alternative for education and group work."

It may be that, but neither the National Education Association, nor the National Association of Social Workers, has given credence to the strategy. There are psychologists who have bestowed a guarded approval to challenge/adventure noting "the intensive group experience is inherently neither good nor bad . . . if properly handled, however, the experience may be a valuable adjunct to personal development."

Critics have accused the movement of everything from lack of certified leadership, to poor safety practices, to unethical practices, and to negative emotional impact. More traditional outdoor educators

strained rhetoric: 'Organized thought control and behavior programming . . . a perversion of group therapy that makes healthy minds sick . . . Obvious degeneracy . . . '"

have warned that the challenge facilitators are often guilty of negative environmental impact, as they emphasize psychosocial goals and pay no heed to environmental balances.

ENCOUNTER, 1970:

" . . . The very eclecticism of the human potentials movement has brought it criticism even from within its own ranks. Robert Driver, founder and operator of Kairos, San Diego's human growth center, has compared it to "a tree which is growing too fast without putting down proper roots." The movement also attracts a great many persons who join it for the wrong reasons: "Already," says Driver, "we see some growth experiences that are used merely to blow out the tubes every six months or so . . . "

" . . . There is genuine concern as well as the lack of follow-up research to determine the long-term effect of the encounter experience. Says Psychologist Richard Farson, an Esalen advisor, "All research shows that people have the most tremendous subjective reaction after it is over. As a rule, more than 80% say they are overwhelmingly responsive. But the objective results (test data) show virtually no lasting effects. It is difficult to show as much as 5% change in anybody even after the most intense encounter . . . "

EXPERIENTIAL, 1990:

The very eclecticism of the adventure/ challenge movement has brought criticism from within its own ranks. The most knowledgeable have compared the tremendous expansion of the methodology to "a tree which is growing too fast without putting down proper roots." The movement also attracts a great many persons who join it for the wrong reasons. It is difficult to train appropriate leaders who are there for the right reasons, let alone those adventure seekers who are involved to meet their own needs.

There is genuine concern as well as the lack of follow-up research to determine the long-term effect of the challenge experience. Psychologist U. R. Long* reports, "All research shows that people have the most tremendous subjective reaction after it is over. As a rule, more than 80% say they are overwhelmingly responsive. But the objective results, test data, show virtually no lasting effects. It is difficult to show as much as even 5% behavioral change in anybody after even the most intense challenge.

ENCOUNTER, 1970:

" . . . The human potentials movement cannot be dismissed as a passing fad. It is too soon to assess the true value of the movement. In education, where man's affective aspect is largely overlooked, the movement is probing long neglected areas. Max Birnbaum, Associate Professor of Human Relations at Boston University, sees the day when the learning experience will involve a group of peers, "in contrast to the traditional classroom, with the teacher as an authority figure and the students as charges." According to Donald Clark, the movement "does not lead to old answers but to new puzzles, new problems, new models of experience, new perspectives, and subsequently may provide a possible—though not guaranteed—footing from which one may reach for new answers and new skills . . . "

EXPERIENTIAL, 1990:

The experiential, challenge, adventure movement cannot be dismissed as a passing fad. It is too soon to assess the true value of the movement. In corporate training and development, where man's affective aspect is largely overlooked, the movement is probing long neglected areas. Richard Wagner, Assistant Professor of Management at the University of Wisconsin-Whitewater, sees the day when the learning experience will involve a group of peers, "in contrast to the traditional classroom, with the teacher as an authority figure and the students as charges." According to Wagner, the movement "does not lead to old answers but to new puzzles, new problems, new models of experience, new perspectives, and subsequently may provide a possible—though not guaranteed—footing from which one may reach for new answers and new skills."

SUMMARY

What appears to be a parallel, in fact, can be viewed as an evolutionary form and improvement of application of a process that began to clarify in the 1970s, needed some time and distance in order for objectivity and analysis to occur, and is now re-formed and re-applied with modifications to experiential learning. It is the theoretical application of Kolb's Learning Cycle on a wider, organizational (rather than individual) scale.

The Providers of Outdoor-Based Training

Todd Miner, Ed.D.

Challenges of Researching Providers of CEL and OBT

One of the major challenges facing research into experiential learning is trying to differentiate Corporate Experiential Learning and Outdoor Based Training. The definition provided earlier, "Corporate Experiential Learning represents models, methodologies and processes that focus on individual, team and organizational development. Corporate Experiential Learning utilizes both indoor and outdoor learning environments with action-oriented activities, exercises and simulations which incorporate review, feedback and action planning. CEL includes, but is not limited to, "Outdoor Adventure" models such as ropes courses, rock climbing, rappelling, mountain climbing, sailing and rafting." This article is based on a survey of "outdoor-based training" providers, primarily outdoor training programs, but not necessarily the Outdoor Adventure variety as defined above.

The models and methodologies are new and rapidly changing, therefore creating another challenge for researchers. Like many new innovative training approaches, providers appear and disappear on a regular basis. Only twenty percent of provider organizations appearing in a 1989 national listing of OBT providers (Garvey, 1989) remained in the 1993 edition (Agran, Garvey, Miner & Priest, 1993).

Providers of OBT Survey Results

Using surveys, national listings, and a number of articles, a profile of OBT providers emerges. There are well over 100 providers of OBT in North America. This number does not include the large number of training and development professionals not considered OBT providers, but who use some experiential techniques.

In a 1991 survey, OBT providers reported that the single most important factor in an effective program is the skill of the facilitator/trainer (Miner, 1991a). This was corroborated by Wagner & Roland (1992). To try to determine the characteristics of an effective facilitator, Miner (1991a) asked providers what they valued in (their) facilitators. Organizational development skills were listed first, followed by outdoor/technical skills

173

and then training and personnel experience. Interestingly, business experience was rated second lowest, just above counseling/psychology skills.

Aronson (1991) found that facilitators averaged 46 hours of annual or seasonal training. Other than the 100 percent of respondents receiving CPR training, types of training were not assessed. Given recent attention to safety in Outdoor Adventure CEL (Miner, 1991b) and recognized professional standards (Priest & Dixon, 1990), documenting more advanced safety training will be important for the industry. A review of the literature indicates that minimal attention has been paid to safety instruction in OBT staff training.

Little variety appeared in surveying philosophy or theory (Miner, 1991a). Many of the practitioners responded that their philosophy depended on the client and that Kolb's Experiential Learning Cycle (see Chapter 1) was the theoretical basis of their training. Other influences or theories which were cited were Outward Bound, Inc., Project Adventure, Inc. and various leadership, team development and organizational development theories.

Goals

Providers of outdoor-based training apply these techniques to a wide variety of personal and organizational development purposes. Miner (1991a) found that in North America the most common goal of OBT programming is team building, followed by leadership development. Wagner, Baldwin & Roland (1991) reported that team building was a goal more common to "outdoor centered programs" in the United States, while individual growth tended to be the goal of "wilderness programs." Providers reported that they spent slightly over half of their programming time focused on team building. Approximately a quarter of their programs dealt mainly with leadership and less than 20% of time was spent on personal development.

In contrast, Great Britain reported personal development as the most important benefit of OBT (commonly labeled "Outdoor Management Development," Bank, 1985).

Activities and Settings

The image of OBT as principally rock climbing and ropes courses is ingrained in the public view. However, reality is quite different than that perception. Providers reported that 30% of all program time was spent in discussion, during framing and debriefing (Miner, 1991a). Only about 20% of program time was spent on rock climbing, rafting, canoeing, sailing, or mountain climbing. Nearly 50% of actual activity time was spent on problem-solving and team-challenge initiatives. Ropes courses accounted for almost 33% of the actual activity time.

Providers of outdoor-based training use settings ranging from corporate on-site, to wilderness areas, to resort conference centers. About one third of the program time was spent at the providers' facility and slightly less than one third was spent at a retreat or training center. Less than 25% of training time was spent in backcountry or wilderness areas (Wagner, Baldwin, and Roland 1991).

Clients

Several North American studies have analyzed the individual participants and/or the client organizations of OBT. Miner (1991a) reported that the largest percentage of participants, over one third, were low-to-mid level management. Twenty-five percent of OBT participants were executives and 20% were intact work groups with mixed management levels of participants. While managers may be the most commonly served group, Wagner, Baldwin, and Roland (1991) showed that executives and middle managers tend to participate in the more remote and more expensive "wilderness programs," while a wider range of hierarchical levels tend to use the "outdoor-centered" programs. Aronson (1991) reported that OBT providers serve a wide variety of organizations: over one half worked with non-profits and educational institutions. About 60% of the providers served corporations and governmental agencies and half served hospitals. Miner (1991a) found that only 10% of OBT providers' business was with non-profits. Sixty percent of business was with private sector companies of 50 or more employees. The discrepancy between the results of Aronson and Miner is based on the survey respondents and cannot draw a conclusively detailed picture of a single typical client.

In a recent survey of leading U.S. corporations, thirteen percent reported doing some form of OBT (Wagner & Fahey, 1992). Estimates of the number of individual participant/clients range from 100,000 to 200,000 (Miner, 1991a).

Types of OBT Providers

There are two categories of OBT providers: outdoor and corporate (Miner, 1991a). Providers from an outdoor background generally have worked in other applications of Outdoor Adventure, including education, therapeutic settings, or human service organizations. The outdoor providers often serve other clients in addition to corporate work, such as youth, or adults in recovery from substance abuse. These providers represent a majority of members in the Association for Experiential Education (AEE), according to the 1993 directory of programs (Agran, Garvey, Miner, & Priest, 1993).

"Corporate" provider organizations often have traditional training and development, management, or business consulting experience. They commonly use other kinds of traditional training and consulting techniques in addition to experiential learning. They often hire staff with technical outdoor skills for the outdoor adventure segments of their programs. Approximately 25% of the providers listed in AEE's directory are corporate providers. Undoubtedly, this percentage would be higher if analyzing the membership of the American Society for Training and Development (ASTD).

Recommendations for Further Research

Periodic surveys (annual or bi-annual) would reflect current situations and build on the work completed to date. For example, information from mainstream training and development providers regarding their use of corporate experiential learning models would help to more accurately assess the popularity and efficacy of these techniques.

Additional research on the variety of program goals is warranted. This will improve the evaluation of effectiveness based on clearly articulated goals.

To date, there has been little research on staff development of experiential learning providers. Other than safety training, this issue is seldom mentioned, much less investigated. One of the few studies found that staff training significantly improved effectiveness (Wagner & Roland, 1992). Further detailed research on the type, duration, and/or sequence of staff development will benefit professional development within the field.

Several additional questions to be investigated include: How is effectiveness related to the credentials of a provider? Does an exclusive focus on experiential learning techniques enhance effectiveness? What are the differences between the effectiveness of providers who use experiential learning occasionally as compared to providers who use experiential learning exclusively?

Conclusion

In a field where as much as $250 million is spent annually, research is important to both providers as well as client organizations. The safety, efficiency, and effectiveness of corporate experiential learning depends on who provides it and how well they do it.

CROSSING THE LINE: PSYCHOLOGICAL PERSPECTIVES

THOMAS E. SMITH, PH.D.

Corporate training and development has been one of the major growth areas in experiential education. Another major growth area is individual and group therapy. More psychotherapists, social workers, activity therapists and family therapists are using experiential methods with clients suffering from chemical dependency, depression, eating disorders, etc.

The relationship between corporate training and psychotherapy is of greater concern in the CEL movement as illustrated in Figure 7-1:

Figure 7-1

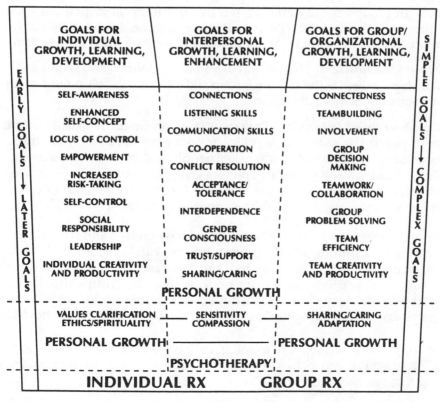

This table presents an overview of program development using experiential methodologies. The model suggests that the lines dividing typical CEL goals and those of psychological or personal growth domains are blurred. This paper sets forth guidelines on when and how to cross over that line between corporate training and personal growth goals.

There are, in fact, two different "lines" to consider. The first separates programs of basic awareness and enrichment from personal growth; the second separates personal growth from the domain of individual and group therapy. The latter line received considerable attention in the late 1950s and 1960s when the procedures of personal growth groups (like laboratory training groups, T-groups, sensitivity groups and encounter groups), were introduced as education and training methodologies. There are a number of distinctions between those models and the more traditional psychotherapeutic models including:

1. *Time Limits.* The personal growth groups were usually of limited duration, often in 3-day, 4-week, or 20 session packages. The traditional psychotherapy group was typically longer.

2. *Focus.* Individual and group therapy tends to deal with the inner reasons or the "whys" of behavior. The training groups focus more on behavior patterns and thus, attend to the "hows" of behavior (Shepard and Bennis, 1966).

3. *Leadership*. T-groups, sensitivity groups, encounter groups, and personal growth groups could be facilitated by educators, management trainers, and other "people-workers." Therapeutic intervention, both individual and group, was offered by professional psychologists, social workers, and counselors.

4. *Time Orientation.* Therapy involves past problems and issues and past relationships, whereas the training group and personal development group tended to focus on the here-and-now.

5. *Concentrated Intensity*. Therapeutic involvement is usually offered on an hour-per-day, 2-3 sessions weekly, or once-a-week basis. Thus, the client has considerable interaction with other people and must focus on events outside the group between sessions. Training groups, on the other hand are typically offered in concentrated blocks of time (hours, days), which means that the client is totally involved with the experience for a given period of time.

Even while noting the "distinctions" between therapy groups and training groups, the two procedures are different points on a continuum with considerable overlap. There are therapy groups of time-limited duration, and there are training groups that unfold as a series of separated sessions. There are personal growth groups that become quite intensive and provide clients with opportunities to explore past relationships and personal conflicts; and therapy groups that are structured to focus on the "here-and-now."

The distinction between education, training, enrichment, leadership development and team-building programs and personal growth groups is equally unclear. Again, they are points along a continuum.

There is generally an overlap of the three tracks shown in Figure 7-1. Often, programs have goals on all three tracks. Typically, in psychiatric settings there is greater emphasis on the goals of individual development, and programs would tend to move across the "lines" into the domain of values clarification, personal growth, psychological adjustment and psychotherapeutic intervention. Programs for adjudicated youth and youth-at-risk often deal a bit more with the goals of interpersonal development, steering clients towards improved communication, cooperation, and social adjustment. Often, however, leaders of such groups have been advised to steer clear of that "line" which would open up the psychological domain. Leadership training manuals for experiential leaders often emphasize the point that "we are not psychologists—we are not therapists." Some training programs even provide suggestions for handling "psychological emergencies" until the client can be referred to a professional therapist.

Some corporate training programs have emphasized goals of personal development (e.g., empowerment, enhanced risk taking, leadership). In the corporate setting there has been only limited support for crossing the line into the domain of personal growth. Some corporate clients express great skepticism about moving to that "touchy-feely stuff," as they had negative experiences—or have heard/read about negative experiences with the T-groups, sensitivity groups, and encounter groups in the 1960s. Such corporate attitudes are shared by many individuals within the corporation, who feel that the work setting is not a place to get too close to others or share personal feelings, confusions, and pains.

As programs move toward the more advanced goals highlighted on the three tracks of Figure 7-1, and into the complex arenas of personal growth, there is an interconnectedness. Whether the goals involve individual growth and development, interpersonal development, or group/organizational development, a move into value clarification, enhancement of compassion/sensitivity, and basic sharing/caring of others, they are involved with some aspect(s) of personal growth.

At the most complex levels of psychotherapeutic intervention, there may be some differences in the specific objectives of individual or group counseling, but the basic goal is always improved psychological and social functioning, and enhanced adjustment. Likewise, the basic goals of personal growth are similar, whether derived from the individual-, interpersonal-, or group-development track.

Many suggest that the appropriate education and training goals for corporate programs are those that do not cross the line. Certainly, that has been the more typical historical pattern for corporate training and development programs.

On the other hand, others argue that the most appropriate way to achieve the corporate goals of improved communication, cooperation and increased productivity is to cross the line and, facilitate personal growth in group experiences. Perhaps corporations can meet the requirements of a multi-cultural world economy, and the necessary balance between productivity and harmony, only if their employees become more self-actualized and personally fulfilled. Personal growth goals should be *emphasized*, not avoided.

Acceptance, and "total positive regard" (Carl Rogers), for clients (i.e., individuals, groups or corporations), leads to an ever deepening search to develop their own potential for personal fulfillment. Whether or not we start with an agenda that includes personal growth goals, corporations (which are, after all, collections of individuals) may increase awareness of the value of those goals.

If/when the corporate clients of CEL begin to set personal growth goals, how should experiential leaders meet the challenge? Should that work be reserved for professional psychologists and counselors?

Certainly, the experiential learning professionals working in mental health and rehabilitation settings have become adjunct therapists, and have offered their methodology as a "primary therapy" (Gillis, 1990). As corporations move toward valuing and incorporating personal growth goals in their education and training programs, CEL professionals will need to develop programs that focus on these goals. In this case, a number of questions to be considered include:

- How will this affect the training of CEL leaders ?
- What will the client and facilitator requirements for pre-program involvement be (assessment, orientation, etc.)?
- How will post-program follow-up change?
- What are the ethical issues of such programming?
- How will group processing adapt to these changes?

Ropes Courses—Misconceptions and Applications

Warren Cohen

Ropes and challenge courses account for nearly one-third of CEL program time (T. Miner). Other indications of the popularity of ropes courses are the development and continued growth of the Association for Challenge Course Technology (ACCT), Challenge Course Installation Standards (1994), and the publication of a ropes course-specific training and development text, *Using Ropes Techniques* (Snow, 1992).

Ropes courses allow participants to challenge themselves and their teams physically, emotionally and intellectually. Ropes courses are "hot" all over the world: outdoors, indoors, in urban and wilderness settings. But ropes courses are also hotly debated. At the Texas Experiential Ropes Association conference in 1992, Brian Jackson stirred up much discussion and debate with his paper "Debunking the Mystique of the Ropes Course." Jackson exclaimed, in one of his challenging statements:

> There is a growing pre-Copernican mentality within elements of the training field, as well as parts of corporate America, that outdoor-based programs revolve around the epi-center of a 'ropes course'. The very name is a misnomer, and it's high time we reexamine the use of these steel and chemically-coated abominations that are, conceivably, destined to become the Edsels of the experience-based training and development field (p. 2).

So What Are These Ropes Courses ?

As Jackson accurately states, the actual label "ropes course" is a misnomer. Today's high technology ropes course utilizes little, if any, *rope*. Materials include galvanized aircraft cable, pressure treated wood and various hardware items (e.g., Crosby clips, stand-vices, swaged eyes, drop plates, figure eights, Sticht plates, dynamic belays, static belays and shear reduction devices).

Another misconception is that there is a single product called a "ropes course" or a "challenge course." In reality, there are different types of courses including: "high ropes," where activities take place well above the ground; and "low ropes" course activities which rarely get higher than eye level. They can be used for team or individual problem solving (Wagner, Baldwin & Roland, 1991, p. 53).

How relevant are ropes courses to the business world? Are they "torture devices," (Paul Stoltz, Chapter 1), or the "chemically-coated abominations" as described by Jackson?

Background

Outdoor experiential education consultant Lee Snooks was one of the first to utilize ropes courses as a relevant educational tool. In 1972 he worked with the Battle Creek, Michigan school district and promoted outdoor education as an ideal teaching media to address racial conflict and segregation as major causes of under achievement among students.

It was Snooks' belief that an outdoor/off-site format would remove students from highly influential school, community and family situations that permitted racial separatism and inhibited communication between African-American and white students.

A proposal, Project BACSTOP (Better Acquisition of Cognitive Skills Through Outdoor Programming), was submitted to the Michigan Department of Education (MDE); and upon approval, was validated and classified by the MDE as a Demonstration Site. The Project was funded to assist interested and qualified school districts in adopting/adapting BACSTOP programming and methodology. Since then, many companies have developed similar programs for use with educational and corporate clients.

Snooks tried to remind those presenting these programs that; "While the ROPES (Resourcefulness, Opportunities, Perseverance, Encouragement, Skill) course and allied initiatives are often perceived as excitingly glamorous and captivating, it is essential to emphasize that these adventure oriented activities are a small part of a total delivery system commonly referred to as, "adventure/experiential education" (Lipsitz & Miller, 1987).

The adventure (risk-taking), aspect of the ropes course often overshadows the educational thrust that the original program was meant to address. This has led to a skeptical view of experiential learning with critics calling it, "at best, a waste of time and at worst, harmful to managerial effectiveness" (Wagner, Baldwin & Roland, 1991).

In addition, the general lack of knowledge about this unique training tool by clients and deliverers alike, has resulted in misconceptions and poor application. Yet, despite these obstacles, it has also been used very successfully as a process for examining behavior, as a technique to identify critical issues for both individuals and work groups.

Scene: Executive Staff Meeting

Head Honcho:

"In order to survive in today's work force and compete on all levels of production, we have to act and work more as a team. I decided to investigate one of these outdoor training places. So, I went on this wild rafting/outdoor challenge trip out west and thought it was a great team building experience for everyone who was on it. I mean, we *really* worked together well, it was a lot of fun and I'll tell you honestly, I felt terrific afterwards.

It was so great that I've decided that in order for us to become a team just like that one, we're all going to go through one of these outdoor ropes courses and participate in an executive challenge program. So, what do you think, people?"

*What the Staff is **Thinking:***

"What the hell is a ROPES course?"

"I hate the woods."

"Huh?"

"I'm not climbing any mountain!"

"Who wants to go through another obstacle course—I did that in the army!"

"Oh great, another fad. What a waste of time!"

*What the Staff **Says:***

"Sure. Great idea H.H.!!!"

Learning Points and Section Goals

Notice that the Head Honcho speaks of this wonderful training experience in the past tense. "Worked together well," "had fun," "felt great," were spoken as if everything that built *that* team was left at *that* site. Many times this is exactly the case.

What did H.H. learn and were those processes applied to the work place once he returned? What were the benefits? What barriers to change will a program such as this face when one person's moments of exhilaration are forced on the others? It was a terrific experience for Head Honcho, but what about his staff? Is it necessarily the right program for them? And who should participate in making these decisions?

Practitioners' Program Promotion

Another barrier to successful corporate experiential learning processes is the provider's marketing philosophy an organization takes in presenting it's product. Many programs focus on the slam-bang impressive excitement of the ropes course itself, replete with promises of transformation in beliefs, team metamorphosis and/or redefinition of the purpose of life! During or immediately after the program itself, these promised results may be realized. But, what a provider promises in a brochure or presentation may not be what they deliver to the actual work setting.

In one study, Stoltz (1992) investigated the effectiveness of a program's efforts to develop leadership skills through experiential learning. He suggests that the gap between, " . . . promises and reasonable expectations should be a primary concern to client and provider alike." He adds that the vagueness, " . . . in promotional materials highlights the discrepancy between those promises and more skill-specific, bottom-line client needs" (p. 370-371).

Unfortunately, for the purposes of "getting them in the door," the comments of participants describing the initial excitement generated from the event is what is published. The actual activities themselves and the resulting long-term behavioral changes and benefits are, more often than not, ignored.

It is the long term lessons learned, the solidified planned action steps and resulting accountability for the behaviors promised that must be in place if new skills and processes are to be continued back in the home or worksite. This is where real success is measured and program credibility maintained. Yet, specific measurable behaviors are not always part of the program's promotional strategy.

Recreation or Education

Requests for an experiential learning program sometimes stem from the positive excitement generated from an experience. One person recommends the idea of a ropes course to a corporate colleague or client based solely on their (limited), personal experience and perceptions. This is not a solid reason for attempting the course if an organization is expecting significant change or long term learning from their staff. If the organization is looking for recreational activity to "break up" conference monotony, a wide variety of simple interactive group actions can be arranged. But, if the provider comes to the experiential program with an educational-based approach, these recreational goals may be in conflict. The customer will either be extremely surprised and pleased with the "bonus information," or be disturbed and unhappy because the "games" that were promised, "weren't supposed to make us think."

If, however, the intent of the organization is to educate and develop the staff into a more cohesive team through an experiential education process, then a more appropriate approach can be selected, designed and presented. The true team goal must be determined up front, so that the facilitator can apply an appropriate process focused on team issues and concerns.

Initial Stages of Assessment

Wagner, Baldwin and Roland (1991, p. 55) state that, "the success or failure of outdoor training can be determined only if the purpose of the program is known. Unfortunately, most outdoor training programs apparently do not start with any clear objective."

What are the customer's needs? What do they want to focus on? Without these answers, the needed processes cannot be identified. And if these needs are not identified, how can the experience effectively translate and be incorporated into the work setting?

Processing and Debriefing

Wagner, Baldwin and Roland (1991) consider debriefing or processing, "the most crucial part of a [CEL] program . . . (it) is a qualitative discussion period that allows participants to analyze their efforts to solve problems and act cohesively as a team. It is a critical step in applying the outdoor experiences to the work place" (p. 54). Teachings, lessons and behavior transfer converge with the facilitator. Debriefing or processing the experience by skilled facilitators is the key (Chapter 3).

Conclusion

"Ropes courses can easily become a 'vacation' or a 'fun break' from the routine of work. In some programs, trainees take part in a series of unique outdoor activities that are independent and disconnected. They come away from such experiences with good feelings, but with few new insights or skills" (Buller, Cragun and McEvoy, 1991, p. 58). They suggest that sound learning theory, support and sponsorship by top management, linking the program to organizational strategic goals, skilled facilitation, transfer of learning and skills to the work setting, follow-up and networking and program evaluation are extremely important if this unique training tool is to be successful. Yet, much of these necessary areas are not even addressed by ropes course practitioners.

"Preliminary evaluations of program outcomes are positive, but some practitioners still ignore the conceptual and practical base for effective program implementation . . .Without that kind of sound foundation, Ropes courses will not yield positive results; it will likely become just another fad" (Ibid.).

Physiological Perspectives

Camille Bunting, Ph.D.

Anyone who has participated in an Outdoor Adventure (OA) experiential learning program can attest to some degree of physical and emotional arousal. In fact, it is arousal upon which some trainers capitalize to help their clients "grow" through the training process. The Theory of Optimal Arousal (Duffy, 1957; White, 1950; Yerkes & Dodson, 1908) is a hallmark of Outdoor Adventure ranging from Outward Bound Inc., and the Boy Scouts to personal and corporate training and development. The theory postulates that positive benefits accrue through an increase in stress up to a certain optimal point, and that this point varies from individual to individual. If stress increases beyond this point, then positive benefits drop sharply and can even move to a negative outcome (see Figure 7-2).

Figure 7-2

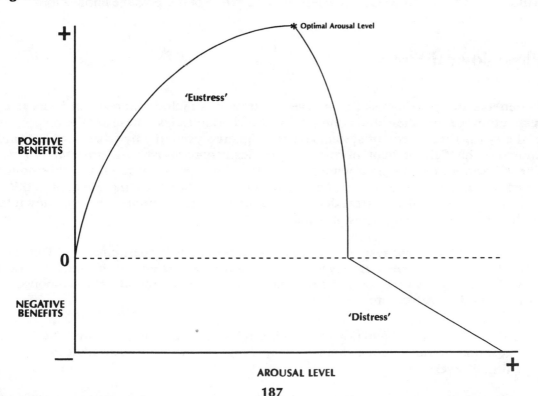

Hans Selye (1950) theorized that everyone needs some level of "creative tension" (stress), to function at an optimal level. Within a group, the problem is that some individuals never reach their optimal level while others go beyond and have negative or "distressful" experiences. Only within the past few years has the research and data gathering been focused on the physiological considerations of Outdoor Adventure programming. To date, most of the information collected has concentrated on "high impact" activities such as high ropes course events, rock climbing, rappelling, white water canoeing, etc.

Volumes of anecdotal information collected over the years describe experiential learning in glowing "life enhancing" terms, adding further credibility to the Optimal Arousal Theory and the benefits of CEL/OA programs. Many believe that "eustress" (the positive euphoric type of stress that accompanies activities like Outdoor Adventures), is nothing but positive and contributes only positively to a person's well being. Growing evidence suggests this may not be the case for everyone. *Stress* is one of the risk factors for heart disease. Most of the research on stress has been conducted in laboratories under controlled stress conditions. But the field studies of paratroopers in training (Bloom, von Euler, & Frankenhaeuser, 1963; Hansen, et al., 1978), public speaking (Taggart, Carruthers, & Somerville, 1973; Dimsdale, & Moss, 1980), medical students taking final exams (Doornen, 1986), and individuals at work (Frankenhaeuser, 1981) corroborate the laboratory research. It is likely that the only difference between 'eustress' and 'distress' is the perception of the individual. If that is true, then the physiological responses to stress might be the same. These field studies may be only remotely related to Outdoor Adventure training but CEL and particularly Outdoor Adventure trainers must be aware of the possible implications.

Physiological Stress

In general, the physiological responses to stress can include increase in heart rate, respiration, perspiration, and contractility of certain muscles. These are the responses of the sympathetic nervous system and are triggered primarily by what have become known as the 'fight or flight' hormones, specifically *epinephrine* and *norepinephrine*. These hormones of the neuroendocrine system (the system of regulatory hormones which influence vital responses, i.e., heart rate, blood pressure, muscle contractility, etc.) have been studied in great detail in relation to stress response, and are known to be elevated with varying types of stress.

Most, if not all, of these responses have been experienced by participants of Outdoor Adventure activities whether they were enjoying their experience or having a dreadful time. Three studies describe the cardiovascular and/or neuroendocrine response to various Outdoor Adventure activities:

> **Study 1**—heart rate and urinary catecholamine (i.e., fight or flight hormones) response to novice rock climbing, rappelling, and belaying as influenced by fitness level.

Study 2—heart rates elicited by various high ropes course events.

Study 3—heart rate and plasma catecholamine response to the "Pamper Pole" (high ropes challenge) as influenced by fitness level.

Cardiovascular Response

Heart rates increase not only as a *result* of participation in Outdoor Adventure activities, but also in *anticipation* of the designated activity. When heart rates were measured in college-age males before and after introductory rock climbing and rappelling, there were notable increases. There were also significant differences in heart rate response between aerobically high and low fit subjects, with higher heart rates exhibited by the aerobically less fit subjects (Fig. 7-3). When comparing Day 1 and Day 2 climbing and rappelling heart rates, it seems that experience ameliorates reactivity. Day 2 heart rates for both activities are lower than those on Day 1, especially for the low-fit subjects. (Bunting, Little, Tolson & Jessup, 1986).

Figure 7-3

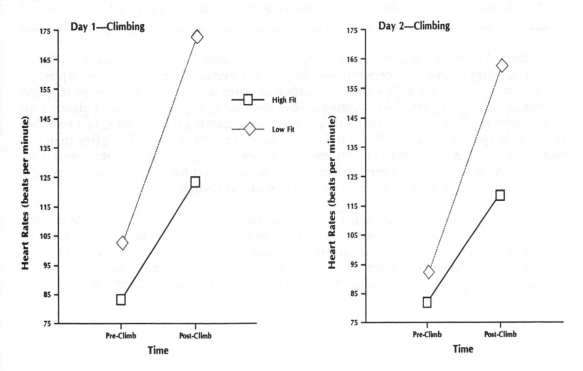

This is consistent with laboratory studies using physical tasks in which low fit subjects have higher heart rates than high fit subjects. Typically, individuals with a higher level of physical fitness will have lower resting heart rates as well as lower exercise heart rates. This is due to increased efficiency of the overall cardiovascular system, such as the heart being able to eject a greater volume of blood with each contraction. Heart rate responses to various high challenge course events are shown in the following table. College age males and females, all in average to above average physical condition, volunteered for this project. Therefore, the high heart rates cannot be attributed to a low level of physical fitness (Little, Bunting, & Gibbons, 1986).

Heart Rate Means					
	High Beam	**High Tension Traverse**	**Heeby Jeeby**	**Zip Line**	**Pamper Pole**
Total Time (sec.)	130.79	105.79	142.36	209.71	146.30
Beginning HR	111.79	152.71*	114.29	114.29	119.07
Ending HR	161.71	179.14	175.20	180.14	179.86
Maximum HR	170.79	180.21	182.00	190.71	200.93**

*   Indicates a significant difference between *beginning* heart rates at p<.01 level.
** Indicates a significant difference between *maximum* heart rates at p<.01 level.

As indicated in the table above, the Pamper Pole elicited the highest maximum heart rate. The Pamper Pole is a telephone-type pole set vertically in the ground, approximately twenty feet tall with a diameter tapering from ten inches at the base to eight inches at the top. A participant climbs up the pole using pegs and stands balanced on top. The next challenge is to dive out and attempt to catch a trapeze or ring a bell that is hanging approximately 7'6" out in front of the pole and about 4'6" higher than the top of the pole. A safety system of harnesses, ropes and other equipment is used. College age males were volunteer subjects. They were tested for aerobic fitness using a treadmill stress test, and six high-fit and six low-fit individuals were selected.

Heart rates were measured immediately prior to climbing to the top of the pole (which was made less physically strenuous with the use of an extension ladder that went to within two feet of the top), at the time of the jump, and after being back on the ground. Near maximum heart rates have also been recorded for participants of varying ages and physical fitness levels during other high, but less acute, challenge course events.

Summary

This study clarifies the critical importance of knowledgeable activity sequencing and design. CEL/OA leaders must be aware that many of the activities used are capable of triggering extreme cardiovascular and neuroendocrine responses. These responses could be hazardous to the well being of certain participants. The following are essential when planning any CEL/OA program:

- Outdoor Adventure activities can elicit significant physiological stress responses.
- Low fit participants exhibit greater heart rate and neuroendocrine system increases than the more highly fit.
- Experience (familiarity) with the activity seems to decrease heart rate response in low fit participants.

For most people, the combined physical and emotional challenge in a unique natural environment seems to be a psychological *dis*tress reliever. However, in cases where coronary artery disease is present, whether diagnosed or not, the elicited physiological stress responses may trigger acute coronary problems, just as it can in other athletic or recreational sports participation.

Recommendations for Corporate Experiential Learning/Outdoor Adventure Programs

1. All participants should be informed that many of the activities cause sudden elevation in heart rate, both from physical exertion and psychological anxiety and/or excitement. The fact that individuals with an average or below average level of physical fitness exhibit higher heart rate responses than high fit individuals should also be explained.

2. Each participant should be encouraged to use personal judgment in deciding whether or not to participate in the various activities. This should be done for each activity, and those activities with the greatest potential for eliciting acute (sudden) responses should be pointed out by the staff.

3. CEL staff should be familiar with participants' health history, and participants with known cardiovascular problems should not be allowed to do the 'high impact' activities. These would include the activities most likely to elevate heart rates to a near maximal level, i.e., high challenge course events, difficult climbing and rappelling with considerable exposure (situations that are both high and vertical with uninhibited views so that the "feel" of being unprotected is increased), and situations of increased physical risk where direct safety systems are not possible.

4. Participants should be informed of the physiological considerations prior to training. Providers can discourage those with currently diagnosed cardiovascular problems by substituting less physiologically stressful activities that will meet the same learning objectives. If they insist upon participating in the "high impact" activities, they must agree to a physician monitored stress test or other appropriate medical certification, and *with written approval of their doctor*, and verify insurance coverage of the program and the individual, be allowed to participate.

5. CEL staff should be aware that experience can reduce the degree of heart rate elevation. Beginning the adventure training with "high impact" activities will probably elicit higher heart rates than if such activities are sequenced after activities with gradually increasing intensity. For example, heart rates would probably be greater in individuals participating on the Pamper Pole as their first adventure activity rather than following a series of activities with incrementally more intense challenges.

To date, adequate data has not been collected on the low impact challenge course events such as All Aboard, Low Tension Traverse, Trust Fall, Spider Web, etc. This project is currently underway, and may show that some of the activities trainers now view as low impact may not be so. Typical responses to these activities seem to be less anxiety-producing than the high-impact events, and therefore are less likely to elicit near maximal heart rates. The Wall (12-14 feet high) initiative is also being studied, and is expected to elicit heart rates somewhat higher than initiatives conducted at lower heights.

The intensity of a CEL/OA program is determined by its emphasis on Outdoor Adventure activities, the sequence of activities, and the time devoted to physical challenges. At the 1992 Ropes Course Symposium, Siewers (1992) suggested requiring all individuals over the age of 40 who did not exercise regularly at a vigorous level, to have an exercise stress test prior to participation on high challenge course events, as well as all individuals with known cardiovascular or pulmonary abnormalities, or two (or more) major coronary risk factors. This would be the most conservative approach.

In light of this information, outdoor CEL trainers must assess the potential physiological impact of their programs, consider the recommendations listed above, as well as Siewer's suggestions, and make prudent adjustments.

LEGAL CONSIDERATIONS

BETTY VAN DER SMISSEN, RE.D., J.D.

Although outdoor adventure programs (wilderness, high ropes, etc.), are often appealing, numerous issues and concerns involving liability have been voiced (Kezman & Connors, 1993), especially regarding several deaths that have occurred at high ropes courses (Ryan, 1991). This paper provides an overview of the complexities of legal liability as it relates to the more outdoor adventure CEL models.

Who is Liable? The Doctrine of Respondeat Superior

One must distinguish between the corporation contracting for an outdoor adventure training program and the provider of the service. The contract should be clear that the *provider* is responsible for the conduct of the training program activities, including dealing with environmental conditions such as weather and maintenance of equipment. However, the corporation takes some responsibility for the general behavior of their employees, for transportation to the training site, and other non-activity-related logistics and amenities. There should be a mutual agreement regarding emergency procedures (including emergency transportation and medical attention) and especially, who pays the bills for these services.

The question of liability usually is not between the corporation being trained, and the training provider, but who is included under the doctrine of respondeat superior for the provider. Generally injuries are the result of an action by an individual ("trainer") who has a direct relationship to the participant, usually a face-to-face leadership responsibility. If this trainer was negligent, then he/she usually (but not always) has personal liability; also, under the doctrine of respondeat superior, the negligence of the trainer is transmitted as a corporate entity. The person's supervisor, manager, or administrator is not personally liable for this trainer's negligence; however, such supervisory personnel may be held liable for any administrative or supervisory actions or decisions which they made which enhanced the likelihood of the injury occurring. For example, if a person was placed in a leadership role for which they were not qualified, then the supervisor would be said to have negligently assigned leadership and thus enhanced the likelihood of injury or death. The provider company (corporate entity), either includes all employees and volunteers in their insurance policy or makes specific provision for indemnification when such persons are acting within the scope of their responsibilities.

The negligence of all persons working in behalf of the provider, includes not only the aforementioned face-to-face leadership and administrative/supervisory personnel, but also maintenance staff, drivers of vehicles, and any other personnel, and is transmitted to the corporate entity (provider company). Because of the doctrine of respondeat superior, "let the superior respond," it is very important that one have orientation and in-service education for *all* persons associated with the training program: volunteers, trainees or interns receiving only room and board, an aid, or paid employees.

The Standard of Care

In any insurance claim for injury or law suit, the critical question is "what was the *standard of care* given in the conduct of the program?" The standard, from a legal perspective, usually is defined in the negative, i.e., "not to expose participants to unreasonable risks." What is "unreasonable" usually is what a trial is all about! The provider is not an insurer of safety and the "unreasonable risk" or possible harm must be reasonably foreseeable. However, just because one does something recommended does not necessarily mean that it was appropriate. Practices must be modified in accordance with situational circumstances.

There are three components that determine the situational appropriateness of the standard of care: (1) the activity, (2) the participants, and (3) the environmental conditions. How difficult is the activity relative to the participants, their physical condition and emotional state, their background and experience (cultural, language), their general motor skill capability and level of maturity? What are the environmental conditions including the weather (e.g., humidity, heat, rain, wetness from dew, lightning), terrain, and the maintenance of equipment and facility/area?

Desirable practices must relate to *all* three determinants (of the standard of care), and the leadership must be competent in implementing the necessary practices. Too often CEL/OA program leaders are skilled in the activity itself, but have only minimal or limited experience relating and working with participants of particular characteristics within unique corporate cultures.

Two operational plans related to standard of care are often overlooked, but may be critical in a court of law to "prove" that the program was conducted using desirable practices. In addition to specific supervision of an activity, a *general supervisory plan* provides for systematically overseeing the entire area and being alert for types of situations which might be considered dangerous or hazardous, including failure of leadership to carry out desirable practices and observation of participant behaviors. A general supervisor should be able to anticipate dangerous situations and plan ahead to eliminate or ameliorate them. Normally an activity is not dangerous in and of itself, but becomes so because of the situation or conditions within which it is conducted. A general supervisor must be experienced in order to perform the above functions. The plan must set forth specific duties and responsibilities, and how they will be accomplished by and for each individual. The plan is usually written, providing the documentation often needed in court.

The other operational plan is a *maintenance inspection plan*. Being alert to maintenance needs is everyone's responsibility and includes four aspects:

1. leaders' "eye-balling"—the responsibility of the direct leaders conducting the activity. Every time an activity is conducted there should be certain equipment and facility/area checks. Specific items to be checked should be part of the orientation and in-service education program.

2. written, daily/weekly check-off of maintenance "surveillance"—regular, systematic physical evaluation of equipment and facilities check-off, note any needs, date, and sign.

3. critical parts check—requiring special expertise, for example, an engineer may be needed to check the ropes course, or a tree specialist to check the condition of trees in the area. This should be done periodically, as required by which elements need this type of review.

4. external inspector—it is desirable that every couple years either an outside consultant perform a site review, or that peers from another program reciprocate with each other in checking the site in order to avoid overlooking what is too familiar to the owner or manager of a facility.

Doctrine of Comparative Fault

Almost all states have modified the concepts of assumption of risk and contributory negligence and now have some form of the doctrine of comparative fault, also referenced as comparative negligence. Under this doctrine the fault of the provider (defendant) is compared to the fault of the participant (injured plaintiff), and the damages award, if any, is reduced in accord with state law. That is, what did the injured and the provider do that increased the likelihood of injury and to what extent did that act cause the injury? Some states have a "pure" ratio of percentage. That is, for example, if the plaintiff was 60% at fault and the defendant 40%, the plaintiff would receive only 40% of the award. The majority of states, however, have some variation of the "50/50 rule", which provides that if the plaintiff's fault is equal to or greater than the defendant's fault, the plaintiff receives no award at all.

Documentation. Because the damage award is directly related to percentage of fault of the plaintiff, it therefore is essential that the provider maintain excellent records of the conduct of the program and the behavior/performance of the participants. This requires a documentation system. Not only the policies, but also the procedural practices in the conduct of the program are very important; and it is not enough to have them written. The supervisor/director/administrator *must* see that such are carried out in every detail. The performance of staff, whether paid or volunteer, must be supervised. Further, it is very important that *all* staff receive, as part of their orientation/in-service education, an emphasis on the safe and proper conduct of the activity. Most programs have an orientation (content of which should be in the file), but often do not follow up with supervision and further in-service education.

Often, there is inadequate documentation of the behavior/performance of the participant and the procedures if an injury should occur. Documenting the behavior/performance of the participant, as related to comparative fault, means observing and recording the actions of the participant which may be contributing towards the possible occurrence of injury. For example, did the participant follow the instructions of the leader? Were the safety precautions adhered to? Were the sequences of activities followed? Did the participant check equipment as directed?

Warnings. One of the most important elements in establishing fault of the participant (injured) is that of "Warnings." What warnings were given to the participant and what was the response of the participant? This includes warnings related to the performance of the skill, to the environmental conditions, and to the interactions of the participants. Warnings are cautions and if the participant does not heed such, then such participant is considered to have enhanced the likelihood of injury and is contributing fault in terms of the doctrine of comparative fault. In what form must these warnings be given? The transmittal of the warning to the participant will vary, depending upon the nature of the risk or hazard of the warning. Sometimes a warning will be part of the instructions of the leader to the participant; or it may be a sign posted at the site of the ropes course; or it may be embodied in the printed literature.

The essence of a warning is effective communication with the individual participant. Here are several guides to effective communication of warnings:

- ◆ obvious and direct, not subtle!
- ◆ language understandable to the participant (to the person being warned);
- ◆ specific to the risk or hazard so that the participant can make an informed decision as to whether or not to do something or to do it in a certain way;
- ◆ signs located at the point of the hazard whenever possible.

Emergency plan. The conduct of the program also must include detailed procedures if an injury should occur. In a number of legal cases, the issue was not the initial injury, as much as the failure to properly take care of the injury in a timely manner. An emergency plan should include:

1. An individual skilled in basic first aid, that is, in the basic life saving/survival techniques, should be part of every group of participants. The first aid most apt to be needed should be reviewed as a part of the orientation and in-service education of the staff. Immediacy of response is often critical and even though a person may hold a valid first aid certificate, there still should be a review.

2. Determine where and how the next level of treatment is obtained? Is there an EMT, paramedic, nurse, or physician immediately available? If not on staff, appropriate arrangements must be made to obtain such services in an emergency. The next level can be calling the 911 emergency service. If away from an urban area, proper arrangements, with the nearest transportation needed and a medical facility, should be in place.

3. Who is in charge of public relations, specifically notifying the company employing the individual involved, contacting the next of kin, and handling the media? The latter is often overlooked and is very important. What is reported in the newspaper, radio or television depends on this plan. There should be a spokesperson for the sponsor of the activity.

Of course, the emergency procedures for any injuries should be planned jointly with the corporation being serviced. Many have their own systems of emergency care, insurance, and public relations.

Assumption of Risk

Understanding the concept of *assumption of risk* is essential. The impact of comparative fault on assumption of risk varies from state to state; in some instances it has become a part of the continuum of fault, while in others there is a distinction between implied assumption of inherent risks and express (usually written) assumptions of risk and sometimes referred to as a waiver. However, there are some important essentials which impact upon the conduct of programs as related to assumption of risk.

In most jurisdictions the mere participation in an activity no longer infers assumption of the inherent risks of an activity. Inherent risks are those which are the essence or nature of the activity and do not include risks or potential injury due to the negligence of the leadership or sponsor. For there to be an assumption of risk, the participation must be voluntary, and in some corporate training programs, the participation is not truly voluntary, but is expected and, often, with considerable management pressure. In addition, three criteria generally must be met before a participant assumes the inherent risks; and, it is essential that the sponsors of an activity conduct the program so that these three criteria are met:

1. The participant must be knowledgeable about the activity. There must be information given regarding the nature of the activity to be conducted and under what circumstances.

2. The participant must understand the nature of participation in terms of one's own capacity to do the activity. What is required in terms of physical skill and emotional/psychological suitability?

3. The participant must appreciate the possibility of injury—from small bumps and bruises to the extreme (death, brain damage or quadriplegia). Care should

be taken that one does not "scare" the participants, for indeed there are very few injuries. It could be stated that "there are few injuries, even small ones, but in any physical activity there is always the possibility for injury/accident regardless of the care that's taken."

Just because participants are mature, intelligent individuals, it should not be assumed that they "know, understand and appreciate." Special attention must be given by the leadership, to inform through literature, orientation prior to the outdoor experience, and both verbal and expected skill performances during the experience. On the positive side, the liability of a provider is reduced on the basis of assumption of risk where a participant is "experienced," for such experience does indicate that the participant has or should have (greater) knowledge, understanding and appreciation of the activity and the potential for injury.

Exculpatory Clauses—Waivers

A waiver is a contract between the provider offering the program and the participant. Many providers of outdoor programs, or for that matter, any leisure pursuit offered by private enterprise or a public entity, believe that waivers are essential as a protective device and indiscriminately have all participants sign a form. The true function and intent of a waiver is that the provider is relieved of responsibility for any injury which occurs due to the provider's negligence; however, many offering programs/services are really not aware of this and that the actual effect is to lower the standard of care required of the provider from that of ordinary negligence to gross negligence. Because of this, although an individual has the right to so contract against their own personal interest, some individuals feel that it is unethical to ask any participant to sign an exculpatory clause or waiver. In a corporate training program, if the participants are "required" or urged to participate by management, there is real question whether or not the basic criterion for validity is met, that of voluntary signing, but rather that the form would be considered an *adhesion contract*, a form signed by a person who did not believe there was really any other choice.

Also, many of the forms include a statement of "assumption of risk" and a clause stating that the participant will "hold harmless" the provider. Regarding assumption of risk, see the discussion following, on Agreements to Participate. A signed form accepting the risks inherent really is not necessary because such acceptance is part of the common law practiced in most all states. Further, as a contract, the company/employer cannot sign for the individual; all assumption of risk and waivers must be signed by the individual.

There are two applications of "hold harmless," often termed *indemnification*. One is in contract with the corporation, which is appropriate to shift liability. Certainly, in the contract with the company there should be a statement that the company will indemnify, (hold harmless), the provider for any legal action taken regarding injuries to the employees. The company also should accept responsibility for the general behavior and conduct to the participants.

Agreement to Participate Form

It is recommended that participants sign an *agreement to participate* form. The purpose is *not* to contract away one's rights if injured (see discussion on waivers), but rather to establish some documentary evidence regarding efforts to meet the requirements for assumption of risk and contributory fault. It also establishes the responsibilities of the participant and is excellent public relations in that there is information regarding the nature of the experience. The form does not have to be long, but must be signed by the individual participant; the corporation cannot sign on behalf of all employee participants. Such a form should have several parts or "types" of content. (Parts do not have to be segmented as such, but may be sequential paragraphs.)

Part A: Nature of activity—a brief description to provide a basis for knowledge about and understanding of the activity.

Part B: Possible injury consequences—one effort to inform so that the participant may "appreciate" such possibilities. Often when one uses a "waiver form," this statement of possible injury consequences only is used; for better legal defense, it should be used in conjunction with the nature of the activity and list some of the possible injuries.

Part C: Expectations of the participants—what is the expected behavior and performance from the participants? Are there special rules and regulations, protective equipment or appropriate dress desirable? This section should also place some responsibility upon the participant, such as indicate when they are having difficulty with a skill, perhaps when they are not feeling well or are fatigued, check equipment as directed, call attention to any situation which they perceive to be a potential danger to themselves or others, etc. It can be stated that they should feel free to ask any questions, and also the company should permit voluntary withdrawal when the circumstances so indicate.

Part D: Condition of the participant—if a certain physical condition or performance level in a skill is required or desirable, this should be stated. Also, it is important that the leader know of certain participant conditions, such as allergies (especially bee stings), epilepsy, diabetes, physical disabilities, etc.

Following this section, there can be a brief statement regarding the arrangements in case of injury, particularly who pays for the ambulance, if needed, and if such injury is within the company's medical coverage. There also needs to be information provided by participants, regarding emergency contacts, phone numbers, etc. The individual participant should sign and retain a copy of the agreement.

Chapter 7 Summary

The high profile of Outdoor Adventure models has caused problems and made it enigmatic for current and potential users of CEL. Some of the confusion stems from the perception that all CEL is Outdoor Adventure. CEL is also sometimes confused with fire-walking, combat flying, bungee jumping and parachuting.

Because of the variety among CEL providers, there is no one clearly defined methodology. Some providers do not consider business experience necessary for successful program implementation. Others value organizational development experience as a most important element.

Ropes courses and other outdoor adventure models are not for everyone. However, with prudent design, the use of these models and techniques can be relevant and powerful. Providers must expand their awareness into the physiological, psychological and legal issues.

CHAPTER EIGHT

TRANSFER ISSUES AND CONCERNS

RICHARD J. WAGNER, PH.D., CHRISTOPHER C. ROLAND, ED.D.

Transfer of training or transfer of learning is defined by many researchers and practitioners as the degree to which trainees effectively apply the knowledge, skills, attitudes and behavior gained in a training context (Gibson, 1994). One of the key elements for transfer to take place is a high level of trainee buy-in and commitment to learn. As Peter Senge (1990) notes, "The organizations that truly excel in the future will be the organizations that discover how to tap peoples' commitment and capacity to learn."

While trainers are always concerned with how well training programs transfer to the work setting, there appears to be particular concern with new and controversial training methodologies, including various forms of experiential training. Many of the 350 Corporate Training Directors surveyed by Wagner, Baldwin & Roland (1991), expressed some serious concerns about experiential training, particularly the out-of-doors variety. Some of these concerns are evident in the comments below:

- ◆ "Expensive, trendy gimmick"
- ◆ "Fluff"
- ◆ "No concrete basis to support my positive impressions"
- ◆ "Interesting and entertaining, but not relevant"
- ◆ "Too costly"
- ◆ "Not serious training"
- ◆ "The cost-benefit analysis is doubtful"

Despite the above, a large number of training directors commented on the effectiveness and usefulness of CEL for their organizations. Transfer to the work setting is clearly controversial, and subject to individual interpretation.

Kolb's Learning Cycle

In an attempt to clarify the issue of how well experiential training transfers to the work setting, it should be helpful to look at its theoretical underpinnings. David Kolb's Learning Cycle is the most commonly used theory of experiential learning (Chapter One). The impressions of experiential training differ from person to person, and often are at the extreme ends of the spectrum; some people swear by it, and others swear at it.

In addition to the concerns expressed in the survey responses and in meetings with our training colleagues around the world, there is a set of less obvious, but perhaps more serious problems, linked to Kolb's Model. These problems limit the effectiveness of the transfer to the work setting.

Kolb's model suggests that experiential learning involves an immediate (1) *concrete experience*, which is the basis for (2) *observation and reflection,* that is then organized or (3) *assimilated into a theory*, from which new hypotheses or implications lead to (4) *active experimentation*. While most experiential programs claim to be based on this model, many programs actually stop far short of using the model appropriately.

Concrete experience: In an effective training program, the activity, or concrete experience, is linked to the objectives of the training program. But, sometimes the activity, planned for two hours, actually takes three hours, or more, to complete, as often happens with many management simulations and activities. The group gets side-tracked and makes the activity a lot tougher than anticipated, or an inexperienced trainer allows the group to get off track. The result may be that the group never finishes the activity, or that the trainer fails to step in and guide the group to some conclusion, thus breaking the cycle of learning.

In Chapter One, Stoltz refers to the "sin" of "putting the event before the learning." The events must be linked to the learning objectives for successful transfer of learning to the work setting. All too often activities are selected because they are fun and enlightening, not because they relate to the learning objectives of the client. The choice of concrete experience must be linked to the learning objectives of the organization. *Relevancy* is the key (Mironoff, 1988; Payne, 1991).

Observations and reflections: The process of considering what happened during the concrete experience takes *time* and skillful encouragement by the program facilitator. Often the facilitator leaves insufficient time for the observation/reflection process. Many program designers are very good at developing "activities" (management games, computer simulations, role plays, or outdoor events), but have little interest in moving the learning cycle beyond the activity itself.

Debriefing an activity gives the facilitator the opportunity to focus the group's attention on observing, reflecting, sharing and commenting on the experience. The focus on proper debriefing has become more important in the last few years. When the debriefing process is skillfully handled by the facilitator, it strengthens the second step of Kolb's learning cycle. Experienced facilitators are careful not to dominate this portion of the program, "telling" the participants what happened; rather, they encourage and draw out participants' observations and reflections on what they experienced.

Learning will occur *only* if there is time for the learner to observe and reflect. Learners need to consider what went wrong, and what went right in the process. Simply being "told" what did not work, or not taking the time to observe and reflect will minimize the lasting effects occurring from the experiential activity.

Taking the time to observe and reflect on the experience should lead directly to the third step of Kolb's Learning Cycle, *assimilating the observations and reflections into a theory*, from which new hypotheses can be formed. While the debriefing process can allow participants to observe and reflect on their experience, this reflection does not complete the transfer of learning. Participants must be encouraged to formulate a "theory" of behavior change so that the learning transfers to the work setting.

This developing theory must take into account the norms, values, beliefs and attitudes of the organization, i.e., the culture. If not, the theory will not be meaningful in real life. Organizations are as different as individual people, and what works in one organizational culture may not work in another. Because of the differences in the cultures of organizations, a "one-size-fits-all" program will not be effective; and the design appropriate for one organization will not be usable in another organization with different needs and/or culture(s).

The theory-building step is really the critical step to the transfer of learning. After the group has "formed a square while blindfolded," the skilled facilitator guides the group to develop a "theory" of problem solving that is based on what was experienced (the importance of planning, for example), leading to the expansion of this theory to the work setting. It is necessary that facilitators gain sufficient knowledge of the client organization to be effective guides for the group making these generalizations and transfers to the work setting.

The final step of Kolb's Learning Cycle involves *active experimentation*, or actually testing the theory in the work setting. As Kolb's model suggests, without active experimentation in the work setting, the one-shot type of training program may be a temporary experience, and may not result in actual lasting change. Too many providers of experiential programs base their program design on this ineffective approach. To expect lasting, meaningful change from a simple program (one-day of team building or a five-day wilderness experience), is unrealistic. The theory developed from the experience, observation and reflection should lead to active experimentation on the job, thereby increasing the opportunities for transfer. Latham & Saari (1979) agree and note that including ample opportunity for practice in a given model may result in a relatively permanent change in employee behavior. This practice results in new *concrete experiences*, which continue the learning cycle.

Follow-up (Chapter 3), or "maintenance" (Michalak, 1981) is a key element in the active experimentation phase that reinforces transfer of the training experience to the work setting. Michaleak, in *The Neglected Half of Training*, suggests the use of "maintenance of behavior" concepts, defined as "anything which keeps an acquired skill or knowledge up to a performance standard." Contrary to popular opinion, the "anything" does not necessarily mean training. Following through on action plans (Youker, 1985) which can include following structured work habits and patterns (Kushell, 1979), can be immensely helpful. The use of learning partners or anchors are examples of *change agents,* advocates of CEL, who see the experiential learning event as part of a long-term process, and encourage the active experimentation phase. Change agents can be internal consultant/trainers, facilitators, senior management or visible individuals committed to the viability of the process and program objectives.

Conclusion

Transfer of experiential learning to the work place typically involves a process that includes pre-work (e.g., need assessment, customized design), program implementation and follow-up. In Kolb's Cycle, the process includes experience, observation, reflection and experimentation. Unfortunately, many external and internal experiential trainers do not follow these processes, believing that transfer of learning will occur automatically upon exposure to the concrete experience. Research, case studies and common sense refutes that belief: a successful training process must include the advance work, the active experiencing and various follow-up efforts. Putting these concepts together will give organizations the best opportunity to get "the biggest bang for their buck."

CHAPTER NINE

MOVING FORWARD WITH EXPERIENTIAL LEARNING

CHRISTOPHER C. ROLAND, ED.D., RICHARD J. WAGNER, PH.D., ROBERT WEIGAND

Corporate Experiential Learning—especially the more action-oriented variety—is becoming a remarkable worldwide movement. This book presents *some* of the many models, applications and issues of CEL. Other important information about this training methodology appears in newspapers, documentaries and professional journals/magazines. Unfortunately, many publications have focused on the unique activities that are often used in CEL processes while ignoring the philosophical and long term benefits.

Professional Associations

Professional associations are another means to promote public awareness and education. The American Society for Training & Development (ASTD) has given some attention to CEL. Two other associations more specifically focused on this form of training are:

The Association for Business Simulation and Experiential Learning (ABSEL)

Founded in 1974, ABSEL is dedicated to training and development, simulation research, experiential learning, learning theory and experiential exercises through effective, innovative methods. The Association hosts an annual conference and publishes conference proceedings as well as a semiannual newsletter. Conferences include workshops on CEL. Beginning in 1995, there will be pre-conference workshop specifically focusing on CEL. [For information contact Hugh M. Cannon, Wayne State University, 5201 Cass Avenue, Suite 300, Detroit, MI 48202-3930.] Currently the organization is on the leading edge of developing and assessing simulations and experiential exercises specifically for the business environment.

The Association for Experiential Education (AEE)

Founded in 1973, "AEE's diverse membership consists of individuals and organizations with affiliations in education, recreation, outdoor adventure programming, mental health, youth service, physical education, management development training, corrections, programming for people with disabilities, and environmental education." AEE hosts an annual conference, publishes the *Journal of Experiential Education* and the newsletter *AEE Horizon* three times per year. [For information: contact AEE at 2885 Aurora Avenue #2, Boulder, CO 80303-2252.]

In Search of Excellence: Some Recommendations

More and more organizations are searching for resources to either begin an experiential program/process or to enhance existing CEL endeavors. Publications and professional associations are good resources to augment the many consultants and consulting companies. In addition to outdoor program providers and corporate program providers an increasing number of traditional organizational development consultants now include experiential methods in their organizational development and training work.

In order to maximize a program's potential for success, a partnership must be developed between the consultant and client so that all phases of an experiential program/process are collaboratively designed and executed. Therefore, selecting a consultant should be a careful, methodical task with a demand for quality and results. Potential service providers should expect to answer these additional questions in a Request for Proposal (RFP):

♦ How do you conduct a needs assessment?

♦ What is your training background?

♦ Given a set of desired expectations and outcomes, what is the suggested approach?

♦ If an outdoor training approach is suggested, why?

♦ What approach is suggested to reach the "Doubting Thomas's?"

♦ How are corporate, management and training group expectations managed?

♦ What type of follow-up will sustain the learnings and the learning environments?

♦ What is the program/process design for multi-cultural teams?

♦ How can impact of the training program/process be measured?

Train-the-Trainer Programs

Experiential activities and exercises can be successfully *integrated* within existing training programs, curricula and organizational development strategies. This integration process is often conducted by in-house trainers and consultants. As organizations discover the potential return of CEL, the demand for transfer of skills to internal training and development staff, often accomplished by "training the trainers," is increasing.

On-site Ropes Courses

Many organizations are installing ropes courses on-site: e.g., GTE Data Services, Arthur Andersen, Saturn Corporation and the Federal Aviation Agency. This decision must take into account the potential uses of course elements, and the corporate message the on-site course sends to employees. An anonymous internal memo from an employee of a Fortune 500 organization illustrates some of the problems employees perceive with these courses (Wagner, Ryan & Roland , 1992):

> "The placement of this equipment is already a source of emotional stress to employees who want to continue working for [this organization] but do not want to risk being paralyzed or killed just to keep a desk job . . . even if, and I think it is a big if, no one is hurt out there, just installing military training equipment sends a message to employees that we are no longer respected by upper management for our intelligence, but only value our ability to do physical labor, (p. 252)."

To avoid such a misunderstanding, an in-depth needs analysis prior to deciding on an on-site ropes course should include the following:

1. Does the organization really need a ropes course? What are the specific goals and objectives? Are there suitable alternatives to a ropes course?
2. Is there a specific plan to educate all employees regarding the ropes course?
3. Many ropes course "packages" include a Train-the-Trainer program. What is the program's focus? Who are the facilitators?
4. Can the ropes course be used year-round? Will employees (and trainers) be comfortable in extreme temperatures?
5. If a high ropes course is being considered, what are the physiological considerations for participants who may be less than optimally fit?
6. What are the legal considerations?

Conclusion

This book is intended to be a resource to those individuals and organizations that are either investigating the possibilities of using corporate experiential learning or attempting to enhance existing programs and processes. Individuals and organizations must ask themselves, their colleagues, their employees and their consultants difficult questions. CEL has the potential to become a demanded methodology because it is conducive to learning and can transfer learning to the work place. Certain models and methodologies will prove to be stronger and more effective than others; and those that are indeed more effective will represent some of the most exciting, relevant and effective training technologies ever known.

Appendix A

Biographical Sketches

MICHAEL O. BLACK, Ph.D.

Dr. Michael Black has been involved in experiential training and development since 1988, as program designer, facilitator, trip leader, safety technician, and researcher. He earned his doctorate in counseling psychology from the University of Utah, where his research focused on experiential training and development, as well as experiential therapeutic interventions. He has been a staff member at the University of Utah, Northern Arizona University, and the Colorado Outward Bound School. He is currently a consultant with Somerville & Company in Denver, Colorado.

HEATHER BROWN

Heather Brown is currently an Instructional Designer with Telecom Australia, where she designs Management Development Programs, administers needs and competency analyses and program evaluations. Her experience includes Outdoor Management Specialist for Mountaincraft Australia and other outdoor development providers. In the UK, she also lectured in Further and Adult Education Colleges, and directed courses for teachers in hillwalking and navigation. She is the recipient of the Duke of Edinburgh's Award for expedition skills and personal development using the outdoors.

Heather has a degree in French and a Post Graduate Diploma in Training Management.

CAMILLE J. BUNTING, Ph.D.

Dr. Camille J. Bunting is the director of the Outdoor Education Institute and Associate Professor in the Health & Kinesiology Department at Texas A&M University. She received her Bachelor and Masters degrees from Baylor University and her Ph.D. from Texas A&M University with an emphasis in exercise physiology. She has been actively engaged as an experiential educator since 1974, and has been conducting outdoor adventure physiology research since 1979. Dr. Bunting has published a participant ropes course manual as well as articles in both scientific and educational journals. She was the 1991 recipient of the Reynold E. Carlson Award for distinction in outdoor environmental education, and a 1993 recipient of the Julian W. Smith Award for contributions to the field of outdoor education.

JOHN CAMPBELL

John Campbell, M.Phil., ACISA, MITD, had 15 years experience as Production General Manager and Regional Director in the brewing industry before joining Executive and Staff Training (EAST), North Yorkshire, UK, as Managing Director in 1986. He has a wealth of practical experience in sales and marketing, retailing, wholesale distribution, production and human resource development.

He has designed and led programs for companies both in the UK and overseas, addressing issues such as corporate vision and values and harnessing the potential of multicultural teams, as well as developing core competencies.

CHRISTINE CLEMENTS, Ph.D.

Dr. Christine Clements is an assistant professor of management at the University of Wisconsin—Whitewater. She received her undergraduate and MBA degrees from the University of Wisconsin, and her Ph.D. in Business Administration from the University of Arkansas. She has authored several articles on leadership education, work-family role conflict and organizational theory, and has presented numerous papers at the regional and national levels. Dr. Clements' background and interests are primarily in the organizational behavior area, including experiential training in team building, leadership development and gender issues in management. In addition to consulting, she teaches courses in Organizational Behavior, Leadership and Organization Theory & Effectiveness. Chris has been actively involved on state and university committees to improve teaching methods, curriculum development and student learning.

WARREN E. COHEN

Warren E. Cohen is an Associate in the University of Michigan office of Human Resource

Development, the training and development area of UM's Personnel Department. As one of UM's internal organizational development consultants, Warren works with executives, administrators, managers, supervisors, faculty and staff as an intervention specialist, program designer and workshop presenter. In addition, he coordinates HRD's Team Development curriculum, and the University's New Employee Orientation program.

Warren is also an organizational development and management consultant designing and facilitating strategic planning, team building, management and group development programs for organizations in the private and public sector. He has been involved in the experiential education field since 1976 focusing on individual and organizational development. He has a BA in Psychology from the University of Michigan, with emphasis on human resource administration training and development. His MS is in Industrial/Organizational Psychology from Purdue University.

MADELINE G. CONSTANTINE

Madeline is the Program Coordinator at Stony Acres, a Wildlife Sanctuary/Recreation Facility owned by the students of East Stroudsburg University, Pennsylvania. For the past eleven years Madeline has managed, programmed and trained staff on the 35-element ropes course at Stony Acres. Serving many groups, profit and non-profit, from all walks of life, the Stony Acres Ropes Course annually logs more than 12,000 participant hours. Stony Acres has been the arena for research projects on self-efficacy, self-concept and adventure based corporate training. Madeline earned her Master's of Education in Health and Physical Education at East Stroudsburg University.

LEONARD D. DIAMOND

Leonard Diamond is a Managing Partner at Roland/Diamond Associates, Inc., an organizational development consulting company. He has more than twenty years of management experience in a variety of corporate settings, including information systems, research and development, real estate and fixed income investments, portfolio management and strategic planning. Before joining Roland/Diamond Associates, he held executive management positions at Aetna Life & Casualty in Hartford, Connecticut, and General Motors in Flint, Michigan.

Len specializes in creating programs for groups and individuals using highly customized experiential learning models. He has considerable experience in transitional management, group dynamics, team development, conflict management, staff selection and training & development. He has a B.S. in Business Administration from Ithaca College, Ithaca, New York.

ELAINE M. HATALA

Elaine has been providing adventure based programming and training for eight years. As the Director of Outreach Programs at Bowling Green Adolescent Center in Berlin, NJ, Elaine regularly provides seminars, workshops and training for a wide variety of organizations at the local and state level. Elaine specializes in on-site adventure based training and also trains at several Ropes Courses throughout New Jersey and Pennsylvania. Elaine earned her M.A. from New York University and is currently pursuing an Ed.D. at Temple University.

DONALD L. KIRKPATRICK, Ph.D.

Dr. Donald Kirkpatrick is Professor Emeritus at the University of Wisconsin. He was Professor of Management at the University of Wisconsin-Madison for eleven years and the University of Wisconsin-Milwaukee for twenty-two years. Prior to his teaching posts, he was Personnel Manager for Bendix Products Aerospace Division and Training Director for International Minerals and Chemical Corporation.

Don is currently an international management and training consultant, having conducted seminars in India, Australia, Hong Kong, Taiwan, Thailand, Japan, Malaysia, Fiji Islands, Singapore, Venezuela, Mexico and Saudi Arabia. His seminar topics include: Leadership and Motivation, Effective Communication, Managing Conflict, Managing Change, How to Conduct Productive Meetings, Selecting and Training Supervisors, Evaluating Training Programs, Performance Appraisal and Coaching, Participative Management Effectively and Empowerment and Team Building. He is past President of the American Society for Training & Development (ASTD).

Dr. Kirkpatrick is the author of six books: *How to Train and Develop Supervisors* (AMACOM), *How to Plan and Conduct Productive Business Meetings* (AMACOM), *No-Nonsense Communication* (Kirkpatrick), *How to Improve Performance through Appraisal* (AMACOM), *How to Manage Change Effectively* (Jossey-Bass) and *Evaluating Training Programs: The Four Levels* (Berrett-Koehler). Don has also authored eight Supervisory/Management Inventories on: Communication, Human Relations, Safety, Managing Change, Time Management, Modern Management, Performance Appraisal and Coaching, and Leadership, Motivation and Decision-making.

DAVID A. KOLB, Ph.D.

Dr. David A. Kolb is the E. Mandell de Windt Professor of Leadership and Enterprise Development in the Department of Organizational Behavior at the Weatherhead School of Management at Case Western Reserve University. Dr. Kolb received his Ph.D. in Social Psychology and his M.A. from Harvard University. He served as the Chairman of the Department of Organizational Behavior in the Weatherhead School from 1984-1991. He has received honorary degrees from the International Management Center, Buckingham, U.K., the University of New Hampshire and Franklin University.

Dr. Kolb has authored numerous books, articles, and monographs. His book, *Experiential Learning: Experience as the Source of Learning and Development* (Prentice-Hall) is an integrative statement of 15 years' research on learning styles and the learning process. Dr. Kolb was also a principal investigator for a major research project funded by the National Institute of Education and the Spencer Foundation concerning experiential learning and adult career development, focusing on mid-career changes in managers and on the role of professional education in preparation for a career of life long learning.

His other books include *Organizational Behavior: An Experiential Approach to Human Behavior in Organizations* (Prentice-Hall) and *Organizational Behavior: Practical Readings for Managers* (with I. Rubin & J. Osland, Prentice-Hall). Forthcoming publications include *Innovations in Professional Education: Steps in a Journey from Teaching to Learning* (with R.E. Boyatzis & S.S. Cowen, Jossey-Bass) and *Perspectives on Experiential Learning: Preludes to a Global Conversation on Learning* (with M. Keeton, et. al., Council for Adult & Experiential Learning).

MARIO KÖLBLINGER, Ph.D.

Dr. Mario Kölblinger is a Management Development Facilitator and Personnel Consultant for Dr. Strasser & Partner in Munich, Germany. With Dr. Strasser, he pioneered outdoor management development in Germany in the early 1970s. He designs and facilitates outdoor and indoor-based courses on project management, change management, process management and total quality management throughout Germany, Austria, Scotland, Switzerland, Sweden and Spain.

Dr. Kölblinger is an associate of Augsburg University and a board member of the German National Association for Adventure Education (Bundesverband Erlebnispadagogik e.v.)

Mario is currently involved with a research study on the state of experiential learning in German corporations and focuses on the implementation of action learning methods at the work place. He studied economics and psychology at Ludwig Maximilian University in Munich and was an Assistant Professor of Business Administration. He holds a Master's Degree in Business Administration (Dipl,kfm.) and received his Ph.D. (Dr. rer. pol.) at Munich University.

RON LEWIS

Sergeant Ron Lewis is a Course Researcher/Coordinator responsible for the Senior Police Administration Course (SPAC) delivered at the Canadian Police College, Ottawa, Canada.

He is a 25 year member of the Royal Canadian Mounted Police (R.C.M.P.) and has spent the last 10 years in a training function. Five years were devoted to drug enforcement training for members of the R.C.M.P. and various international police agencies, while the past five years involved management training at the Canadian Police College.

Sgt. Lewis introduced experiential training into the SPAC curriculum several years ago and is a strong advocate of this method of delivery for management training.

TOCK KENG LIM, Ph.D.

Dr. Tock Keng Lim is a researcher and lecturer in Quantitative Psychology in the Masters of Education Programme at the Center for Applied Research in Education (CARE), National Institute of Education, Nanyang Technological University. Her experience in education includes teaching of economics, research and testing and administration in staff development and training of school leaders. While in Staff Development and Training, she developed an assessment centre package for the selection of school leaders.

Currently in CARE, her research activities include cognitive and personality tests, computerized adaptive testing, thinking skills, school leadership, stress management and experiential training.

Dr. Lim holds a Bc in Economics from the University of London, an M.Phil. in Economics from the University of Auckland, New Zealand and an M.A. and Ph.D. in Educational Psychology from the University of Texas at Austin.

MICHAEL MAIN

Since 1981, Michael Main has directed his own Gaborne-based company in Botswana where he facilitates in-house management skills training courses for all levels of management from supervisors to the most senior staff. He also organises and facilitates leadership courses utilizing the wilderness environment to help provide "hands-on" learning to enhance people skills.

Michael's background includes Group Operations Manager for the Kgalakgadi Management Services, Gaborne; Video Presenter for Agricor (of the former Bophutjatswana Republic in South Africa); National Security Manager for Delta Corporation in Zimbabwe, Harare and Police Officer with the British South Africa Police in Southern Rhodesia (now Zimbabwe).

Mr. Main is currently conducting field research for various government and non-government agencies in Botswana. Projects have included assistance on several archaeological surveys, participation in two sociological surveys among the San (Bushmen) and assistance with a tourism survey for the Government of Botswana.

Michael is the author of five books on the sub-region: *Kalahari: Life's Variety from Dune to Delta; Visitor's Guide to Botswana* (with John & Sandra Fowkes); *Zambezi: Journey of a River; On the Edge of Africa: A Guide to the Kasane Region;* and *Botswana Guide for HATAB* (Southern Book Publishers).

TOM McGEE

Tom McGee worked for the Crane Division, Naval Surface Warfare Center from 1968 until his retirement in 1994. While working for this large Navy industrial complex, he held various positions in the personnel field and was the Training Director of the Division upon his retirement. Tom holds an undergraduate degree from the University of Notre Dame, a Masters degree from Indiana University and a Public Management Certificate from Indiana University.

RITA MILLER

Rita Miller, R.N., C.B.S. is a certified mental health nurse-therapist with fifteen years experience in group and individual therapies. She is the former director of the Group Center, an acute, adult, partial-hospitalization program at the Center for Mental Health of the Reading Hospital in Reading, Pennsylvania.

Ms. Miller has presented workshops and lectures to the medical/mental health professional community, as well as to business and industry and the public on Stress Management and Humor Skills. She developed a free consultation and referral service for women through the hospital's Women's Center. This service was feature in *The Ireland Report*, a national journal of women's health care.

RUSSELL B. MILLHOLLAND

Russell Millholland is Director of Human Resources for Saint-Gobain Advanced Materials Corporation (formally Norton Company of Worcester, Massachusetts). Mr. Millholland has twenty years with Norton Company with responsibilities in financial, accounting, production planning, materials management, plant management, information systems, organizational development, research and development management and human resources.

Mr. Millholland previously designed and coordinated the Total Continuous Quality Improvement efforts for the Advanced Ceramics SBU. He was instrumental in the development and implementation of outdoor-based training strategies that reinforce typical classroom methodologies. He has designed a wide variety of learning modules with outdoor components including problem solving, communication, and continuous quality improvement.

Mr. Millholland has a Bachelor of Science Degree in Finance & Banking and an MBA from Suffolk University. He has also completed several management programs at Pennsylvania State University, Babson College and the Massachusetts Institute of Technology (MIT), Senior Executives' Program.

TODD A. MINER, Ed.D.

Dr. Todd Miner is the Coordinator of Alaska Wilderness Studies and an Assistant Professor in the School of Education at the University of Alaska, Anchorage. Todd has lived in Alaska for nearly 20 years, in which time he has climbed Denali (Mt. McKinley) and many of the other major peaks of the state. He has explored the far corners of Alaska by foot, ski, kayak, and raft and led numerous climbing expeditions to Mexico and South America.

Dr. Miner received his doctorate in education from Boston University in 1993. His dissertation explored the effectiveness of experiential training and development using isomorphic versus traditional facilitation styles for team building. He has written several articles on experiential learning and on Alaska. Todd's current research interests include safety and adventure education applications with Native Americans.

RODNEY NAPIER, Ph.D.

Dr. Rod Napier is a management consultant serving a wide-range of clients in business and industry. He is the Co-Director of The Tamagami Wilderness Experience, a leadership development program that provides individuals with a wide-range of emotionally and physically challenging events keyed around community building in a wilderness setting. He is Co-Director of the Small Group Facilitators Internship Program training and enhancing skills in small group diagnoses, intervention and design.

For twelve years Rod was a Professor in the Department of Psychoeducational Processes at Temple University, Philadelphia, Pennsylvania. He is now an Adjunct Professor at Temple where he has taught various courses including Group Management and Practice, Learning Theory, Organizational Development and Group Dynamics.

Dr. Napier is author of a variety of books including *Groups: Theory and Experience* (with M. Gershenfeld, Houghton Mifflin) and *Making Groups Work* (with M. Gershenfeld, Houghton Mifflin). Rod received his MA from the University of Chicago and his Ph.D. from the University of Wisconsin.

IRIS RANDALL

Iris Randall is President and Founder of Roah, West & Randall, Inc., a consulting firm specializing in training programs and products to help organizations manage transition. Having substantial experience in the area of personal and professional development, she has designed and presented workshops on life and career planning, management of diversity, time management, sales training and effective communications.

Iris is affiliated with The Institute for Managing Diversity at Morehouse College as an Advisory Board member, workshop facilitator and guest lecturer. Based on the principles that diversity is beyond race and gender, the Institute works with organizations to bring about behavioral and cultural changes. Her multi-cultural and international experience included Director of Training Operations with responsibility for three continents. One of her specialties is in identifying the strengths of a diverse group of people and helping them become an effective team.

Iris is a Field Manager, Training Associate and Distributor for Carlson Learning Company, Minneapolis. Her education includes a B.A. from Marymount College, courses at the University of Michigan Graduate School of Business Management and Special Teaching Certification in Remedial Reading from the University of Connecticut. She is the author of *Getting Unstuck,* a desktop seminar in self development based on her own experiences; and also writes regularly for *Black Enterprise, Managing Diversity Newsletter,* and *Learning 2001.*

CHRISTOPHER C. ROLAND, Ed.D.

Dr. Christopher Roland is a Managing Partner at Roland/Diamond Associates, Inc., an organizational development consulting company. For the past twelve years he has partnered with a wide range of organizations in the development and implementation of change strategies. Chris has extensive background in designing stand-alone experiential programs as well as integrating experiential segments within existing training curricula. His background also includes teaching, guest lecturing and workshop facilitating at various universities including Boston University, Indiana University and the University of Muncton (New Brunswick, Canada). He has published in various professional journals including *Training & Development Journal* and *Journal of Experiential Education*. He is also co-author of The *Theory and Practice of Challenge Education.*

Chris received his B.Ed. and M.Ed. from Keene State College, New Hampshire, and his doctorate from Boston University. His dissertation was *The Transfer of an Outdoor Managerial Training Program to the Work Place.*

ROSEANN RYBA

Roseann Ryba is a Manager in Andersen Consulting's Change Management Practice. She holds a Master's Degree in Human Resource Development from the American University and has over fifteen years experience in the field.

As a consultant, she has assisted clients in the design and delivery of experiential training and development programs. As a manager, she has facilitated as well as collaborated with providers in the coordination, design, and delivery of experiential training.

Prior to joining Andersen Consulting, Ms. Ryba managed a consulting practice specializing in Human Resources, Training and Organizational Development. Previously, she served as a Human Resource Manager at AT&T Bell Laboratories where she assisted in the coordination of, and participated in, a major change effort involving experiential training. She has scaled the wall, climbed the pole, bared the soul, and slain the dragon with the help and guidance of some of the best providers in the field.

PENNIE S. SEIBERT, Ph.D.

Dr. Pennie Seibert is an Associate Professor of Psychology at Boise State University, Boise, Idaho. This position includes teaching psychology and interdisciplinary courses, conducting an active program of research, consulting, student advisement and community service. Her teaching responsibilities include courses in general psychology, industrial/organizational psychology, cognitive psychology, interdisciplinary humanities and advanced research. She is a founder and researcher with the Applied Cognition Research Institute at BSU.

Dr. Seibert has been an Instructor at the University of New Mexico as well as a Special Research Assistant to Henry C. Ellis, Distinguished Professor of Psychology, University of New Mexico. She was also a National Public Relations Representative for Frederick Chusid & Company (Chicago) and an entertainment booking agent in Saigon, South Vietnam.

Pennie has published numerous articles in a variety of journals including *Training & Development Journal, Environment and Behavior, Bulletin of the Psychonomic Society,* and *Memory and Cognition.* She had made presentations at the American Psychological Society, the Interdisciplinary Humanities Conference, Western Psychological Association and the Rocky Mountain Psychological Association.

TOM SMITH, Ph.D.

Dr. Tom Smith is a retired clinical/school psychologist and experiential educator. He is Founder and Director of the Raccoon Institute in Cazenovia, Wisconsin offering consultation and training in experiential education, challenge education and challenge therapy.

His books include: *Wilderness Beyond . . . Wilderness Within, 2nd edition; The Theory and Practice of Challenge Education* (with C. Roland, M. Havens, & J. Hoyt: Kendall/Hunt) and *Incidents in Challenge Education: A Guide to Leadership Development* (Kendall/Hunt). He has published over one hundred professional papers, and is a frequent presenter at regional, national, and international conferences on experiential education and leadership training.

Tom has studied with and about the Native American Indians, and in recent years has made two trips to China to study and present training workshops. He says, "The older I get, the more I see the wisdom of historical traditions." His next book is *Challenge Education and Native American Indian Traditions.* Tom received his Ph.D. from the University of Wisconsin.

PAUL G. STOLTZ, Ph.D.

For five years, Dr. Paul Stoltz was an Assistant Professor at Northern Arizona University in Flagstaff, Arizona where he designed and directed an undergraduate level Training and Development program that has become a benchmark for universities around the world.

Currently, Paul, a nationally recognized consultant, trainer and speaker, is President of PEAK Learning Corporation. He has trained executives, managers and students in a variety of areas of performance enhancement including: self-development, leadership, cultural diversity, teamwork, sales, motivation, time management and communication skills.

In addition to various published articles, Dr. Stoltz is the author of *The Complete Guide to Sales Training* (AMACOM).

MARK J. SULLIVAN

Mark Sullivan supervised North American field personnel for a computer accessories manufacturer prior to managing sales training programs for the world's largest airline at their Executive Sales Institute. His responsibilities included developing and training front-line customer contact employees and management teams in 16 countries on four continents.

Mark was selected as one of seven American business executives under the Reagan Administration to represent U.S. industry in a three month Japanese government sponsored, business study tour in Tokyo. Subsequently, he consulted extensively with sales, purchasing, finance, operations, and field service managers in both the Pacific Rim and European markets. He has conducted more than 300 skill building seminars in negotiating, consultative selling, team building, and conflict management. He has also been involved in the Institute of Cultural Affairs, the Gestalt Institute of Cleveland and the Wharton School strategic planning simulation training program.

Mr. Sullivan has conducted conflict and change management interventions for both military and a Supreme-Soviet sponsored think tank in Moscow. He has trained Outward Bound Survival Wilderness School instructors at their international headquarters in Aberdovey, Wales. Additionally, he has trained U.S. flight crews in survival techniques, emergency procedures, and hostage negotiating.

Mark received an Ed.M. from Harvard University and is presently working on a Ph.D. in Organizational Behavior at Case Western Reserve University (Weatherhead School of Management). There, he is investigating the role of family dynamics in large second and third generation family businesses.

MARY TEETER

Mary Teeter is a licensed Occupational Therapist in private practice in Pennsylvania. She had been director of the Day Treatment Center at Reading Hospital and Medical Center, Reading, PA and Assistant Director of Occupational Therapy at Wernersville State Hospital.

With over twenty five years of experience leading groups, she has a particular interest in group dynamics and the role of activities and interpersonal behavior.

Mary is committed and enthusiastic about the power of groups to educate, heal, support and problem solve and currently leads educational workshops and bereavement groups.

RICHARD WAGNER, Ph.D.

Dr. Richard Wagner is an Assistant Professor of Management in the School of Business and Economics at the University of Wisconsin—Whitewater, Whitewater, Wisconsin. Dick received his Ph.D. in Organizational Behavior from Indiana University, an MBA from Gonzaga University in Spokane, Washington and a B.S. in Geology from Union College in Schenectady, New York. His background includes ten years as Corporate Training Director with Texaco, Inc., SCOA Industries and TSC, Inc.

Dr. Wagner's primary research interests are in the area of human resource training and development. He has published his work in a number of professional journals including *Training & Development Journal, Journal of Small Business Management, Sales & Marketing Management, Journal of Management Development* and *Journal of Healthcare Education & Training*. He has presented papers at a number of professional meetings, including the Academy of Management, the Association for Experiential Education, the Society for Industrial/Organizational Psychology, the Society for Human Resource Management and the American Society for Training and Development.

At the University of Wisconsin—Whitewater, Dick teaches a number of undergraduate and graduate level courses in the Personnel and Human Resource Management field. Some of these courses include: Human Resource Management, Training and Development, Compensation and Selection Systems and Employment.

ROBERT WEIGAND

Robert Weigand is the Manager of Training and Development at St. Luke's Hospital in Bethlehem, Pennsylvania. His responsibilities include the design, development and implementation of management education. Experiential and outdoor-based training are processes used at St. Luke's to foster the growth of a multi-disciplinary management team. This process supports a continued focus on critical thinking, problem solving and change management.

Bob has over fifteen years of experience in the healthcare environment as a therapist and manager. He co-authored the paper "How Effective is Outdoor-based Training in Improving Management Behaviors: A Healthcare Application" in *The Journal of Healthcare & Training*.

BETTY VAN DER SMISSEN, Re.D., J.D.

Dr. Betty van der Smissen is Professor/Chair of the Department of Park, Recreation and Tourism Resources at Michigan State University, Lansing, Michigan where she teaches both undergraduate and graduate courses on legal aspects of recreation and experiential programs. She is admitted to the State of Michigan Bar, and is a member of the American Bar Association.

Betty is the author of a three-volume reference text: *Legal Liability & Risk Management for Public & Private Entities.* She speaks and conducts workshops widely on risk management and legal liability.

CHARLES J. WOLFE

Charles J. Wolfe is President of Wolfe & Associates, an organizational and management development consulting and training firm. He is the former Director of Management Development for the ITT Hartford in West Hartford, Connecticut. There he conceptualized, developed and implemented a world class system of competency performance planning, development, appraisal and succession driven by business plans. His work has been recognized in Tom Peters' newsletter *On Achieving Excellence, The Bricker Bulletin on Executive Education,* and was selected as one of the "Best of America" human resource practices by Lakewood Publications. Chuck also designed, developed and delivered a management leadership curriculum for the Hartford organization and a series of team building workshops for the Chief Executive Officer and his team.

Mr. Wolfe currently consults with clients focusing on core competency development, managing cultural change, strategic training needs analysis, team building and one on one leadership coaching.

Chuck holds a B.A. degree in Psychology and an M.Ed. degree in Counseling from Northeastern University. He is an Ed.D. Candidate at Harvard University where his doctoral dissertation will link business plans to employee development/planning.

APPENDIX B

SAMPLE QUESTIONNAIRE

(1) = Disagree Strongly
(2) = Disagree Moderately
(3) = Disagree Slightly
(4) = Neither Agree Nor Disagree

(5) = Agree Slightly
(6) = Agree Moderately
(7) = Agree Strongly

Here are some statements about you and your fellow workers. Please check only one box.

	1	2	3	4	5	6	7
I consider myself to be close to other members of the group . . .	1	2	3	4	5	6	7
Friendly relationships exist among group members . . .	1	2	3	4	5	6	7
Other members of the group know what I think and value . . .	1	2	3	4	5	6	7
I'm familiar with members of this group as individuals with lives outside the group . . .	1	2	3	4	5	6	7
Members of the group are willing to seek assistance from others when they need it . . .	1	2	3	4	5	6	7
Members of the group demonstrate a willingness to listen to the ideas of others . . .	1	2	3	4	5	6	7
I feel that other members of the group are open to new ideas . . .	1	2	3	4	5	6	7
I feel safe in sharing my thoughts and opinions with other members of the group . . .	1	2	3	4	5	6	7
I can say almost anything to any member of the group without fear of reprisal. . . .	1	2	3	4	5	6	7
Members of the group understand my messages as I intend them . . .	1	2	3	4	5	6	7
Disagreements over group activities are not taken personally by group members . . .	1	2	3	4	5	6	7
Members of the group talk freely about any topic . . .	1	2	3	4	5	6	7

APPENDIX C

SAMPLE INTERVIEW QUESTIONS

How have your behaviors changed at work since you attended the CEL program? Be specific. Give an example of each of these behavior changes.

What is the most memorable experience from your training program?
Why was this experience so memorable?
Has this experience effected your work behaviors?
If so, how? Be specific, and give examples.

Have your noticed any changes in your fellow participants since the program?
What changes? Be specific.

Have your interactions with your co-workers changed since the training program?
With whom have they changed (peers, subordinates, etc.)?
If so, how have they changed? Be specific.

What would you have done differently if you were running the CEL program?

Why would you have done it this way?

How would this have changed the outcomes from this program?

How would *you* define teamwork?

What, in your opinion, are the key elements involved in teamwork at your organization?

Has the CEL program had any impact on any of these elements?

If so, how? Be specific and give examples.

We discussed "risk-taking" behavior in our meetings with you. How would *you* define "risk-taking" behavior at work?

Give an example of high risk behavior.

Give an example of low risk behavior.

Has CEL had any effect on your willingness to engage in "high risk" behavior at work?

If so, give an example of when this happened.

Exactly how do you think that CEL caused this change in you?

REFERENCES

Adamson, P. (1993) Executive Director, Adventure West, Perth, Australia (personal interview).

Agran, A., Garvey, D., Miner, T. & Priest, S. (1993). *Experience-based Training and Development Programs, (3rd Ed.).* Boulder, CO: Association for Experiential Education.

Argyris, C. & Schon, D.A. (1974). *Theory into Practice.* San Francisco: Jossey-Bass.

Aronson, R. S. (1991). Participant Liability Study. Unpublished Manuscript.

Athos, A. & Pascale, R. (1981). *The Art of Japanese Management.* New York: Simon and Schuster.

Bacon, S. (1983). *The Conscious Use of Metaphor in Outward Bound.* Denver, CO: Colorado Outward Bound School.

Baldwin, T.T. & Ford, K.J. (1988). Transfer of Training: A Review and Directions for Future Research. *Personnel Psychology,* 41, 63-105.

Bandura, A. (1977). Self-Efficacy: Toward a Unifying Theory of Behavioral Change. *Psychological Review,* 84(2), 191-215.

Bank, J. (1985). *Outdoor Development for Managers.* Aldershot, England: Gower.

Baron, R. A. (1983). *Behavior in Organizations: Understanding and Managing the Human Side of Work.* Boston: Allyn and Bacon.

Basarab, D. J. & Root, D. K. (1992). *The Training Evaluation Process.* Boston, MA: Kluwer Academic Publishers.

Beeby, M. & Rathborn, S. (1985). *Developing Training Using the Outdoors: A Pilot Programme.* South West Regional Management Centre, UK, 11-14.

Beer, M., Eisenstat, R. & Spector, B. (1990). *The Critical Path to Corporate Renewal.* Boston: The President and Fellows of Harvard College.

Black, M. O. (1993). Outdoor Experiential Management Training: A Substantive Grounded Theory about Process and Outcomes in One Training Program. Doctoral Dissertation, University of Utah.

Bloom, G., Euler, U. S. von & Frankenhaeuser, M. (1963). Catecholamine Excretion and Personality Traits in Paratroop Trainees. *Acta Physiology Scandinavia,* 58, 77-89.

Bolman, L. G. & Deal, T. E. (1991). *Reframing Organizations Artistry, Choice and Leadership.* San Francisco: Jossey-Bass.

Boud, D., Cohen, R. & Walker, D. (Eds.) (1993). *Using Experience for Learning.* Buckingham, UK: SRHE and Open University Press.

Boud, D., Keogh, R. & Walker, D. (Eds.) (1985). *Reflection: Turning Experience Into Learning.* New York: Nichols Publishing.

Bowman, B. (1987). Assessing Your Needs Assessment. *Training,* 24(1), 30-34.

Buller, P. F., Cragun, J. R., & McEvoy, G. M. (1991). Getting the Most Out of Outdoor Training. *Training and Development Journal,* 45(3), 58-61.

Buller, P. F. (1986). The Team Building-task Performance Relation: Some Conceptual and Methodological Refinements. *Group & Organization Studies,* 11(3), 147-168.

Buller, P. F. & Bell, C. H. (1986). Effects of Team Building and Goal Setting on Productivity: A Field Experiment. *Academy of Management Journal,* 29, 305-328.

Bunting, C., Little, M., Tolson, H. & Jessup, G. (1986). Physical Fitness and Eustress in the Adventure Activities of Rockclimbing and Rappelling. *The Journal of Sports Medicine and Physical Fitness,* 26(1), 11-20.

Campbell, A. & Main, M. (1991). *Western Sandveld Remote Area Dwellers. Report on the History of Local Governments and Lands.* Government of Botswana.

Caudron, S. (1994). Volunteer Efforts Offer Low-Cost Training Options, *Personnel Journal,* June, 38-44.

Cheffers, J., Brunelle, J. & Von Kelsch, R. (1978, Sept). Measuring Student Involvement. Paper presented at the AIESEP International Conference, Magglingen, Switzerland.

Cline, E. B. & Seibert, P. S. (1993). Help for First-time Needs Assessors. *Training & Development Journal,* 47(5), 99-101.

____. (1992). *Guidelines for a Versatile Needs Assessment Procedure.* Paper presented at the meeting of the Rocky Mountain Psychological Association, Boise, Idaho, April 24-26.

Conger, J. (1993). Personal Growth Training: Snake Oil or Pathway to Leadership? *Organizational Dynamics,* 22 (Summer), 19-30.

Consalvo, C. M. (1993). *Experiential Training Activities for Outside and In.* Amherst, MA: HRD Press.

Covey, S. R. (1991). *Principle-Centered Leadership.* New York: Simon & Schuster.

____. (1989). *The 7 Habits of Highly Effective People.* New York: Simon & Schuster.

Cray-Andrews, M. (1985). Experiential Education—One Reality. *The Journal of Experiential Education,* 8(3), 13- 18.

Csikszentmihalyi, M. & Csikszentmihalyi, I. S. (1988). *Optimal Experience.* New York: Cambridge University Press.

Csikszentmihalyi, M. (1975). *Beyond Boredom and Anxiety.* San Francisco: Jossey-Bass.

Davies, B., Massey, B. H., Lohman, T. G. & Williams, B. T. (1977). Urinary Excretion of Free Noradrenaline and Adrenaline in Trained and Untrained Men. *British Journal of Sports Medicine,* 11, 94-98.

Deal, T. E. & Kennedy, A. A. (1982). *Corporate Cultures.* Reading, MA: Addison-Wesley.

Dewey, J. (1938). *Experience and Education.* New York: Collier Books.

Dick, R. (1991). *Helping Groups be Effective,* Queensland, Australia: Interchange, Chapel Hill.

Dimsdale, J. E. & Moss, J. (1980). Plasma Catecholamines in Stress and Exercise. *Journal of the American Medical Association,* 243(4), 340-342.

Doornen, L. van (1986). Sex Differences in Physiological Reactions to Real Life Stress and Their Relationship to Psychological Variables. *Psychophysiology,* 23(6), 657-662.

Duffy, E. (1957). The Psychological Significance of the Concept of Arousal or Activation. *The Psychological Review,* 64(5), 265-275.

Evaluation Process. (1992). Boston, MA: Kluwer Academic Publishers.

Ewert, A. (1985). Outdoor Experiential Education: Its Power and Pitfalls. *The Outdoor Communicator.*

Flanagan, J. (1954). The Critical Incident Technique, *Psychological Bulletin,* 51, 327-358.

Flor, R. (1991). Building Bridges Between Organization Development and Experiential/Adventure Education. *Journal of Experiential Education,* 14(3), 27-34.

Frankenhaeuser, M. (1971). Experimental Approaches to the Study of Human Behavior as Related to Neuroendocrine Functions. In L. Levi (Ed.), *Society, Stress, and Disease,* Vol. 1, London: Oxford University Press, pp. 22-35.

____. (1975). Experimental Approach to the Study of Catecholamines and Emotion. In L. Levi (Ed.), *Emotions, Their Parameters and Measurement,* New York: Raven Press, 209-234.

____. (1978). Psychoneuroendocrine Approaches to the Study of Emotion as Related to Stress and Coping. In H. E. Howe & R. A. Dienstbier (Eds.), *Nebraska Symposium on Motivation 1978,* Volume 26, Lincoln: University of Nebraska Press, 123-161.

____. (1981). Coping with Stress at Work. *International Journal of Health Services,* 11(4), 491-510.

Frick, W. (1990). *Personality Theories: Journeys Into Self.* New York, NY. Teachers College Press.

Freire, P. (1970). *Pedagogy of the Oppressed.* London: Penguin.

Froiland, P. (1993). 1993 Industry Report. *Training,* May, 29-65.

Fyffe, A. & Peter, I. (1990). *The Handbook of Climbing.* New York, NY: Penguin Books.

Gager, D. (1977). As a Learning Process It's More Than Just Getting Your Hands Dirty. *Voyageur.*

Galagan, P. (1987). Between Two Trapezes. *Training & Development Journal.* 4(3), 40-50.

Gall, A. L. (1987). You Can Take the Manager Out of the Woods, but . . . *Training & Development Journal,* 41(3), 54-59.

Garvey, D. (1989). *Experience-based Training and Development: Domestic and International Programs (2nd Ed.).* Boulder, CO: Association for Experiential Education.

Gavanglia, P. L. (1993). How to Ensure Transfer of Training. *Training & Development Journal,* 47(10), 68.

Gibson, J. (1994). Training: The Name is the Same, the Game Has Changed. Masters Project, University of Hartford.

Gilley, J. W. & Eggland, S. A. (1989). *Principles of Human Resource Development.* Reading, Boston, MA: Addison-Wesley.

Gist, M.E., Bavetta, A.G. & Kay, C. (1990). Transfer Training Method: Its Influence on Skill Generalization, Skill Repetition, and Performance Level. *Personnel Psychology,* 43, 501-523.

Glass, A. L., & Holyoak, K. J. (1986). *Cognition (2nd Ed.).* New York: Random House.

Glorioso, J. E., Sr. (1991). Assessing Your Training Needs. *Security Management,* 35(1), 87-90.

Going Out on a Limb to Build Teamwork. (1994). *USA Today,* April, p. 5E.

Goldstein, I. L. (1993). *Training in Organizations (3rd Ed.).* Pacific Grove, CA: Brooks/Cole Publishing Company.

Grundy, S. (1982). Three Modes of Action Research, *California Perspectives,* 2-3, 23-34.

Grundy, S. & Kemmis, S. (1982). Educational Action Research in Australia: The State of the Art (an Overview). In D. Boud, R. Keogh & D. Walker (Eds.). *Reflection: Turning Experience into Learning.* New York: Nichols Publishing.

Guy, V. & Mattock, J. (1991). *The New International Manager.* London: Kogen Page.

Habermas, J. (1974). *Theory and Practice.* London: Heinemann.

Hansen, J. R., Stoa, K. F., Blix, A. S. & Ursin, H. (1978). Urinary Levels of Epinephrine and Norepinephrine in Parachutist Trainees. In H. Ursin, E. Baade, & S. Levine (Eds.), *Psychobiology of Stress,* New York: Academic Press, Inc., 63-74.

Holcomb, J. (1993). *Make Training Work Every Penny.* Del Mar, CA: Wharton Publishing.

Horne, D. (1964). *The Lucky Country.* Melbourne, Australia: Penguin.

Hofstede, G. (1984). *Cultures Consequences.* Newbury Park, CA: Sage.

Human Potential: The Revolution in Feeling. (1970). *Time Magazine,* November 9, 54-58.

Isenhart, M. W. (1983). An Investigation of the Interface between Corporate Leadership Needs and the Outward Bound Experience. *Communication Education,* 32.

Jackson, B. (1992). Debunking the Mystique of the Ropes Course. *The OTRA Journal,* 1(1), 2-3.

Jackson, L. & Caffarella, R. (Eds.). (1994). *Experiential Learning: A New Approach.* San Francisco: Jossey-Bass.

James, T. (1980). *Education at the Edge.* Denver: Colorado Outward Bound School.

Johnson, K. (1994). Corporate Conscience, Insurer Gives Retreat a Social Mission. *The New York Times,* Saturday, July 2, pp. 22;24.

Kahneman, D. (1973). *Attention and Effort.* Englewood Cliffs, NJ: Prentice Hall.

Kaufman, R. (1987). A Needs Assessment Primer: A Ten-step Approach to Help Even Beginners with this Necessary, Yet Often Dreaded, Task. *Training & Development Journal,* 41(10), 78-83.

Kezman, S. W. & Connors, E. K. (1993). Avoid legal pitfalls in nontraditional training. *HR Magazine,* 38(5), 71-74.

Kirkpatrick, D. L. (1994). *Evaluating Training Programs: The Four Levels.* San Francisco, CA: Barrett-Koehler Publishers.

——. (1993). *How To Train and Develop Supervisors.* AMACOM. New York: American Management Association.

Knapp, C. E. (1984). Idea Notebook: Designing Processing Questions to Meet Specific Objectives. *The Journal of Experiential Education,* 7(2), 47-49.

_____. (1985). The Science and Art of Processing Outdoor Experiences. *The Outdoor Communicator,* New York State Outdoor Education Association, XVI, No.1.

Knight S. (1990). *The Selling of the Australian Mind.* Melbourne, Australia: Heinemann Australia.

Kolb, D. (1991). Adventure-based Professional Development: A Theory-focused Evaluation. Doctoral Dissertation, Cornell University.

Kolb, D. A. (1984). *Experiential Learning: Experience as The Source of Learning and Development.* Englewood Cliffs, NJ: Prentice Hall.

Kolb, D.A. (1976). Management and the Learning Process, *California Management Review,* 18(3), 21-31.

Kolb, D. A., Rubin, I.M. & Osland, J. (1991). *Organizational Behavior: An Experiential Approach (5th Ed.).* Englewood Cliffs, NJ: Prentice Hall.

Kölblinger, M. (1994). Perspectives in Corporate Adventure-based Training in German Management Education. Unpublished Manuscript.

Kushell, R. E. (1979). Teaching Daily Work Habits and Patterns Aids Transfer. *Training,* December.

Laabs, J. J. (1991). Team Training Goes Outdoors. *Personnel Journal,* June, 56-63.

Latham, G.P. & Saari, L.M. (1979). The Application of Social Learning Theory to Training Supervisors through Behavior Modeling. *Journal of Applied Psychology,* 64, 239-246.

Laurent, A. (1986). The Cross-cultural Puzzle of International Human Resource Management, *Human Resource Management,* 25(1), 91-102.

Lewin, K. (1936). *Principles of Topological Psychology.* New York: McGraw-Hill.

Limerick D. & Cunnington B. (1993). *Managing the New Organisation.* Chatswood NSW, Australia: Business and Professional Publishing.

Linder, D. E. & Linder, M. J. (1972). *Experience and Change: A Psychometric Assessment of the Impact of Outward Bound Courses. An Evaluation Report.* Minnesota Outward Bound School.

Lipsitz, J. & Miller T. G. (1987). *B.A.C.S.T.O.P. Manual.* Battle Creek, MI: Battle Creek Public Schools.

Little, M., Bunting, C. & Gibbons, E. (1986). Heart Rate Responses to High Ropes Course Events. *The Texas Association for Health, Physical Education, Recreation, and Dance Journal,* 55(1), 38-39; 42.

Long, J. (1987). The Wilderness Lab Comes of Age. *Training & Development Journal,* 41(3), 30-39.

Mackay, H. (1993). *Reinventing Australia,* Sydney: Angus and Robertson.

Main, J. (1987). Trying to Bend Managers' Minds, *Fortune,* November 23, 95-102.

Manning, C. (1963) *A Short History of Australia,* Chicago: Mentor. March, 30-39.

Marmer S. C. (1993). Simulation Training Builds Teams Through Experience. *Personnel Journal.*

Marsh, H. W., Richards, B. E. & Barnes, J. (1984). Multidimensional Self-concepts: The Effect of Participation in an Outward Bound Program. ERIC Index # ED 251271, June 7, Rev. Sept. 29.

Marx, R.D. (1982). Relapse Prevention for Managerial Training: A Model for Maintenance of Behavior Change. *Academy of Management Review,* 5, 361-367.

Mertes, B. F. (1974). The Non-traditional Student's Non-traditional Classroom, *Junior College Journal,* 42(5), 29-32.

McCauley, L. (1994). On Default Modes and Anchors. *Harvard Business Review,* March/April.

Michalak, D. F. (1981). The Neglected Half of Training. *Training & Development Journal,* 35(5), 22-28.

Miner, T. A. (1991). A Descriptive Analysis of the Experience-based Training and Development Field. In C. Birmingham (Ed.), *Association for Experiential Education: 1991 Conference Proceedings and Workshop Summaries Book.* Boulder, CO: Association for Experiential Education, 59-66.

_____. (1991). Safety and Experience-based Training and Development. *Journal of Experiential Education,* 14(3), 20- 25.

Mironoff, A. (1988). Teaching Johnny to Manage. *Training,* March, 48-53.

Mitchell, C., Ferrier, D., & McDaniel, M. (1991). Outdoor Training Companies. *Training & Development Journal,* 45(3), 63-65.

Morgan, G. & Ramirez, R. (1983). Action Learning: A Holographic Metaphor for Guiding Social Changes. *Human Relations,* 37(1), 1-28.

Morganthau, T., Frons, M. & Smith, V. (1979). Risky or Reckless? *Newsweek,* p. 79.

Mulligan, J. & Griffin, C. (Eds.). (1992). *Empowerment through Experiential Learning.* London: Kogan.

Mumford, A. & Honey, P. (1986). *Manual of Learning Styles.* London: Haney.

Nadler, R. & Luckner, J. (1992). *Processing the Adventure Experience.* Dubuque, Iowa: Kendall/Hunt Publishing Company.

Napier, R. & Gershenfeld, M. (1983). *Making Groups Work.* Boston: Houghton Mifflin.

Neuber, K. A., Atkins, W. T., Jacobson, J. A. & Reuterman N. A. (1980). *Needs Assessment: A Model for Community Planning.* Beverly Hills, CA: Sage Publications.

Payne, T. (1991). The Fallacy of "How To" Training. *Training,* October.

Peters, T. (1992). *Liberation Management.* New York: Alfred A. Knopf.

Phalon, R. (1987). Hell Camp, Malibu Style. *Forbes,* December 28, 110-112.

Phillips, J. J. (1991). *Training Evaluation and Measurement Methods (2nd Ed.).* Houston, TX: Gulf Publishing Company.

Priest, S., Attarian, A. & Schubert, S. (1993). Conducting Research in Experience-Based Training and Development Programs: Pass Keys to Locked Doors. *The Journal of Experiential Education,* 16(2), 11-20.

Priest, S. & Dixon, T. (1990). *Safety Practices in Adventure Education.* Boulder, CO: Association for Experiential Education.

Priest, S. & Baillie, R. (1987). Justifying the Risk to Others: The Real Razor's Edge. *Journal of Experiential Education,* 10(1), 16-22.

Priest, S. (1985). Outdoor Leadership "Down Under." *The Journal of Experiential Education,* 8(1), 13-16.

_____. (1984). Effective Outdoor Leadership: A Survey. *Journal of Experiential Education,* 7(3), 34-37.

Reeve, D. (1982). Revitalizing Managers by Training Outdoors. *Personnel Management,* 14(40), 34-37.

Rhoades, J. S. (1972). The Problem of Individual Change in Outward Bound: An Application of Change and Transfer Theory. Doctoral Dissertation, University of Massachusetts.

Rogers, C.R. (1969). *On Becoming a Person.* Boston: Houghton Mifflin.

Roland, C. C. (1992, April). Facilitators: One Key Factor in Implementing Successful Experience-based Training and Development Programs. Paper presented at the Coalition for Education in Outdoors Research Symposium, Bradford Woods, IN.

_____. (1985). Outdoor Managerial Training Programs: Do They "Work"? *The Bradford Papers,* 5, Indiana University Press.

_____. (1983). Style Feedback for Trainers: An Objective Observer System, *Training & Development Journal,* 37(9), 76-80.

_____. (1982). Supplement Your Program Evaluation—Try Observer Systems! In G. Robb (Ed.) *The Bradford Papers, Vol. III,* Bloomington, IN: Indiana University Press.

_____. (1981). The Transfer of an Outdoor Managerial Training Program to the Work Place. Doctoral Dissertation, Boston University.

Rosset, A. (1991). The Challenge of Needs Assessment. *Supervisory Management,* 36(5), 4.

_____. (1990). Overcoming Obstacles to Needs Assessment. *Training,* 27(3), 36-41.

_____. (1989). Assess for Success. *Training and Development Journal,* 43(5), 55-59.

Ryan, B. (1991). Ropes Course Related Accidents, Injuries and Deaths. *Proceeding of the 3rd. Annual Ropes Course Symposium,* Ashland, MA: Association for Challenge Course Technology.

Schneier, C. E., Guthrie, J. P., & Olian J. D. (1988). A Practical Approach to Conducting and Using the Training Needs Assessment. *Public Personnel Management,* 17(2), 191-205.

Schwartz, G. E., Davidson, R. J., & Goleman, D. (1978). Patterning of Cognitive and Somatic Processes in the Self-regulation of Anxiety: Effects of Meditation Versus Exercise. *Psychosomatic Medicine,* 40, 321-328.

Scovel, K. (1990). Executives Take to the Hills. *Human Resource Executive.* August., 28-31.

Selye, H. (1950). *The Physiology and Pathology of Exposure to Stress.* Montreal: ACTA Inc., Medical Publishers.

Senge, P. (1990). *The Fifth Discipline; The Art and Practice of the Learning Organization.* New York: Doubleday.

Shepard, J.A. & Bennis, W.G. (1966). A Theory of Training in Group Methods. *Human Relations,* 9, 403-414.

Siewers, R.D. (1992). Cardiovascular Stress in Ropes Course Participation. *Proceedings of the 3rd Ropes Course Symposium,* Ashland, MA: Association for Challenge Course Technology.

Smith, T. (1994). *Incidents in Challenge Education: A Guide to Leadership Development.* Dubuque, Iowa: Kendall/Hunt Publishing Co.

Smith, T., Roland, C., Havens, M., & Hoyt, J. (1992). *The Theory and Practice of Challenge Education.* Dubuque, Iowa: Kendall-Hunt Publishing Co.

Snow, H. (1992). *The Power of Team Building: Using Rope Techniques.* San Diego, CA: Pfeiffer & Co.

Sorohan, E.G. (1993). We Do; Therefore We Learn. *Training & Development Journal.* 47(10), 55.

Spielberger, C. D., Gorsuch, R. L., & Lushene, R. E. (1970). *Manual for the State-Trait Anxiety Inventory (STAI).* Palo Alto, CA: Consulting Psychologists Press.

Spitzer, D. R., (1985). 20 Ways to Energize Your Training. *Training,* June.

The Stateless Corporation. (1994, April). *The Guardian,* p. 16.

Stoltz, P. G., (1992). An Examination of Leadership Development in the Great Outdoors, *Human Resource Development Quarterly.* 3(4), 357-372.

_____. (1989). Developing Communication Skills Through Outdoor Experiential Training: A Quantitative and Qualitative Analysis. Doctoral Dissertation, University of Minnesota.

Stowell D. M. & Smith H. S. (1991). The Quality Interview. *Quality Progress,* 24(6), 38-41.

Taggart, P., Carruthers, M. & Somerville, W. (1973). Electrocardiogram, Plasma Catecholamines and Lipids, and their Modification by Oxprenolol when Speaking Before an Audience. *The Lancet,* August 18, 341-346.

Taylor, J. A. (1953). A Personality Scale of Manifest Anxiety. *Journal of Abnormal and Social Psychology,* 48, 285-290.

Thompson, B. L. (1991). Training in the Great Outdoors. *Training,* 28(5), 46-52.

Thompson, P. D. (1993). Athletes, Athletics, and Sudden Cardiac Death. *Medicine and Science in Sports and Exercise,* 25, 981-984.

Trompenaars, F. (1993). *Riding the Waves of Culture.* London: Nicholas Brealey Publishing.

Wagel, William H. (1986). An Unorthodox Approach to Leadership Development. *Personnel,* 4-6.

Wagner, R. J., Baldwin, T. T. & Roland, C. C. (1991). Outdoor Training: Revolution or Fad? *Training & Development Journal,* 45(3), 50-57.

Wagner, R. J. & Campbell, J. (1994). Outdoor-based Experiential Training: Improving Transfer of Training Using Virtual Reality. *Journal of Management Development.* 13(7), 4-11.

Wagner, R. J. & Fahey, D. (1992, April). *An Empirical Evaluation of a Corporate Outdoor-based Training Program.* Proceedings of the Midwest Academy of Management. St. Charles, IL.

Wagner, R. J. & Lindner, J. M. (1993). Data on Outdoor-centered Training: Who's Doing What? *Sales & Marketing Management,* 145(2), 39-40.

Wagner, R. J., Ryan, G. M. & Roland, C. C. (1992). Corporate Outdoor Experiential Training & Development. In T. Smith, C. Roland, M. Havens & J. Hoyt, *The Theory & Practice of Challenge Education.* Dubuque, Iowa: Kendall/Hunt Publishing Co.

Wagner, R. J. & Roland, C. C. (1992). How Effective is Outdoor Training? *Training & Development Journal,* 46(7), 61-66.

Wagner, R. J. & Weigand, R. (1993). How Effective is Outdoor-based Training in Improving Management Behaviors: A Healthcare Application. *Journal of Healthcare Education and Training,* 7(3), 1-4.

Webster's Ninth New Collegiate Dictionary. (1989). Springfield, MA: Merriam Webster.

Weick, E. (1979). Cognitive Processes in Organisations. In B. Staw (Ed.) *Research in Organisations,* 1, 41-74. Greenwich, Conn.: JAI Press.

Weigand, R. & Westcott, R. (1994). Communicating about EBTD. In C. Roland & L. Diamond (Eds.) *Frontload: A Periodic Review of Experiential Strategies, Issues and Research.* (Available from Roland/Diamond Associates, Inc., 67 Emerald Street, Keene, NH 03431).

Weil, S. & McGill, I. (1989). Making Sense of Experiential Learning. Buckingham, UK: SRHE and Open University Press.

White, R. W. (1959). Motivation Reconsidered: The Concept of Competence. *Psychological Review,* 66(5), 297-333.

Williams, E. S., Taggart, P. & Carruthers, M. (1978). Rock Climbing: Observations on Heart Rate and Plasma Catecholamine Concentrations and the Influence of Oxprenolol. *British Journal of Sports Medicine,* 12, 125-128.

Winokur, J. (1987). *The Portable Curmudgeon.* New York: New American Library.

Wolfe, D. (1989). Is there Integrity in the Bottom Line: Managing Obstacles to Executive Integrity. In S. Srivastva (Ed.), *Executive Integrity,* San Francisco: Jossey-Bass.

Yerkes, R. M. & Dodson, J. D. (1908). The Relation of Strength of Stimulation to Rapidity of Habit-formation. *Journal of Comparative Neurological Psychology,* 18, 459-482.

Youker, R. B. (1985). Ten Benefits of Participant Action Planning. *Training,* June, 52-56.

Young, B. (1993). Executive Director, Outdoor Management Development. Melbourne, Australia (personal interview).

Zemke, T. (1993). Experiential Learning: There is Room for a Little Altruism in all the Fun. *Training Directors' Forum Newsletter,* p. 7.

Zemke, R. (1988). Raiders of the Lost Metaphor. *Training,* 27(4), 8.

GLOSSARY

ABSEL: the Association for Business Simulation and Experiential Learning

AEE: the Association for Experiential Education

Activity: any event used during a training program to allow trainees to "learn by doing." An experiential activity can vary from role play and management games to backpacking and rock climbing.

Anchor: a colleague who helps an employee follow through with action plans back at work (see *learning partnership*).

CEL: Corporate Experiential Learning represents models, methodologies and processes that focus on individual, team and organizational development. CEL utilizes both indoor and outdoor learning environments with action-oriented activities, exercises and simulations which incorporate review, feedback and action planning. CEL includes, but is not limited to, "outdoor adventure" models and methodologies such as ropes courses, rock climbing, rappelling, mountain climbing, sailing and rafting.

Champion: one or more individuals within an organization who advocate and support various experiential training processes and programs.

Continuous Renewal Training: training which extends over a long period of time, and does not focus on "one-shot" programs, but rather on the total process of change and improvement.

Cross Functional Team: comprised of members from different functional areas to address specific work objectives usually impacting the variety of areas represented.

Design: " . . . a blending of personalities, goals, expectations and past experiences with realities of the environment, time restrictions and the available resources to create an event of meaning and perhaps beauty that can stand alone." (Napier, 1983)

Encounter Group: a small group primary focused on looking inward and exploring one's inner thoughts and feelings.

Experiential Equipment: portable, easy-to-assemble equipment used for various indoor and outdoor exercises.

Experiential learning: uses hands-on, learn-by-doing, out-of-your-seat and on-your-feet methods such as indoor and outdoor group simulations, role plays and community service projects; contrasts with lecturing, reading and other more passive methods.

Facilitator: a person who understands and has experience in corporate training who leads an experiential activity; facilitators are highly skilled in involving groups in the feedback process.

Feedback: providing information or leading a discussion on group performance during and/or after an experiential activity as well as subsequent results at the work place.

Frontload: the element of program design and facilitation that gives activities, simulations and initiatives a framework of logical connections and applications to the work place.

Group Processing: discussing or "debriefing" an activity upon completion; discussion can also occur when the facilitator stops the group mid-way through the activity. The discussion often centers around the issues/topics which have been identified prior to the training session. Group processing is a form of guided feedback.

Guide: A facilitator who "shows the way" by asking thoughtful questions contrasted with an instructor who provides the answers.

High Challenge Course (also known as "High Ropes Course"): a series of challenges constructed from rope, wood and cable reaching heights up to seventy feet. Participants are required to wear special safety harnesses and use special safety equipment.

Initiatives: indoor or outdoor problem solving situations presented to groups or individuals.

Intact Team: a group of people who interact on a regular basis in the work setting with a (clear) common goal, mission or work product.

Journey: a continued course of learning spanning days, weeks, months and even years for individuals, teams and organizations.

Kirkpatrick Model: a model for the evaluation of a training program that utilizes four levels: Reaction, Learning, Behavior, Results.

Kolb Learning Cycle: developed by Dr. David Kolb in 1975, describing the four stages of experiential learning: Concrete Experience; Observation and Reflection; Assimilation in a Theory and Active Experimentation.

Learning Partnership: random or assigned dyads formed during a training process or program that continue back at the work place.

Low Challenge Course (also known as "low ropes course"): a series of physical challenges constructed from cable, rope and wood, no higher than three feet from the ground. Focus is on individual challenge with support from "spotters" (usually other team members).

Metaphor: an experiential activity or series of activities that parallel a real life business issue, e.g., the frustration that evolved from the "Traffic Jam" activity is a metaphor to frustration back at work.

Orienteering: the process of finding one's way on foot across terrain by map and compass often performed in small groups.

Outdoor Adventure: CEL models and methodologies, including, but not limited to, ropes courses, rock climbing, rappelling, mountain climbing, sailing and rafting.

OMD: Outdoor Management Training: term is frequently used in the United Kingdom.

Outdoor-based Training: training programs that are conducted mainly outdoors.

Outward Bound: officially "Outward Bound, Inc.," an international organization known for outdoor activities including but not limited to wilderness backpacking, canoeing, rock climbing and rappelling.

Processing: see "debriefing"

Program: a planned combination of indoor and/or outdoor training experiences that involve a sequence of experiential segments; these segments can be augmented with more traditional lecture, video, role play, etc. Programs can be stand alone "one shot" (e.g., 3 hour, 1 day, 3 day) or part of a longer-term training/organizational development process.

Project Adventure: officially "Project Adventure, Inc.," one of the pioneering organizations that integrated indoor and outdoor experiential "adventure" activities within a high school physical education curriculum.

Provider: an external consultant or consulting/training/organizational development firm providing various experiential training services.

Sensitivity Training (also called "T-group Education"): a training model usually conducted in groups of 8 to 14 during which each individual examines how they are perceived by others in terms of their interpersonal skills.

Sequencing: the arrangement of activities, initiatives and other experiential exercises in order of succession.

Simulation: any activity specifically designed to be similar to an actual work setting.

Teams Course: a series of group-oriented physical exercises usually located outdoors.

Training Process: long-term training/organizational development commitment involving experiential methods/programs, traditional training methods (e.g., lecture, video), coaching and consultation (e.g., co-facilitating meetings).

Tweak: to make small design changes prior to, as well as during a training activity.

WEL: Wilderness Experiential Learning

This book is the product of a cooperative venture between Kendall/Hunt Publishing Company and Roland/Diamond Associates, Inc.

Roland/Diamond Associates, Inc.

11 Sequin Road ◆ West Hartford, CT 06117 ◆ (203) 233-5456
67 Emerald Street ◆ Keene, NH 03431 ◆ (603) 357-2181

Roland/Diamond Assoicates is an organizational consulting and training company specializing in customized services for individual, team and organizational growth. Clients include a variety of fields including higher education, human resources, insurance, manufacturing, health care, government agencies and financial institutions.

Management and Organizational Consulting

- ◆ Conducting cultural and organizational needs assessment
- ◆ Facilitating strategic planning and visioning sessions
- ◆ Individual and team coaching
- ◆ Meeting facilitation

Corporate Experiential Learning Program Design, Delivery and Follow-up

- ◆ Leveraging change for organizational effectiveness
- ◆ Downsizing aftermath for survivors and former staff
- ◆ Leadership effectiveness
- ◆ Team development
- ◆ Continuous improvement
- ◆ Valuing and leveraging differences
- ◆ Creativity and innovation
- ◆ Effective communication
- ◆ Conflict management
- ◆ Cross-functional team collaboration
- ◆ Supplement to internal training/management development curriculum
- ◆ Train-the-trainer programs